High-Impact Assessment Reports
for Children and Adolescents

The Guilford Practical Intervention in the Schools Series

Kenneth W. Merrell, Founding Editor
T. Chris Riley-Tillman, Series Editor

www.guilford.com/practical

This series presents the most reader-friendly resources available in key areas of evidence-based practice in school settings. Practitioners will find trustworthy guides on effective behavioral, mental health, and academic interventions, and assessment and measurement approaches. Covering all aspects of planning, implementing, and evaluating high-quality services for students, books in the series are carefully crafted for everyday utility. Features include ready-to-use reproducibles, lay-flat binding to facilitate photocopying, appealing visual elements, and an oversized format. Recent titles have Web pages where purchasers can download and print the reproducible materials.

Recent Volumes

Promoting Student Happiness: Positive Psychology Interventions in Schools
Shannon M. Suldo

Effective Math Interventions: A Guide to Improving Whole-Number Knowledge
Robin S. Codding, Robert J. Volpe, and Brian C. Poncy

Emotional and Behavioral Problems of Young Children, Second Edition:
Effective Interventions in the Preschool and Kindergarten Years
Melissa L. Holland, Jessica Malmberg, and Gretchen Gimpel Peacock

Group Interventions in Schools: A Guide for Practitioners
Jennifer P. Keperling, Wendy M. Reinke, Dana Marchese, and Nicholas Ialongo

Transforming Schools: A Problem-Solving Approach to School Change
Rachel Cohen Losoff and Kelly Broxterman

Evidence-Based Strategies for Effective Classroom Management
David M. Hulac and Amy M. Briesch

School-Based Observation: A Practical Guide to Assessing Student Behavior
Amy M. Briesch, Robert J. Volpe, and Randy G. Floyd

Helping Students Overcome Social Anxiety:
Skills for Academic and Social Success (SASS)
Carrie Masia Warner, Daniela Colognori, and Chelsea Lynch

Executive Skills in Children and Adolescents, Third Edition:
A Practical Guide to Assessment and Intervention
Peg Dawson and Richard Guare

Effective Universal Instruction:
An Action-Oriented Approach to Improving Tier 1
Kimberly Gibbons, Sarah Brown, and Bradley C. Niebling

Supporting Successful Interventions in Schools:
Tools to Plan, Evaluate, and Sustain Effective Implementation
Lisa M. Hagermoser Sanetti and Melissa A. Collier-Meek

High-Impact Assessment Reports for Children and Adolescents:
A Consumer-Responsive Approach
Robert Lichtenstein and Bruce Ecker

Conducting School-Based Functional Behavioral Assessments, Third Edition:
A Practitioner's Guide
Mark W. Steege, Jamie L. Pratt, Garry Wickerd, Richard Guare, and T. Steuart Watson

High-Impact Assessment Reports for Children and Adolescents

A Consumer-Responsive Approach

ROBERT LICHTENSTEIN
BRUCE ECKER

THE GUILFORD PRESS
New York   London

Copyright © 2019 The Guilford Press
A Division of Guilford Publications, Inc.
370 Seventh Avenue, Suite 1200, New York, NY 10001
www.guilford.com

Printed in Canada

This book is printed on acid-free paper.

Last digit is print number: 9 8 7 6 5 4 3 2 1

Library of Congress Cataloging-in-Publication Data is available from the publisher.

ISBN 978-1-4625-3849-2 (paperback)

About the Authors

Robert Lichtenstein, PhD, NCSP, established the school psychology programs at the University of Delaware and William James College (formerly the Massachusetts School of Professional Psychology). He has served as a school psychologist in three different states; as supervisor of school psychological services for the New Haven Public Schools; as director of training at the Medical–Educational Evaluation Center at North Shore Children's Hospital in Salem, Massachusetts; and as the school psychology consultant for the Connecticut State Department of Education. He is a recipient of the Presidential Award from the National Association of School Psychologists and the Lifetime Achievement Award from the Massachusetts School Psychologists Association.

Bruce Ecker, PhD, is Associate Professor and Director of the child clinical concentration (Children and Families of Adversity and Resilience) in the Department of Clinical Psychology at William James College. He has worked in the Minneapolis, Boston, and Framingham, Massachusetts, public schools as well as at the University of Minnesota Hospitals and at Baystate Medical Center in Springfield, Massachusetts. With degrees in both clinical and educational psychology, Dr. Ecker has assessed and treated hundreds of children, adolescents, and their families, many of whom have experienced psychosocial trauma, chronic psychiatric illness, and developmental and medical difficulties. He is a recipient of the Excellence in Teaching Award from William James College and held the college's Mintz Chair in Professional Psychology from 2014 to 2016.

Preface

Like many mental health professionals, we entered this field with the intention of improving the lives of others. Psychological assessment is a significant professional activity that is intended to serve this purpose.

Highly specialized practitioners devote vast time and effort to assessment. Whether these efforts result in commensurate benefit is a troubling question. A critical look at current assessment practices suggests that we have lost sight of the potential value of assessment, at a great disservice to consumers—children, families, teachers, and service providers.

Our premise in writing this book is that most written and oral assessment reporting falls short in meeting the needs of those best situated to improve the lives of children. We are hardly the first to raise these concerns. For over 50 years, discerning critics have advocated for changes in report-writing practices to better serve users. The research literature in this area, although sparse, has consistently supported these calls for reform.

As trainers and clinical supervisors, we have felt responsible for guiding and influencing the practice of future practitioners. This has forced us to look critically at our own practice and at what we have advised others to do. As a result, our approach has evolved and, in all likelihood, will continue to evolve. Encouragingly, our efforts to effect changes in assessment practices have been supported, and our sense of urgency heightened, by the many practitioners who share our concerns, experience similar dissatisfactions, and wish to modify their report-writing practices. We have also heard from like-minded trainers of school psychologists and clinical psychologists who are trying to impress upon students the importance of a consumer-centric approach. These trainers experience much the same frustrations as we do about trying to make inroads in the face of countervailing influences, most notably (1) the lack of helpful guidance and models in the professional literature and (2) current trends and expectations in school and clinical settings.

This book is an added voice to the chorus of those who call for assessment to be done in a way that regards the needs of the consumer as paramount. We have been heartened by the work of Brenner (2003), Brown-Chidsey and Andren (2013), Groth-Marnat (2009), and Hass and Carriere (2014), who are challenging conventional practice and offering valuable corrective guidance. Most notably, we have admired and been inspired by the work of Virginia Harvey (1997, 2006, 2013), who wrote extensively and eloquently on the topic. We hope to further this agenda by offering not just a call to action, but an instructive how-to guide.

We acknowledge that there is no one "right way" to report assessment findings and that arguments can be made for different approaches. This is why guiding principles and underlying philosophy are so important: they are the benchmarks by which we weigh the adequacy of any given approach. In many respects, we have opted for an approach that is both idealistic and practical, proposing refinements that current practitioners will hopefully regard as both consistent with higher goals and manageable given typical expectations and constraints.

What began as a book strictly about report writing has expanded somewhat to delineate the concept of consumer-responsive assessment more broadly. This was a natural development, given the goal of seeking optimal outcomes. For reporting to have a positive impact presumes that practitioners produce assessments with strong content that emerges from overall sound assessment practices. Equally important, the ultimate value of an assessment depends on the relationships we establish with consumers (children, parents, teachers, etc.) and how we continue to work with them to ensure that findings are understood, accepted, and put to use.

This brings to mind one coauthor's (R. L.) conversation with a fellow school psychology trainer after attending a presentation in which long and comprehensive assessment reports were held up as the paragon of excellence. This colleague spoke of a school psychologist in a small town ("where everybody knows everybody") who operates in a highly personal manner. As explained, her assessment reports are no more than a few pages long and undistinguished. However, to enable the many parents in her district with transportation issues to attend school meetings, this school psychologist will pick up and return parents in her own car, thereby creating the opportunity for private conversations. Knowing about this school psychologist's work, the trainer surmised, "She is doing a world of good for children and families, and I suspect that her brief reports are legally defensible and adequately doing the job." If professional practice were guided strictly by outcomes, this example might be regarded as an inspiration rather than as an outlier.

A comment about testing is in order. It may appear to the reader that we are critical of standardized cognitive testing. Actually, we have genuine respect for the unique information that cognitive tests contribute to an assessment. Unique and valuable findings are generated as examinees respond to unfamiliar, school-like tasks under fixed conditions—findings that supplement what is learned through records, observations, and interviews. We also place a high value on the qualitative data (strategies, reactions, verbalizations, etc.) yielded by standardized testing. Our reservations concern the all-too-common misinterpretation and overinterpretation of test results and the emphasis on test results in oral and written reports that is disproportionate to the relevance of the reported findings.

While proficiency in administering and interpreting tests is a useful skill acquired through substantial investment of time and effort, consumer-responsive assessment involves a much broader and more demanding array of professional skills. Developing the expertise to conduct an effective consumer-responsive assessment requires extended exposure to relevant learning opportunities and a commitment to reflective practice. We hope that this book facilitates your pursuit of this lofty goal.

This book was made possible by the many people we have learned from over the years: our mentors, our colleagues, our students, our clients, . . . and each other.

Contents

1. Assessment Reports That Work for Consumers   1

Consumer-Responsive Assessment: Rationale and Description   2
   Who Are the Consumers?   4
   Types of Assessment Reports   5
   Terms   5
Content Overview   6

2. Understanding Current Practice   8

Current State of the Art   8
   Emphasis on Tests   8
   Readability   11
   Length   13
Why Evaluators Do What They Do   14
   Initial Training   14
   Psychological Terms   16
   Established Models   17
   External Pressures   18
The Challenge for Practitioners   21

3. Assessment Fundamentals   22

Assessment Design   22
   Consent or Contracting   23
   Individualized Assessment   24
   Selectivity   25
   Hypothesis Testing   25
Data Sources   26
   Review of Records   27
   Interviewing   27
   Observation   29

Rating Scales 31

Testing 32

Interpretation and Use of Assessment Findings 38

Integration of Assessment Data 38

Recommendations 40

Professional Writing 41

Assessment in a Multi-Tiered System: The New Normal? 41

Solution-Focused Assessments 43

Implications for Assessment Reports 45

4. The Consumer-Responsive Approach   **47**

Core Principles 48

Collaborative Relationships 48

Emphasize Process, Not Product 48

Relevance 48

Importance of Oral Reporting 49

Accessibility 49

Multiple Sources of Assessment Data 49

Child Focus 49

Collaborative Consumer-Responsive Relationships 50

The Working Alliance in Assessment 50

Elements of a Collaborative Working Relationship 51

Putting the Collaborative Relationship into Practice 52

Consumer-Responsive Practices Over the Course of the Assessment 54

Activities That Precede the Referral 54

Initial Interviewing 54

Relating to the Child 56

Assessment Reporting 61

Follow-Up Contacts 61

Consumer Evaluation 62

Respecting Culture 62

Culture and Trust 64

Culture and Communication 65

Bridging School Requirements and Parent Needs 67

5. Consumer-Responsive Report Writing   **69**

Characteristics of Consumer-Responsive Reports 70

Selectivity 70

Theme-Based Organization 71

Child Focus (vs. Test Focus) 72

Presentation of Data 73

Language and Writing Style 83

Report Structure 85

Identifying Information 88

Reason for Referral 88

Assessment Procedures 89

Background Information 89

Intervention History 91

Interviews 92

Behavioral Observations 93

Assessment Results 94

Clinical Impressions 98

Summary 99

Recommendations 100
Data Summary 103
Concluding Comments 104

6. Straight Talk: Oral Communication of Findings   105

Interpersonal and Communication Skills 105
Feedback Meetings 106
  Team Meetings 107
  Individual Meetings 109
Conveying Findings 110
Communicating with Different Consumers 111
  Communicating with Parents 111
  Communicating with Teachers 113
  Communicating with Children and Adolescents 115
In Conclusion 115

7. Variations on a Theme: Reports for Special Purposes   117

School-Based Assessment Alternatives 117
  Screening and Progress Monitoring 117
  Special Education Re-Evaluation 123
  Assessment of Children with Severe Intellectual Disabilities 125
Other Assessment Alternatives 127
  Independent Evaluation 127
  Assessment for Disability Accommodations 129
  Parent Feedback Letter 130
  Neuropsychological Assessment 131
  Forensic Assessment 133
  Team Reports 134
  Computer-Generated Reports 135

8. Making It Happen: Implications and Impact   137

Individual Practitioner Issues 138
  Ongoing Professional Development 138
  Exercising Flexibility 139
  Consumer Expectations 139
  Issues for Community-Based Evaluators 139
  Phased-In Implementation 140
System Issues 141
  Issues for Schools 142
  Issues for Community Agencies 147
  Issues for Third-Party Payers 147
  Prevention Pays 148
  Consumer Feedback 149
  Issues for Graduate Training Programs 149
A Vision for Future Practice 150
  Toward a Tipping Point 153

Appendix A. Readability Measures   155

Appendix B. Test Administration and Scoring Rubric   157

Appendix C. Psychological Assessment Follow-Up Procedures   161

Appendix D. Sample Assessment Reports and Parent Feedback Letter   164

Appendix E. Background Information Outline and Case Example   191

Appendix F. Data Summary Template   195

Appendix G. Report-Writing Rubric   207

Appendix H. Feedback Conference Simulation   211

References   215

Index   221

CHAPTER 1

Assessment Reports
That Work for Consumers

Every psychological assessment is an opportunity. It is an opportunity to enlighten, to collaborate, and to plan.

Psychological assessment is an opportunity to help the 8-year-old boy who struggles with reading to understand that he is not dumb; to help his parents learn that difficulty distinguishing the sounds that make up words is a common reading difficulty; and to help his teachers understand that an intensive program of phonological training will greatly speed this boy's learning to read. Psychological assessment is an opportunity to help a 15-year-old girl learn that the cuts that stripe her forearms are not a sign of sickness or of sin, but rather of the desperate way that someone her age tries to cope with memories of sexual abuse and feelings of self-hatred. It is also an opportunity for her parents to understand that her isolation is born of shame, for her teachers to understand that the girl is doing all she can and that failing grades will make her worse, and for her therapist to understand that treatment will take time, because it is so hard for her to trust. Psychological assessment is an opportunity for a 3-year-old boy who barely relates to others and has but few words to understand that he is loved by and connected with his family, as his parents learn what an autism spectrum disorder is, become less scared of their son, and learn ways they can help. It is an opportunity for a treatment team to become engaged and give this boy the intensive instruction that will help him and his family for many years to come.

It is through the oral and written reporting of psychological assessment findings that these opportunities are realized. Far too often, however, customary practices fail to take advantage of these opportunities. Findings are reported in ways that are incomprehensible to the primary consumers—parents, teachers, and service providers—who are most able to put them to use. Consequently, parent and teacher involvement in the assessment process is minimized. We respect the capable and compassionate work of practitioners who conduct

1

assessments. However, we believe that the current model of assessment reporting often mystifies and confuses more than it informs and enlightens.

The consumer-responsive approach is a call to change the way we report psychological assessments. It is a call to communicate clearly, directly, and empathically, and thus, with a high impact. Hence, it is a call to operate in the best interests of the child.

CONSUMER-RESPONSIVE ASSESSMENT: RATIONALE AND DESCRIPTION

The purposes of psychological assessment are to describe areas of functioning that are relevant to referral questions, to explain why a client has the related struggles and strengths, and to propose interventions and supports that will help to improve his or her functioning. By doing so, the assessment answers important questions and informs a treatment plan. It can be the basis of powerful collaborative relationships between the evaluator and the consumers of psychological assessment.

Conventional psychological assessment too often falls short in fulfilling these purposes. The relationship between examiner and consumers is business-like and less conducive to real collaboration. There is an overemphasis on tests and an underemphasis on the child's history and his day-to-day functioning. The choice of tests is largely fixed, without sufficient regard for the specific reasons for referral. Results are communicated in technical jargon that is not understood by parents, teachers, and other consumers who stand to benefit most from the findings. Reports are a primary means of communicating with key consumers, yet they are written in a manner that can be understood only by other psychologists. Oral reporting is too often impersonal and delivered only in a large-group setting. Furthermore, there is little if any follow-up to check if recommendations were implemented and whether they were effective. Such critiques have been expressed by many writers over the years (Brenner, 2003; Groth-Marnat & Horvath, 2006; Harvey, 1997, 2006; Hass & Carriere, 2014; Lichtenstein, 2013a, 2014; Ownby & Wallbrown, 1986; Shectman, 1979; Tallent, 1993; Tallent & Reiss, 1959; Wiener & Costaris, 2012).

We propose an alternative model, one that puts the consumers at the center of the assessment enterprise. We do not disregard the value of assessment as currently practiced. Rather, we see assessment's value greatly enhanced when it is embedded in a "consumer-responsive" approach. Our model is guided by the belief that clear and compassionate reporting is in the interest of all consumers, and thus in the best interest of the children who are assessed.

A consumer-responsive approach is informed by 7 principles: (1) the importance of *collaborative relationships*, (2) a *process approach* that begins with prereferral problem solving and extends through follow-up, (3) an emphasis on *relevance* and with it, intervention, (4) an appreciation that the discussion afforded by *oral reporting* makes it as important as written reporting, (5) the critical importance of *accessibility* (i.e., that reporting be done in ways that all consumers can understand), (6) the *integration of multiple sources of assessment data*, and (7) a *focus on the child* rather than on the tests.

Consumer-responsive assessment has several characteristics. First, like assessment of all types, it is conceptually sound and technically correct. By conceptually sound, we mean that it directly answers the referral questions, rather than conveying information in an unfocused or rote manner. By technically correct, we mean that it meets the standards of reliability, validity, and accurate reporting as described in professional guides, such as the *Standards for Educational Testing and Measurement* (American Educational Research Association [AERA], American Psychological Association [APA], National Council on Measurement in Education [NCME], 2014) and the codes of conduct of the American Psychological Association (2017) and the National Association of School Psychologists (NASP; 2010b).

Consumer-responsive assessment aspires to a high bar. It is responsive to consumers both in process and in content. With regard to process, assessment must engage the primary consumers in a collaborative relationship from beginning to end. Consumers must be full partners in creating the questions to be answered, in choosing the procedures to be used, and in devising plans of intervention. With regard to content, assessments must address the specific questions posed by consumers and provide answers that are helpful and practical. Assessments must consider the whole child in his or her environment. Intervention is a key feature in considering what has and has not worked in the past and in planning effective strategies for the future. Assessment questions should be answered through both oral and written feedback, which must be supplied in language that is understandable to the consumers. The characteristics of conventional and consumer-responsive assessment are contrasted in Table 1.1.

These concepts are hardly new. In an incisive article entitled "Consumer-Focused Assessment," Brenner (2003) applies four criteria to psychological assessment: relevance, response, relationships, and results. *Relevance* and *response* refer to identifying the consumer's needs and producing a solution. This solution includes individualized testing, assessment of strengths as well as deficits, reports that are understandable and meaningful, and recommendations that are concrete and specific. Regarding *relationships,* Brenner (2003) calls for building lasting alliances with consumers. This is accomplished throughout the assessment process by collaborating to develop referral questions, creating rapport while the assessment is proceeding, and giving personalized oral feedback. Brenner's fourth criterion, *results,* involves the continual assessment of consumer satisfaction, to distinguish between what we do that is helpful and what we do that is not.

The expectation that psychological assessment reports are useful, individualized, and understandable is reinforced by statutes and regulations. Central to the special education process is the school-based team responsible for the individualized education program (IEP) of eligible children. This IEP team explicitly includes both parents and school personnel as core members. Federal regulations spell out the rights of parents to receive all pertinent information and participate in educational decisions, and to be fully informed of these rights. Thus, there is the clear and well-conceived expectation that all members of the team will collaborate. If planning is truly to be team based, then all members of the IEP team, including parents and older students who are invited to participate, must understand the information on which decisions are based. This includes the parent who struggled to finish high school, as well as the parent with a graduate degree. It includes the blue-blooded American whose family has spoken English for generations, as well as the new immigrant from Central America, China, or the Middle East. It includes the 14-year-old with disabling sickle cell anemia, as well as the 18-year-old senior who struggles with test taking.

TABLE 1.1. Characteristics of Conventional and Consumer-Responsive Assessment

Characteristic	Conventional assessment	Consumer-responsive assessment
Referral questions	Determined by referral agent	Determined by parents, teachers, service providers, and evaluator, as well as referral agent
Initial parent interview	Focuses on history for purpose of obtaining background information	Focuses on history as well as on building a collaborative working alliance; additional assessment questions and planned assessment procedures are discussed
Choice of assessment procedures	Often a standard battery	Individualized for each case
Role of testing relative to other procedures	Testing is most important source of assessment data	Testing, record review, interviews, and observations have comparable importance
Written report: Organization of results	Results reported test by test	Results reported by theme or functional area
Written report: Language	Graduate school reading level with jargon and unexplained technical terms	High school reading level with everyday language
Written report: Interpretation Interpretations/Conclusions	Discusses test findings	Integrates findings from all sources
Oral reporting	Presentation in large-group (e.g., IEP team) meeting	Presentation in large-group meeting and separate discussion(s) with consumers
Follow-up	Not done	Done routinely

Essential to this approach is communicating assessment findings in a way that users can understand. This point is so important that it is codified in the NASP (2010b) *Principles for Professional Ethics:*

> **Standard II.3.8.** School psychologists adequately interpret findings and present results in clear, understandable terms so that the recipient can make informed choices.

Who Are the Consumers?

In identifying the consumer as the primary audience for our reports, we had best be clear about who the term refers to. First and foremost, it refers to parents and parental caretakers, who have so much at stake and are most affected by assessment outcomes. Assessment findings and recommendations can have a long-term impact on the child and family. In addition to parents, school teachers, and administrators, other service providers, such as pediatricians, speech-and-language clinicians, and psychotherapists, are primary consumers. Assessment results change how they think about the child and, in many cases, how they provide or facilitate help. Regardless of the setting where the assessment is conducted—school, clinic, hospital, or private practice—all relevant consumers should be involved as important collaborators. Of course, the child or adolescent is the ultimate beneficiary. While usually affected indirectly through the actions of significant adults, the child may also be a consumer of assessment findings through direct communication with the evaluator. Successful assessment reporting must inform, enlighten, and guide these primary consumers.

Types of Assessment Reports

Since the great majority of assessments of children and adolescents are conducted by school personnel to determine a student's educational needs and special education eligibility, the primary focus of this book is the work done in schools by school psychologists. Such work typically includes traditional norm-based measurements of cognition, emotions, behavior, and learning. However, other types of school-based assessment are considered here as well. They include curriculum-based assessment (CBA) and progress monitoring measures used within the framework of multi-tiered systems of support (MTSS). A consumer-responsive approach is also applicable to assessment in other settings, such as hospitals and clinics, to the assessment of adults, and to specialized approaches, such as neuropsychological and forensic assessment. The problems with assessment as typically practiced are similar across settings and with different populations. The solutions that we propose are similar as well.

Terms

For efficiency, we use the term *psychological assessment*—often shortened to assessment—to refer to formal evaluations of individual children that include testing, observation, and other data gathering, and are completed by all types of psychologists and school psychologists. The term psychological assessment encompasses psychoeducational assessment, neurodevelopmental assessment, and neuropsychological assessment, among others. The term may also be applied to solution-focused data collection activities, such as progress monitoring and functional behavioral assessment, which we address at later points in the book.

It is common to use the term *client* to refer to the child or adolescent who is assessed. In our view, this usage would create confusion. We recognize that various people—the child, parent, teacher, and school administrators—may be clients and consumers, even if the child is the person who is assessed. Thus, we refer to these various individuals by their role—child, parent, teacher, and so on. And, rather than use the more precise but cumbersome "child or adolescent" each time, we refer to the assessment subject using the more generic *child* or *children*. Similarly, when referring to a parent or parents, these terms should be understood to encompass guardians or other primary caregivers as well.

We call the person who conducts the psychological assessment the *evaluator*. We came to this decision by process of elimination, since the term *examiner* conjures the image of someone who dispassionately dissects, and the term *assessor* evokes associations with real estate and taxes. Referring to evaluators as psychologists would not do justice to the applicable array of other roles and disciplines, such as school psychologist, neuropsychologist, psychotherapist, and educational diagnostician.

In many instances, we use the term *reporting* rather than *report,* because we wish to convey the broader set of activities involved in communicating results, both in written and oral forms. We use a verb to focus more on the process than the product.

We use the convention of capitalizing the names of major sections of an assessment report (e.g., Reason for Referral, Background Information) to make clear that the reference is to the written report.

For clarity and consistency with the current literature, we refer to MTSS as the overarching service delivery model that subsumes a response-to-intervention (RTI) model and its related components (e.g., benchmark assessment, curriculum-based measurement (CBM), and progress monitoring). MTSS is understood to be applicable to both academic and behavioral goals and to be distinct from the assessment procedure used for identification of learning disabilities.

We alternate the gender of pronouns, rather than use the cumbersome "he or she" every time we make such a reference. The children we assess and the adults we interact with are both male and female, as acknowledged by this alternation.

CONTENT OVERVIEW

This book is intended to be a practical guide to conducting high-impact assessments and writing consumer-responsive reports. We examine the problems inherent in current assessment practices and offer conceptual and practical solutions.

In Chapter 2, we consider the current state of the art and common shortcomings of assessment reports and examine the reasons for common practices. Having thus outlined the scope and the foundations of the problem, we devote the remainder of the book to solutions.

Chapter 3 is dedicated to universally applicable best practices, since consumer-responsive reporting rests on a foundation of fundamentally sound data collection and interpretation. We emphasize individualized assessment procedures, use of multiple sources of data, consideration of measurement error, integration of assessment data, and meaningful recommendations.

In Chapter 4, we elaborate on the core principles of consumer-responsive assessment and describe how they are manifested in the relationships that we establish with consumers. We discuss what consumers want, and when and how to include them in the assessment process. We also discuss the role of culture as it applies to the evaluator–consumer relationship and to communication between the evaluator and consumer.

Chapter 5 is the heart of the book, where we describe the essential elements of consumer-responsive reports and how they translate into report-writing practices. We present specific guidance on how to organize content, present test results, integrate and summarize findings, and formulate recommendations. The chapter includes examples of consumer-responsive writing.

Equally important is Chapter 6, which describes consumer-responsive oral reporting. We discuss the relational skills needed, the choice of information to present, and ways to convey findings both in team meetings, and separately with parents, teachers, and children.

In Chapter 7 we apply a consumer-responsive perspective to reports for special purposes, including screening and progress monitoring reports, educational re-evaluations, assessment of severe intellectual disability, independent evaluations, assessment for disability accommodations, neuropsychological assessment, forensic assessment, multidisciplinary team reports, and computer-generated reports.

Chapter 8 concerns issues in adopting a consumer-responsive approach, noting systemic challenges and how they might be addressed. We also present an idealistic vision for the future, one in which practice is driven exclusively by the goal of optimal benefit to all parties (i.e., consumers, evaluators, and the systems that make use of assessments).

Many of the proposals in this book are based on clinical experience—both our own and that of other authors, since a number of key issues concerning assessment reporting have not been sufficiently studied. Both to highlight this need and to encourage future work in this area, we have proposed research studies in boxes that appear throughout the book.

The appendices should be helpful to readers as they learn or transition to a consumer-responsive approach to assessment. Appendix A provides an explanation of widely used readability measures that can be used to gauge the reading difficulty of a report. Appendix C describes procedures for conducting follow-up contacts with consumers and for requesting their postassessment evaluative feedback. Sample assessment reports and a parent feedback letter are provided in Appendix D. Appendix F is a template for the Data Summary section of an assessment report. Appendix G, a rubric for evaluating assessment reports that incorporates consumer-responsive principles, was developed for graduate student training. Appendix H, a training exercise for oral presentation of assessment findings, contains guidelines and a rubric that emphasize responsiveness to consumers.

Some appendices are applicable to assessment practices in general. Appendix B is a generic rubric for evaluating adherence to essential test administration and scoring procedures. Appendix E provides a recommended structure for the Background Information section of a report, along with a case example. Purchasers of this book can download Appendices B, F, G, and H from the Guilford website and use them freely with attribution (see the box at the end of the table of contents).

CHAPTER 2

Understanding Current Practice

"If it ain't broke, don't fix it," the saying goes. However, current practice in report writing is indeed "broke," having lost sight of the primary purpose of psychological and psychoeducational assessment: to inform decision making. This chapter examines the nature of current practice and how it has come about.

CURRENT STATE OF THE ART

Conventional assessment reports tend to be overly focused on standardized tests, replete with extraneous information and written in a manner more suited to psychologists than to parents or teachers. Deficits are emphasized, while strengths are overlooked or minimized. Assessment data are reported and analyzed in isolation, rather than integrated with other data sources to highlight convergent findings. Referral questions and other key findings get lost in the process of reporting unselectively on every test and subtest administered, leaving readers at a loss to understand their relative importance or to make sense of seeming inconsistencies. Such reports miss the opportunity to meaningfully inform and engage the very consumers—parents and teachers—who are most able to make use of findings for the benefit of the child. Rather, the tone and content of traditional reports largely serve to document that a school district has fulfilled its special education mandate or that the practitioner has done his data-based due diligence in arriving at a diagnosis and recommendations.

Emphasis on Tests

Standardized testing is one of the most significant contributions to the field of psychology. In fact, the discipline of psychology originated with efforts in the late 19th century to assess mental abilities with scientific objectivity. The psychometric underpinnings of psychological and educational tests—reliability, validity, and standardization—have contributed mightily to the central role of tests in assessing human characteristics. The number of tests in print continues to grow; the Buros Center for Testing's *Twentieth Mental Measurements Yearbook* (Carlson, Geisinger, & Jonson, 2017) provides information on approximately 3,000 tests. Tests have been developed to measure every conceivable type of trait and function, including cognitive and neuropsychological abilities, academic skills, adaptive behavior, social and emotional functioning, executive functions, school environment, and family relations.

In the course of their professional training, psychologists devote much time and effort to acquiring test administration and scoring skills. Psychological testing also assumes an exalted status by virtue of its being an illustrious contribution and a distinguishing hallmark of psychologists. Accordingly, they tend to regard standardized testing as the key component of psychological assessment and to emphasize test results in their written and oral reports. As one indication of the extent to which assessment and testing are regarded as synonymous, both evaluators and the general public refer to the enterprise as *testing* (as in "I understand you referred your child for testing"), rather than as assessment (as in "Let's discuss the assessment that I will conduct"). Another indication is that evaluators equate designing an assessment with identifying the battery of tests to be administered. Accordingly, evaluators document the date(s) when the child was tested in the heading of an assessment report, without citing the date when a parent interview or a classroom observation was conducted.

All too often, psychological reports focus more on the tests administered than on the person who was evaluated. A common practice is to provide all test scores in tables in the body of a report and to discuss these results at great length. Citing all scores in the body of a report implicitly creates pressure to explain and make sense of each finding. This information adds considerable length to the Test Results section and elevates its seeming importance. Yet, many test findings discussed in a report do not relate to referral questions or have a bearing on the recommendations (see Research Idea 2.1). Furthermore, including all test scores inclines the evaluator to try to extract more meaning from psychological tests than what is empirically defensible by drawing attention to differences between scores that are not statistically significant or offering convoluted interpretations when related measures yield inconsistent findings.

Tests of general intelligence assess multiple factors, some of which will have little bearing on the referral question or on understanding the child. Nevertheless, the evaluator who uses a standard report format devotes attention to every area of functioning assessed. Consider, for example, the child's performance on the working memory scale of an intelligence test, even though memory was not an area of concern and the level of performance is consistent with the child's overall functioning. Since a working memory score was obtained, the evaluator provides a detailed account of performance in this area, thereby implicitly conveying that memory is relevant to an understanding of the child. Addressing all scores in the report becomes especially problematic when scores are inconsistent or there is no interpretable pattern. The evaluator might then provide a contorted or tenuous explanation or report the inconsistent scores without resolving the contradictions for the puzzled reader.

RESEARCH IDEA 2.1. Relevance of Reported Test Findings

Research question: To what extent do the test findings discussed in assessment reports address referral questions and inform major findings and recommendations?

Traditional assessment reports discuss the results of standardized tests at length, without regard for their relevance. It is hypothesized that a large proportion of reported test results prove to have little relevance. This study would analyze a random collection of school- and community-based psychological reports to determine what percentage of test findings discussed in the report narrative actually address referral questions or inform major findings (i.e., those noted in a Clinical Impressions, Conclusions, or Summary section) or recommendations.

The hypothesized study results would have implications for evaluators to consider the need for greater selectivity in reporting and analyzing test results.

A preferable alternative is for the evaluator to report test results selectively, thereby signaling to the reader what is clinically meaningful. After all, evaluators are selective in reporting other types of assessment data. The evaluator who observes a child for an hour only reports what is noteworthy. In reporting on an interview with a teacher and parent, key points are noted, while trivial and irrelevant information is excluded. It stands to reason that the same kind of selectivity should be applied to test findings as well.

While psychological tests contribute a unique and valuable source of information, their contribution to the overall picture is arguably no greater than the other major sources of assessment of data—records, interviews, and observations. Key findings and consequent recommendations emerge from the convergence of data sources. Test results cannot be meaningfully interpreted without considering factors such as environment, prior experience, emotional status, cultural and language differences, and situational influences. Often, these factors carry so much explanatory power that test findings are uninterpretable or of lesser value.

The importance of cognitive testing is the subject of no small controversy. In conducting a fine-grained interpretation of cognitive test scores, evaluators implicitly subscribe to the logic of *aptitude-treatment interactions* (ATIs), the strategic matching of aptitudes with instructional approaches. The ATI premise is that a particular Intervention A will work best for an individual with a given profile of cognitive abilities, whereas Intervention B will work best with some other cognitive profile. However, despite a long history of attempts to establish such relationships, there is little empirical evidence to support the assumption that patterns of cognitive test scores correctly inform interventions (Cronbach & Snow, 1977; Fletcher & Miciak, 2017; Kranzler, Floyd, Benson, Zaboski, & Thibodaux, 2016). Such findings are elusive, in large part, because it is tenuous to rely on test scores alone. A given set of test results will not have the same implications for each child. Interpretation will be affected by variables such as learning opportunities, cultural and language differences, parent and teacher expectations, motivation, persistence, and emotion regulation. Cronbach (1975, p. 119) recognized this fact with his widely quoted conclusion about ATIs: "Once we attend to interactions, we enter a hall of mirrors that extends to infinity," which is to say, the interpretability of assessed abilities is vastly complicated by the multitude of impinging variables.

The ATI literature is instructive about the role of cognitive testing in some respects, but is also subject to misleading conclusions. The null findings in the search for ATIs serve as a caution against overinterpreting a pattern of cognitive test scores in isolation. Researchers rightfully question the extent to which cognitive and neuropsychological test scores can inform educational interventions (Consortium for Evidence-Based Early Intervention Practices, 2010; Floyd, 2010; Gresham & Witt, 1997; McDermott, Fantuzzo, & Glutting, 1990). It is unfair, however, to read ATI research as an overall indictment of cognitive testing. Testing can help the evaluator narrow down the hypothetical causes of learning and behavior problems to determine the appropriate focus of intervention: Is an intelligent child performing poorly in the classroom because of boredom, emotional distractors, or information-processing difficulties? Is a child not complying with teacher requests in order to get attention, to avoid challenging work, or because of oral communication deficits? Does the child struggle with reading because of deficits in vocabulary, memory, fluency, or phonological processing? Testing adds significant value when it helps identify the core difficulty to which an effective intervention can be applied. In most cases, differentiating between alternate interventions is not the primary outcome of an assessment

Furthermore, in citing quantitative ATI research, critics of cognitive testing disregard the importance of *qualitative* findings. Standardized cognitive tests provide rich clinical information as the examinee provides a wide sample of behaviors and verbalizations in responding to a fixed array of tasks and questions. The skilled evaluator understands that these qualitative findings impact the interpretation of test scores. Correspondingly, the value of cognitive testing should not be judged solely by its implications for curriculum and instruction. Much of its value emanates from its applicability to interventions of a psychological nature since findings about attitude and effort, priorities and preferences, and self-image and self-expectations have major implications for school performance. (See Box 3.4 in Chapter 3 for examples.)

The key here is to assign standardized testing to its proper place—not as a sole determinant of diagnostic formulations and recommendations, but as a unique contributor to the problem-solving process. This source of assessment data should neither be the predominant focus of an assessment, nor jettisoned as lacking value.

Readability

Harvey (1997) conducted readability analyses of practitioner reports, analyzing 40 assessment reports of school-age children: 20 by school psychologists and 20 by psychologists working in independent practice, clinics, and hospitals (see Table 2.1). The average reading difficulty of the school psychologists' reports was at college level, "the level at which writing is in danger of being misunderstood or ignored" (p. 272)—with a mean Flesch–Kincaid grade level of 13.6 and a mean Flesch reading ease score of 33. (As explained in Appendix A, the Flesch reading ease scale measures readability on a scale from 0 to 100, with scores below 30 rated as extremely difficult.) The average for the 20 clinical psychologists was at

TABLE 2.1. Reading Difficulty of Practitioners' Reports

	Flesch–Kincaid grade level		Flesch reading ease	
	Mean	SD	Mean	SD
School psychologists	13.6	2.1	33.3	10.2
Clinical psychologists	15.0	2.1	25.1	11.6

Note. Adapted from Harvey (1997).

an even higher level of difficulty, at the advanced college level, with a mean Flesch–Kincaid grade level of 15.0 and mean Flesch reading ease score of 25. Although there was a fair amount of variability within the sample, the reading level of almost every report was more difficult than what the general public would expectedly understand.

Weddig (1984) obtained similar results in analyzing the reading levels of 50 randomly selected psychoeducational assessment reports. The average report was written at mid-college level reading difficulty, and 30 percent of reports measured at the upper limit of the scale, grade 17+. (These findings cannot be directly compared with those of Harvey, as Weddig used a measure of reading difficulty other than the Flesch or Flesch–Kincaid scales.)

Demonstrating the close connection between readability and value to consumers, Hite (2017) conducted a study in which parents who had prior experience with psychoeducational assessments were asked to compare a consumer-responsive and a traditional version of the same assessment. The 153 participants each rated one of two sets of matched pairs of reports on a 10-item "usefulness" scale. Each pair of reports contained the same data, conclusions, and recommendations, but differed in reading level and amount of technical content. As shown in Table 2.2, participants rated the consumer-responsive versions as significantly more useful ($p < .001$), with effect sizes of over 0.7 for each pair.[1]

TABLE 2.2. Parents' Evaluation of Consumer-Responsive and Traditional Reports

	Flesch–Kincaid grade level	Flesch reading ease	Usefulness Scale		
			Mean	SD	Cohen's *d*
Comparison 1 (*n* = 80)					
Consumer-responsive report	8.3	58	55.73	12.14	0.71
Traditional report	13.3	33	45.80	15.69	
Comparison 2 (*n* = 73)					
Consumer-responsive report	8.9	56	53.67	12.28	0.71
Traditional report	15.9	28	43.99	14.85	

Note. Adapted from Hite (2017).

---

[1]Cohen's *d* was calculated for this table; Hite (2017) reported effect size using a different statistic.

Recent books on report writing by Hass and Carriere (2014) and by Schneider, Lichtenberger, Mather, Kaufman, and Kaufman (2018) have raised concerns about the accessibility of psychological reports and have proposed strategies to make them more readable. Whether calls for reform—this book included—will influence prevailing practice remains to be seen.

Length

Modern life moves at an increasingly fast pace, and there is stiff competition for limited attention spans. Much critical information is conveyed by concise email and text messages, and day-to-day comments are condensed into Twitter messages of 140 or 280 characters. Job applicants are advised to limit their résumés to a single page. Television news programs summarize current events in 60-second reports, punctuated by 10-second sound bites. Yet psychological assessment reports are lengthy and detailed, sometimes exceeding 30 pages. There is good reason to suspect that there is a marked discrepancy between what is written and what actually gets read.

Donders (2001) reported that the average length of a psychological report is five to seven single-spaced pages, although Groth-Marnat and Horvath (2006) note that report length will vary considerably according to the setting and purpose. Ackerman (2006) indicated that comprehensive reports used for forensic purposes are likely to run from 10 to 50 pages. Donders's (2001) estimate of five to seven pages seems low compared to the norm in our part of the world (New England). As a quasi-scientific check, we examined the sample psychoeducational reports submitted by licensed school psychologists as part of their applications for admission to a doctoral program in school psychology. (Granted, this was a limited and perhaps biased sample of aspiring practitioners who selected their work samples with the intent to impress.) The mean length of these 29 reports, not including data summary appendices, was over 10 single-spaced pages. Particularly striking was the wide variation, ranging from 2.5 to 19 pages, with a standard deviation of 4.8 pages.

The length of psychological reports is an outlier compared to the norm for other health and mental health disciplines. Physicians especially spend little time writing diagnostic evaluations. Why is that? In all likelihood, physicians would assert that the time devoted to documentation comes at the expense of direct contact with patients for diagnosis and treatment. They regard their time as too precious to spend writing detailed assessment reports—or even reading long psychological evaluations, for that matter. Stout and Cook (1999), in noting that "long narrative reports are of little pragmatic value to most non-psychiatric physicians" (p. 803), recommended that psychological reports for medical settings be limited to one or two pages, focusing on diagnosis and treatment. The implicit message is that highly trained professionals, whose time is valuable and in short supply, should parse their time strategically to optimize the benefit for the people they serve. Why would this logic not be applicable to school psychologists and clinical psychologists? (We return to this issue in Chapter 8.)

In considering what is needed to correct current trends in report writing, it helps to understand the influences that have sustained current practice.

WHY EVALUATORS DO WHAT THEY DO

Various explanations have been proposed for the persistence of difficult reading levels, overly technical language, and lack of clarity in psychological assessment reports (Groth-Marnat & Horvath, 2006; Harvey 2006, 2013; Ownby, 1997; Schneider et al., 2018). Notable influences include initial training, the use of technical language in academic settings, time constraints, and external pressures resulting from system expectations.

Initial Training

The process of becoming an accomplished evaluator is long and arduous. As Wiener and Costaris (2012) noted,

> Report writing is frequently difficult for graduate students in school psychology and clinical psychology. In addition to formulating the case, they need to think about how to communicate their ideas effectively. They typically have to adapt to the demands of different practicum supervisors who have different ideas about the nature of a good psychological report, some of which are contrary to the research evidence. (p. 120)

Graduate-level psychological assessment courses tend to focus on tests, which can skew the focus of initial report-writing efforts. Yet the time and effort devoted to testing is necessary in order to develop test-specific mastery of administration and scoring. Instructors appropriately emphasize that norm-referenced test scores are valid and meaningful only if examiners adhere closely to standardized procedures—verbatim instructions, specified presentation of stimuli, designated prompts and queries, prescribed allowances for feedback, accurate scoring, and so on. The importance of strict adherence to procedures is highlighted by research showing alarmingly high rates of administration and scoring errors by graduate students—*and* by practicing psychologists (Styck & Walsh, 2016). The next phase of acquiring proficiency with standardized psychological tests—figuring out what to make of the results—is a considerably more difficult proposition. Given what is required for graduate students to learn to analyze test results, integrate these results with other assessment data, and determine the meaningful implications of these findings, initial training can make only limited inroads with report writing.

Report writing is an especially imposing task. It requires high-level writing skills, plus sensitivity and judgment about *what* to report, as well as expertise in *how* to organize, interpret, and integrate findings. Inexperienced graduate students, faced with the daunting challenge of writing psychological reports, resort to strategies that are within reach at their present stage of development, such as rote reporting of scores or following examples found in textbooks or school files. These strategies typically result in something that is a far cry from a consumer-responsive approach.

What often gets lost in the process as students learn about standardized testing and report writing is an appreciation of what determines the ultimate value of an assessment: how to establish rapport with children, parents, and teachers, and how to present findings and recommendations in a manner that maximizes the likelihood that they will be accepted and put to use.

Academic Writing

Graduate students are immersed in learning environments where they are regularly exposed to technical material and sophisticated language. In doing so, they develop a sense of how to write in a professional manner. In various courses, they receive feedback from instructors about using APA style, steering clear of colloquial language, and using psychological terms in an accurate manner. Hence, they respond to these expectations when learning to write assessment reports. The result is a written product that looks professional and impressive, but may fail to communicate clearly so as to be of assistance to children and families. As Wiener and Costaris (2012) observed,

> [Students] naturally want their report to be credible and authoritative but sometimes confuse that with being erudite. As a result, they refer to themselves as "the examiner" instead of writing in the first person, use long sentences with passive voice and complex structure, and use long multisyllabic words. Their definitions of technical terms are often more difficult to understand than the term itself. (p. 131)

Harvey (1997) found that in spite of her extensive efforts to have students write simply and clearly, their reports were written at a high level of difficulty. In her graduate assessment course, Harvey emphasized the importance of writing in understandable language for parents. She provided explicit instruction about how to write accessible reports, including tips about how to increase readability. When students submitted assessment reports, Harvey provided feedback in the form of a Flesch grade level. Students who submitted reports with reading levels above grade 13.0 were advised to make revisions to improve readability. Despite these efforts, students made only modest improvements when they resubmitted reports, and the average reading level of reports remained above grade 13.0.

Ironically, overambitious writing can have the opposite effect of what the author intends. Oppenheimer (2006) conducted a series of experiments in which readers—in this case, Stanford University students—estimated the intelligence of the authors of writing samples. Subjects assigned lower estimates of intelligence to authors who used long and complex words that unnecessarily increased reading difficulty.

Turning to Templates

Templates and formulaic approaches have an obvious appeal for struggling graduate students. Their immediate goal is to respond to a challenging assignment, rather than to effect positive outcomes for the child. An instructor's exhortations to organize findings by theme, integrate data sources, and selectively cite test results go for naught when these expectations are beyond the student's current level of expertise. The exemplars that trainees are inclined to emulate are those that simplify the task by indiscriminately inserting task descriptions and test scores into a template.

Psychological Terms

Students in assessment courses are expected to master a lexicon of psychometric principles (e.g., standard deviations, confidence intervals, base rates, significant discrepancies) and psychological constructs (e.g., fluid reasoning, executive functions, phonological processing, working memory). Furthermore, to enable interpretation of test results, students are provided with complex descriptions of the constructs they measure. As examples, the Stanford–Binet Nonverbal Fluid Reasoning subtest measures "induction, general sequential reasoning, deductive reasoning, visualization, cognitive flexibility, and concentration" (Sattler, 2018, p. 573); the WISC Block Design subtest measures "the ability to analyze and synthesize abstract visual stimuli" (Wechsler, Raiford, & Holdnack, 2014, p. 8); and the Woodcock–Johnson Picture Recognition subtest involves "formation of iconic memories and matching of visual stimuli to stored representations" (Schrank & Wendling, 2012). These descriptions help evaluators interpret results, but inserting them uncritically into reports will befuddle most readers. The challenge for evaluators is to identify what aspects of psychological measures are relevant for the particular child and to convey the findings in a meaningful way.

When first learning to write reports, trainees try to get these psychological terms and principles "right" to assure instructors that they understand course content and can apply it as practicing psychologists do. The implicit assumption is that authoritative, technically precise language is expected and desirable—implorations to eschew obfuscation notwithstanding. And so, in conveying assessment findings, students employ the professional language at their disposal from textbooks and class notes.

As trainees become practitioners, the use of jargon and technical terms is not easily unlearned, especially after it has become part of a template or style that facilitates efficient production of written reports. It is no easy matter to replace terms that are applicable and precisely defined, albeit not well known to lay persons, with common words that best approximate the same meaning. There are few models or guides for translating technical terms into "plain English."

Is there something about the nature of psychological constructs that makes them impossible to explain in a straightforward, comprehensible manner? One could pose the same question about theoretical physics. It's not as though the theory of relativity could be expressed in simple language . . . or could it? The renowned astrophysicist Stephen Hawking did just that in his 1988 bestseller, *A Brief History of Time,* in which he explained the origin of the universe and other scientific-frontier discoveries to lay readers. His explanation of Einstein's theory of relativity scored a Flesch–Kincaid grade level of 11.3 and a Readability Ease score of 61, which is within the target range of mass media magazines and newspapers and is much easier reading than the average assessment report. It should be noted that Hawking's intent was not to impress, but to inform—to make complex theories and concepts accessible to non-scientists. Authors of psychological assessment reports might also take inspiration from *Thing Explainer: Complicated Stuff in Simple Words,* in which Randall Monroe (2015) describes the workings of nuclear reactors, tectonic plates, human organs, and the like using only the 1,000 most common words.

Established Models

Faced with the daunting challenge of learning to write psychological reports, trainees and early-career psychologists turn to examples provided in professional textbooks and in the field.

Professional Texts

Textbooks on assessment, with rare exceptions, provide sample reports that are long, technical, and written at a high level of difficulty.[2] Harvey (2006) analyzed the readability levels of 60 sample reports found in 20 professional texts published from 1990 to 2002. Of these reports, the 38 that were psychoeducational in nature had a mean Flesch reading ease score of 27.5 and a mean Flesch–Kincaid readability score of grade 18.5. The other 22 reports were described as clinical, neuropsychological, or forensic, and had a mean Flesch reading ease score of 20.9 and a mean Flesch–Kincaid readability score of grade 20.3. All 60 reports had a Flesch reading ease score below 50—what Flesch (1979) characterized as difficult to very difficult range—and only one report had a Flesch–Kincaid grade-level score below grade 14. Ironically, Harvey (2006, p. 8) reported that all 20 textbooks "recommended that psychologists write reports that are readable."

Lichtenstein (2014) conducted a similar analysis of sample reports in four assessment textbooks published subsequent to Harvey's (2006) study, and found readability levels of these reports to be at college level or above. Informal inspection of sample reports in more recent academic texts (e.g., Flanagan & Alfonso, 2017; Kaufman, Raiford, & Coalson, 2016) reveals that these "best practice" examples continue to be highly technical, replete with jargon, and heavily focused on test scores.

Emulating Current Practice

Challenged trainees and beginning psychologists also look to emulate models that are deemed acceptable in current practice. The formula-driven reports they are exposed to in the field offer a manageable and economical means of meeting coursework or job expectations. Exemplars that can be emulated with relative ease use a formulaic approach that is more descriptive of tests than of children. The typical formula involves (1) organizing findings by the tests that were administered; (2) citing all test scores, along with some indication of level of performance; and (3) describing cognitive testing tasks and what they ostensibly measure. Hence, much of the report is devoted to a Test Results and Interpretations section with passages like the following:

> The Visual–Spatial Index consists of two core subtests, Block Design and Visual Puzzles. On the Visual–Spatial scale, the student scored in the Low Average range, at the 17th percentile. The student scored in the Average range on the Block Design subtest, with a scaled score of 9. Block Design has the examinee view a pictured design and use red and white

---

[2] Sample reports by Hass and Carriere (2014) and by Lichtenstein and Axelrod (2016) are an exception to this trend.

blocks to recreate the design. It measures the ability to analyze and synthesize abstract visual stimuli. The student scored in the Below Average range on Visual Puzzles, with a scaled score of 5. On Visual Puzzles, the examinee works within a time limit to select three shapes from among several pictured options that, when assembled, will construct a given geometric design. This measures nonverbal reasoning and the ability to analyze and synthesize abstract visual stimuli.

Often, this sort of report will conclude with a cogent summary and recommendations that make little or no use of the reported test findings. Arguably, there is no harm done. In all likelihood, the reader could not make heads or tails of the test results section and paid little attention to it. Despite the low value of rote, technical reporting of test findings, the evaluator can continue in this manner because the format and style are consistent with common practice.

External Pressures

There are external influences in play that discourage practitioners from adopting more consumer-responsive report writing practices. Assessment practices are affected by caseload levels, time constraints, funding patterns, state and federal mandates, system requirements and expectations, service models, and adversarial challenges.

Time and Caseload Pressures

One of the most significant constraints on the assessment duties of evaluators is the weight of their assessment caseload. This is a factor for both school- and community-based evaluators. Mental health agencies may assign large assessment caseloads to meet client demands or budgetary targets. Similarly, independent evaluators may accept a high number of assessment referrals because professional services are in short supply or to maintain acceptable income levels.

It is common for school districts to set staffing levels near the minimum necessary to comply with special education mandates. Many states have ratios of over 2,000 students per school psychologist. The national average is around 1,400:1 (Charvat, 2011), which translates to average caseloads of about 50 students a year for re-evaluations alone. Heavy caseloads are especially common in financially strapped school systems, which tend to have disproportionately high rates of children with serious and multiple stressors. Thus, fewer services are available where more are needed.

A survey of over 1,000 school psychologists by Hosp and Reschly (2002) revealed that caseloads are often burdensome. They found that school psychologists devoted an average of 60% of their job-related time to special education eligibility services (conducting assessments, attending meetings, etc.), with averages ranging from 50.8 to 65.6% for different regions of the United States. School psychologists spent an average of 22.2 hours per week on assessments, with regional averages ranging from 18.8 to 26.5 hours. Based on the reported standard deviation of 11.0 hours, it is estimated that about one-quarter of school psychologists devote 30 or more hours per week to assessment. Other studies (Bramlett,

Murphy, Johnson, Wallingsford, & Hall, 2002; Castillo, Curtis, & Gelley, 2012) reflect that the assessment role of the school psychologist has not changed much over time.

Conducting multiple assessments each week does not allow for comprehensive evaluations that encompass the full complement of data sources, let alone thoughtful interpretation and integration of assessment data. Under the pressure of time constraints, overburdened evaluators find ways to make assessment caseloads manageable. What often falls by the wayside are classroom observations and gathering assessment data from teachers and parents (Allen & Hanchon, 2013). Another way to expedite report writing is to use a formulaic approach that relies heavily on stock phrases that are applicable to all children and on rote reporting of test scores with minimal interpretation.

Funding Patterns

Funding pattern can significantly shape the assessment practices of both school- and community-based evaluators. As already noted, school districts that contend with lean budgets by hiring the minimum possible number of school psychologists and other support personnel ensure high caseloads, which results in less comprehensive assessments and easily generated reports.

Community-based psychologists are also affected by funding issues. Reimbursement schedules of third-party payers, both public (e.g., school systems, Medicaid) and private (i.e., insurance companies) impact the nature of assessments because of what is reimbursed and what is not. Standardized testing is routinely reimbursed, while other valuable aspects of an assessment (e.g., observation in naturalistic settings, school visits, participation in school meetings, follow-up consultation with parents) may be excluded or reimbursed at a discouragingly low rate. These funding patterns encourage the use of standardized testing as the primary assessment method and reliance on written reports as the primary feedback mechanism.

Other systemic influences may impact assessment practices as well. This is particularly true for school systems.

School-System Policies and Expectations

Assessment reports are shaped by state and local school-system policies and expectations, both explicit and implicit. These policies and expectations impact the content and comprehensiveness of assessments and the focus and format of assessment reports.

State policies—which are manifested through regulations, guidelines, funding, and technical assistance—and school-system practices reflect their underlying philosophy about intervention, which in turn will promote a particular approach to assessment. A system that relies on special education as the primary means of serving students with academic struggles will emphasize eligibility determinations. Consequently, evaluations are expected to inform disability determinations, and less importance is afforded to recommendations and their subsequent implementation and monitoring. In contrast, a state or school district may rely on an RTI model, which will favor assessments that depend on direct measures of academic performance and behavior, rather than on cognitive and neuropsychological testing, and tend to be less technical.

Some school districts require or expect evaluators to report exact test scores, rather than descriptive ranges or confidence intervals. Although this expectation may be just a function of customary practice, it is likely to foster reliance on test data to inform disability identification, such as IQ and adaptive behavior scores to diagnose intellectual disability, or ability and achievement scores to diagnose learning disability. This practice tends to discount the kind of clinical judgment that evaluators need to apply in integrating assessment findings from multiple sources. The misguided notion that test scores translate directly into disability determinations enables special education administrators and untrained IEP team members to base eligibility decisions on simplistic formulas.

School districts often assign the components of an educational evaluation along discipline-based lines. It may be the special education teacher who assesses academic achievement, the school social worker who conducts parent interviews, and the speech and language therapist who assesses phonological processing. Depending on how and when these various findings are shared, the net effect may be to reduce the school psychologist's opportunity to integrate data sources for optimal interpretation of assessment findings. Alternatively, a school district (or agency) may systematically promote integration of data by ensuring that findings are shared among evaluation team members, perhaps even compiling the assessments of several evaluators into a single multidisciplinary report.

State and federal mandates also play a role. Concerns about being out of compliance are a major concern for school administrators, and are communicated in no uncertain terms to front-line staff. Special education mandates require assessments to be completed within a given time frame—within 60 days of referral (the default per federal regulations) or some other interval specified by state regulations. These regulations can reduce the comprehensiveness of assessments by restricting the time that can be invested in data gathering and report writing, especially during peak referral periods.

Defensive Practice

School district practices are often influenced by the possibility that parents will exercise their due process rights under special education. Only a small percentage of special education cases go to mediations or hearings, but they consume a disproportionate amount of administrators' time and school district dollars. Hence, school district policies and practices may be significantly shaped by the objective of minimizing the district's exposure.

Assessment reports play a significant role in disputes over education plans. When families disagree with the programs or services offered by a school district, they have an array of due process procedures at their disposal, including complaints, mediations, resolution meetings, hearings, and court cases. As specified by federal law (i.e., the Individuals with Disabilities Education Act [IDEA]), IEPs are based on the findings of educational evaluations. A parent may request an independent evaluation either because of disagreement with a school district's evaluation or, more often the case, because new or different input may justify an alternative education plan. The independent evaluation—typically documented with a long and abstruse report—is implicitly pitted against the school district's evaluation. Hence, the threat of due process reinforces the tendency for school reports to be lengthy and technical, ostensibly to measure up to independent evaluations in influencing mediators, hearing officers, and judges.

Consumer Expectations

Community-based independent evaluators are subject to the influence of consumer needs and expectations. When evaluators are engaged by a parent or a social services agency to conduct an evaluation to counter the findings or recommendations of a school system, there is implicit pressure to produce a lengthy and authoritative report.

Independent evaluators may also conduct assessments to document the need for disability accommodations, such as extra time, a scribe, or a private testing room. Individuals with disabilities may be granted these accommodations on high-stakes standardized tests (e.g., the ACT, SAT, GRE, Praxis) or for college or graduate school courses. The written assessment report provides documentation that informs these high-stakes decisions. Lengthy technical reports that exhaustively analyze standardized testing results are presumed to most effectively serve this function. It is questionable, however, whether this assumption is well founded (an issue that we address in Chapter 7).

THE CHALLENGE FOR PRACTITIONERS

Report-writing practices have changed very little despite decades of well-deserved criticism. In conference and workshop presentations on report writing by ourselves and others, we have observed that practitioners nod approvingly and offer supportive comments about a consumer-responsive approach to reporting. Yet, such practices are infrequently seen in the field.

Practitioners have good intentions of applying consumer-responsive practices, but the countervailing forces are considerable. Reform efforts are counteracted by training experiences, school system and agency expectations, time pressures, funding patterns, and human nature. Consumer-responsive assessment requires a high degree of expertise that is attained over an extended period of reflective practice and clinical supervision. For practitioners to adopt a consumer-responsive approach may call for substantial investment in learning new skills or advocating for their acceptance by institutions. As discussed in some of the chapters that follow, it is preferable but challenging to organize reports in a child-centered manner that varies from case to case. Finding clear, straightforward ways to convey complex psychological constructs is a tall order, and illustrative examples and guides are scarce. A simple codebook will not suffice since explanations of constructs should be customized on a case-by-case basis; for example, an explanation of executive functions might be either concise or detailed, and might emphasize either planning, organization, or self-monitoring.

Learning to write consumer-responsive reports calls for flexibility, skill, and patience. It may take years, decades even, for an evaluator to become proficient and efficient at producing clear, informative, high-impact reports. However, trainees and practitioners who hold themselves to high standards will weather the obstacles and resist easy solutions that undermine the path to advanced expertise. If you are up to the challenge, read on!

CHAPTER 3

Assessment Fundamentals

The consumer-responsive principles and practices espoused in this book will help evaluators conduct high-impact assessments and effectively report findings, *provided that* the evaluator applies overall sound assessment practices. This chapter briefly overviews "assessment fundamentals"—what skilled evaluators routinely do in conducting assessments, whether or not they employ a consumer-responsive approach. These fundamental elements include (1) assessment planning and design, (2) the use of multiple data sources, and (3) clinical skills that promote positive interactions with examinees, informants, and consumers. Such material is typically covered at greater length in comprehensive assessment textbooks.

Since psychological and psychoeducational assessments of children are most often conducted for special education purposes, this book uses the terminology of this system. Special education mandates use the terms *evaluation* and *re-evaluation* to refer to the overall process of collecting data to inform IEP team decisions. To plan the evaluation, team members review the initial information on hand (e.g., from school records, a referral form, or previous evaluations) and, on the basis of that review, determine the requisite elements of the evaluation design (see Box 3.1). The evaluation design may call for individual *assessments* in various areas, including but not limited to psychological assessment. Other possible areas include speech and language, occupational, and psychiatric assessments. The psychological assessment may encompass various areas of functioning, such as cognitive skills and abilities, social–emotional functioning, adaptive behavior, and academic achievement.

ASSESSMENT DESIGN

To design a useful assessment, the evaluator must chart a course of action that is guided by a clear sense of purpose. The general purposes for which children are evaluated are fairly standard: (1) to help parents, teachers, and other service providers better understand the

BOX 3.1. Federal Special Education Regulations That Govern Evaluation Design

Federal special education regulations provide specific guidance about the essential purposes and process for designing educational evaluations.

SECTION 300.305 ADDITIONAL REQUIREMENTS FOR EVALUATIONS AND RE-EVALUATIONS

(a) Review of existing evaluation data. As part of an initial evaluation (if appropriate) and as part of any reevaluation under this part, the IEP team and other qualified professionals, as appropriate, must—

    (1) Review existing evaluation data on the child, including—

        (i) Evaluations and information provided by the parents of the child;

        (ii) Current classroom-based, local, or state assessments, and classroom-based observations; and

        (iii) Observations by teachers and related services providers; and

    (2) On the basis of that review, and input from the child's parents, identify what additional data, if any, are needed to determine—

        (i)

            (A) Whether the child is a child with a disability, as defined in Sec. 300.8, and the educational needs of the child; or

            (B) In case of a reevaluation of a child, whether the child continues to have such a disability, and the educational needs of the child;

        (ii) The present levels of academic achievement and related developmental needs of the child;

        (iii)

            (A) Whether the child needs special education and related services; or

            In the case of a reevaluation of a child, whether the child continues to need special education and related services; and

        (iv) Whether any additions or modifications to the special education and related services are needed to enable the child to meet the measurable annual goals set out in the IEP of the child and to participate, as appropriate, in the general education curriculum.

---

child (i.e., his functioning, behavior, circumstances, difficulties, strengths, etc.) and (2) to identify what interventions and supports are likely to produce positive outcomes. These purposes are equally applicable to assessments conducted by school personnel, community agencies, and independent evaluators. However, every referral is unique, and the evaluator must take stock of case-specific purposes and circumstances that will influence how the assessment is approached.

Consent or Contracting

For school-based special education evaluations, the IDEA requires that the school team notify the parent of the proposed assessment design and obtain consent in order to proceed. Federal special education regulations define consent in general terms only (i.e., according to Sec. 300.9, "The parent has been fully informed of all information relevant to the activity for which consent is sought, in his or her native language, or through another mode of communication."). But as Sattler (2018, p. 80) notes, there is more to *informed consent,* which school districts should attend to:

> From both an ethical and a legal perspective, informed consent does not mean merely getting the child and/or parents to sign a form. Rather it involves a thorough discussion in a language they can understand regarding the purposes, goals, and potential uses of the assessment. . . .

The description of the proposed assessment, however, need not be overly detailed. It is sufficient to describe the procedures to be used and the areas to be assessed (e.g., classroom observation, academic achievement tests, parent and teacher behavior rating scales), rather than the names of specific tests and measures. This gives the evaluator the latitude to select the most appropriate measure as the assessment unfolds. If a parent or third party (e.g., advocate, physician) has concerns about the specific tests to be used, the evaluator might indicate the most likely choice and offer to contact the parent if some alternate measure is being considered. The operating principle that governs practice is that consent is not a matter of obtaining a signature on a form, but rather, of conveying the type and extent of information that the consumer needs in order to make decisions.

An independent evaluator is not subject to the same mandates and procedural requirements as school personnel, but should undergo a comparable process of clarifying in advance the focus of the assessment and what data will be collected. This constitutes, in effect, an informal contract with the client.

Individualized Assessment

A psychological or psychoeducational assessment is not a fixed entity. A core principle is that a psychoeducational or psychological assessment is *individualized*—designed to address the referral questions, circumstances, and needs of the individual child. Using a standard assessment battery, rather than one customized for the specific child, is at odds with this principle. As expressed by Cates (1999),

> The appropriate assessment is tailored to the needs of the client, the referral source, or both. A clothing store that offered the customer an expensive one-size-fits-all garment would not long be in business. The temptation to remain with the familiar is an easy one to rationalize but may serve the client poorly. (p. 637)

While best practice calls for individualized batteries, studies of school psychologists' assessment practices suggest that at least one component, intelligence testing, is included in most assessments, regardless of the reason for referral (Shapiro & Heick, 2004; Sotelo-Dynega & Dixon, 2014).

Using the same fixed template for every report is inconsistent with the concept of individualized assessment. It results in reliance on the same array of assessment data (e.g., classroom observations and standardized tests) and similar weighting of different areas of functioning (e.g., cognitive vs. social–emotional), regardless of referral questions. A formulaic approach may expedite report writing, but it is likely to shortchange children, families, and educators.

Designing an individualized assessment is guided by several considerations. First and foremost, the evaluator must have a clear understanding of the referral questions and concerns, such as academic underachievement, misbehavior, emotional distress, difficulty taking tests, or a suspected learning disability (LD). The evaluator should take stock of what is already known (e.g., from school records or prior evaluations) and what information is readily available from those who know the child well (e.g., parents, teachers, and other service providers). Given the referral questions and existing information, the evaluator must determine how best to assess the areas of functioning and the child's circumstances. The evaluator considers not just characteristics intrinsic to the child, but also environmental variables that influence how the child thinks and behaves. How is the child affected by family and cultural expectations? What traits are valued by the child's peer group and teachers? What kinds of academic demands and school climate are the child exposed to?

Situational factors may also affect how an assessment is conceptualized and carried out. Time may be of the essence because a child is out of school or out of control, thereby putting a premium on rapid completion. Workplace diplomacy may be a concern, as in the case of a teacher who is floundering with instruction or behavior management, consequently referring several students who clearly do not meet disability criteria. Consultation with parents may be the critical concern, such as when a parent has difficulty accepting that a child has a serious disability. Such circumstances may dictate the choice of assessment procedures or how extensive an assessment battery to conduct. A short report may be more productive than a long one for conveying just one or two essential recommendations, whereas a long and detailed report may serve best to document a complicated history for the benefit of multiple service providers. The experienced practitioner recognizes that situational factors call for flexibility.

Selectivity

Evaluators should be selective in the choice of assessment procedures. The reasoning behind this goes beyond concerns about relevance and economy of effort. It follows from the premise that every assessment procedure is invasive; by its nature, assessment claims time from the child and parent, imposes on privacy, and may alter the course of the child's and family's life. Such impositions are balanced against the benefits of an assessment: it can inform important decisions and contribute to positive outcomes. An assessment, while valuable, should be limited to procedures that directly address referral questions and concerns.

Hypothesis Testing

Hypothesis testing is critical to assessment design. The evaluator generates hypotheses that may explain the cause or nature of referral concerns, and selects assessment procedures to test these hypotheses. For example, a first grader's struggles with word decoding may be related to phonological processing or to inattention, possibilities that can be investigated by

---

BOX 3.2. Hypothesis-Testing Example

Consider the case of Derek, age 10, who is referred by school personnel because of concerns about inappropriate social behavior. The evaluator may have several hypotheses regarding the cause of his behavior. The assessment is then designed to test each of these possible explanations. The recommended interventions may vary considerably depending on which hypothesis best explains the behavior.

Hypothesis	Assessment data to test hypothesis
Autism	Parent interview; autism rating scale; autism diagnosis test
Thought disorder	Child and parent interviews; broad-based rating scales of behavior and adjustment (parent, teacher, and self); projective testing
Attention-seeking behavior	Functional behavioral assessment
Communication disorder	Standardized testing of expressive and receptive language; speech and writing samples; assessment by a speech and language pathologist

---

standardized testing and by ratings scales, respectively. Or, to pursue a referral question concerning a child's inappropriate social behavior, the evaluator might select measures that explore hypotheses regarding autism, a thought disorder, attention-seeking behavior, or a communication disorder (see Box 3.2).

Hypotheses typically follow from referral questions and concerns, but they also emerge during the course of an assessment. Consider, for example, a referral of a kindergarten child with delayed language development and limited academic skills, with educational performance as the focal concern. Standardized testing confirms the hypothesis that the child has an intellectual disability. However, in the process of data collection, it emerges that the child has been bullied by older children. Now there are other hypotheses to investigate: Does the child respond in a way that encourages the bullying behavior? Are certain settings (e.g., the school bus) in need of closer supervision? Have these incidents contributed to the child's dislike and avoidance of school?

DATA SOURCES

A fundamental principle of assessment is to make use of multiple sources of assessment data. Federal special education regulations (U.S. Department of Education, 2006) explicitly direct school personnel to "[u]se a variety of assessment tools and strategies to gather relevant functional, developmental, and academic information about the child" (Sec. 300.304(b) (1)). Similarly, the NASP (2010b) *Principles for Professional Ethics* state, "A psychological or psychoeducational assessment is based on a variety of different types of information from different sources" (Standard II.3.3).

The acronym "RIOT" is used to identify four major sources of assessment data: Records, Interviews, Observation, and Testing. Each source has unique value as well as limitations. Observations and ratings scales provide "authentic" data—how a child behaves in everyday situations, responding to prevailing environmental influences and expectations. It would seem that actual behavior is indicative of a child's true nature and characteristics, but it is also situation dependent. A child who is faced with different task demands or social situations may display other behaviors and may function less or more successfully. Tests, by comparison, present each child with the same material, administered under the same conditions. Thus, standardized testing yields results that can be objectively compared to that of other children or to some expected level of performance. But tests have significant limitations as well and cannot tell the whole story. They must be interpreted in context, with knowledge of a child's personal, family, and educational history, and with an understanding of current supports, demands, and stressors.

A well-conceived assessment compiles data from multiple sources with an eye toward integrating findings. An isolated finding—an informant's report of atypical behavior, a significantly high or low subtest score—should be regarded as a hypothesis to be tested. When compared with other findings for confirmatory evidence, the hypothesis may be supported or contradicted. The evaluator looks for a pattern of convergent findings to arrive at clinical impressions with a high degree of certainty.

Review of Records

It is usually the case that some relevant information about a referred child has already been collected. The evaluator might access the school file for basic information about the family, performance in past grades, attendance and tardiness, disciplinary actions, health status, and special services provided. Educational, medical, developmental, or psychological evaluations may have been conducted previously. The child may have received services or supports that provide clues as to what has worked and what hasn't. Information from records yields high value for the time invested. This is not a step to be bypassed. In fact, federal special education regulations explicitly direct the school team to review existing data as the first step in designing an educational evaluation (see Box 3.1). School districts typically use a written form to document the reason(s) for referral and summarize pertinent information from existing records.

Interviewing

Interviews provide rich background information, revealing much about the nature of the child and how the child interacts with the environment at home, in school, and in the community. Goldfinger and Pomerantz (2014) identify several types of interviews, each serving distinct purposes: (1) intake interviews, (2) diagnostic interviews, (3) mental status examinations, (4) crisis interviews, and (5) assessment interviews. Interviews with third-party informants serve multiple purposes. In addition to eliciting information, direct contact with key informants helps the evaluator understand the influences and attitudes of significant persons in the child's life and sets the stage for constructive and collaborative problem solving with the evaluator.

Various informants may contribute to background information. Parents and teachers in particular are valuable sources. Parents have the most access to information about the child and have the greatest influence on a child's life. Teachers have a profound, albeit time-limited, impact on a child, and possess unique information about how the child functions in educational and social situations. It is always advisable to interview one or more parents and one or more teachers as part of an assessment. Face-to-face contact is ideal, but given the various circumstances that may pose obstacles (e.g., time pressures, scheduling difficulties), the evaluator may need to consider other possible means of obtaining such information, such as telephone, Internet (e.g., Skype, Viber, Zoom), and written communication.

When a team-evaluation model is used, the role of conducting in-depth interviews may be assumed by one member of the team, possibly someone other than the evaluating psychologist. Nevertheless, the evaluating psychologist should seek some opportunity for direct contact with the parent—at least through a phone call—to introduce herself and the evaluation process, to clarify concerns, and to establish a foundation for subsequent contacts.

There are cases in which direct interaction with a parent or teacher is the most essential aspect of the assessment, for example:

1. When a parent is first confronted with the finding that the child has a serious disability that will have lifelong implications for the child and family.
2. When assessment findings are highly discrepant with the parent's or teacher's perception of the child or understanding of the situation.
3. When the teacher–child relationship or home situation is the crux of the referral question.

There are numerous topics and questions that the evaluator might pursue, some of which are guided by the referral concerns, and some of which are routinely of interest. Texts by McConaughy (2013) and Braaten (2007) are rich sources of interview questions. However, the process—the nature of the verbal interaction—is every bit as important as the content. As noted by Andren (2013, p. 144), "Interviewing requires more than knowing what questions to ask. Listening, establishing a positive relationship, and synthesizing information are essential for successful outcomes." Relational aspects and other consumer-responsive interviewing practices are discussed in detail in Chapter 4.

Types of Interviews

Interviews may be *unstructured, semistructured,* or *structured.* An unstructured interview relies entirely on the practitioner to determine the areas of interest or concern and how to ask about them. Thus, what is covered can vary greatly from one interviewer to another; the focus depends on the interviewer's clinical skills, plus a certain amount of luck. The interview may yield invaluable, in-depth information about some critically important aspect or may overlook a key area.

Conversely, a structured interview asks the same questions in the same way. While this approach ensures comprehensive coverage, it can be time-consuming, since some topics may be irrelevant to the given case. A standard set of questions may be posed more efficiently in a written questionnaire. A broadband questionnaire will ask a parent about a wide range of domains (e.g., family constellation, family history and health, prenatal and perinatal history, primary caregivers, child care, early developmental history, medical history, educational history, friendships, interests and hobbies, behavior and temperament)—far more than could be practically addressed in an interview. Note that any of these domains might become the subject of a paragraph or subsection in the Background Information of a report, or might be omitted because they are uninformative or irrelevant. However, a written questionnaire is not always feasible or desirable. It assumes that a parent is literate, forthcoming, and willing and able to take on this time-consuming task.

A semistructured interview taps the advantages of both structured and unstructured interviewing methods, enabling both broad coverage and flexibility. The interviewer addresses various broad areas (e.g., family structure, medical and developmental history, educational record, social relations, interests, strengths), perhaps with an initial plan about which to prioritize. Domains are introduced with a general, open-ended question, such as "Tell me about Boris's health and medical history," or "What does Natasha do in her free time?" Based on the response, the evaluator may follow up to obtain additional details. A productive strategy when pursuing an area of importance is to request a description of characteristic behavior. When the informant identifies a general concern or issue (e.g., "Elroy doesn't get his work done in class,"; "Judy has problems with other kids on the playground"), the interviewer asks for a specific description of the behavior (e.g., "What does Elroy do during a work period in class?"; "What happens with Judy during a typical recess period?").

Observation

Naturalistic observation of a child in her everyday school, home, or play environment not only provides authentic information about how the child behaves, but it also generates insights into the demands and conditions of the environment and how the child responds to them. Deciding how and when to observe should be guided by the referral questions and concerns. A child with a reading problem might be observed when asked to read aloud, whereas observing a child with aggressive behavior during unstructured time and transitions between activities might be instructive.

The evaluator must choose between a qualitative approach, known as *narrative* or *free* observation, in which the evaluator keeps an open-ended running account of noteworthy behavior, and *systematic* observation methods, in which specified target behaviors are quantified in some way. Narrative observation relies on the evaluator's clinical skills in determining what behavior to record and how to describe it. Wilson and Reschly (1996) found that the narrative method is used by practitioners far more often than systematic observation. Narrative observation allows for rich documentation of the context in which behavior occurs—what is demanded of the child, how others respond, environmental conditions, and so on. This relationship between environmental triggers and the child's behavior may be directed toward a specific behavior of concern using an A-B-C model, documenting the Antecedents that precede the Behavior and the Consequences that follow. These findings can inform interventions that modify the behavior by altering the environmental antecedents and consequences.

Naturalistic observations should be reported in a "low-inference" manner, describing what is observed without making assumptions or attributions about intentions or underlying causes. Rather than say that a child is oppositional or stubborn, the evaluator describes how frequently, and in what manner, he ignores teacher requests. Rather than infer that a child is sleepy or bored, the evaluator reports that she closed her eyes and rested her head on the desk for several minutes at a time. Nevertheless, a certain degree of inference is unavoidable. We trust the evaluator's judgment in reporting that a child looked sad without describing what the sad face looked like (downturned lips, furrowed brow, downcast eyes, etc.).

Systematic observation quantifies preselected behaviors using methods such as frequency, duration, latency, and time sampling. These methods are useful for documenting the occurrence or magnitude of some discrete behavior (e.g., not completing assignments, out of seat, cursing) and establishing a baseline level prior to implementation of an intervention. Time sampling is widely used to estimate the percentage of time that a child is on task, as this *replacement behavior* is a common goal in classroom settings. (A cardinal principle is to set a goal of increasing the positive behavior that should be exhibited, rather than just eliminating negative behavior. A goal that can be accomplished by a dead person is not conducive to personal growth.) Readers are referred to Hintze, Volpe, and Shapiro (2008) and to Gischlar (2014) for informative chapters on systematic observation methods.

Direct observation will yield more data in some situations than in others. Observing in early childhood settings, where children move about and have frequent changes in activity, will dependably yield rich data, while observing middle or high school classrooms in which students do independent seatwork or listen to a teacher lecture may prove a poor use of time. Observation is a critical component when assessing a child referred for externalizing behavior, and is likely to keep the evaluator busy recording relevant behaviors. Observing a child with internalizing behavior may yield far less data, but equally important assessment findings.

As with every type of assessment data, we are concerned with the reliability and validity of observations. When observing in a naturalistic setting such as a classroom or playgroup, there is the implicit assumption that what the evaluator observes is representative of the child's behavior. For adequate reliability, the evaluator should observe the child for the better part of an hour, if not more, and in multiple settings. Since the child's behavior on a given occasion may or may not be a representative sample, greater certainty is gained by asking a teacher, parent, or caretaker who knows the child well whether the observed behavior was typical. Close correspondence between direct observations and teacher information is strong evidence of a robust finding. When the two are discrepant, there are other possibilities to consider, for example, that the child's behavior is situation specific (e.g., the child behaves differently in structured and unstructured situations or with different teachers) or that the child was aware of being observed and altered his behavior. To reduce the likelihood that the evaluator's presence will affect the child's behavior, it is advisable to conduct observations prior to testing or interviewing the child for the assessment.

Even when a representative sample of behavior is obtained, the observed behavior should be regarded as indicative of how the child behaves in that particular situation—as influenced by the teacher and peers and by setting-specific expectations or task demands. Was the child observed in a class on a favorite subject or in the one that plagues her? Was he interacting with a preferred teacher or with an irritating classroom aide? Furthermore, a child's behavior will vary somewhat from situation to situation, and from day to day. Was the child observed on a day that she was extremely stressed or when things were going smoothly?

Assuming the evaluator has obtained a typical sample of the child's behavior, what interpretations should then be made? There are no norms that indicate the extent to which the child should be on task, interacting with peers, or responding to a teacher's directions. This stands to reason, since behavior is highly determined by environmental circumstances. (This is the whole point of *schoolwide positive behavioral supports:* to provide a supportive, reinforcing school environment in which all children behave better!) However, a meaningful basis for interpreting a given child's behavior is noting how other children behave in the same situation. A procedure used by many observational systems is to compare recorded behaviors for the "target" child with that of other children in the same setting.

Observations of a child during testing and interviewing also yield valuable data. These observations may or may not match up with those of the child in a classroom or at home. The assessment session is a unique situation, removed from usual circumstances and expectations—a chance for the child to present a different, and perhaps preferred, impression. The assessment setting also provides rich information because it is standardized in many respects—not just in how testing tasks are presented, but in how the evaluator explains the situation, establishes rapport, asks interview questions, and so on. This enables meaningful comparisons between that child and others who have been presented with the same conditions. Over time, the practitioner develops a personal database—a set of clinical norms that serve as a basis for interpreting behavior during assessment sessions.

Observations during testing may enrich or modify the interpretation of test scores. The evaluator takes note of cognitive characteristics (e.g., problem-solving strategies, quality of language, awareness and self-correcting of errors), as well as attitudinal and behavioral patterns (e.g., social skills, persistence, reaction to failure, affect). Checklists of behaviors to note during testing, such as those provided by Sattler (2018) or included in the records forms of many tests, can be helpful.

As a practical matter, the evaluator's opportunity to observe is limited with respect to both time and settings. Hence, evaluators rely on "secondhand observations"—input from people who have had extended contact with the child, such as a parent, caretaker, or teacher. Their cumulative impressions of a child's behavior or functioning can be objectively assessed using rating scales.

Rating Scales

Ratings scales elicit the observations and impressions of individuals who know a child well. What distinguishes a rating scale from a checklist or survey is the quantifying of responses to yield scores that can be interpreted on a norm-referenced basis. The scores provide an objective basis for determining how a child's behavior compares to others of a similar age and, possibly, of the same gender. To reduce subjectivity, a well-designed rating scale standardizes items by specifying the applicable period of time (e.g., the past month) and the frequency of the observed behavior (e.g., never, rarely, once a week, once a day, multiple times a day). Although rating scales resemble structured interviews with respect to information sources and content, we associate them with tests because they generate norm-referenced scores. Hence, rating scale results are typically included in the Test Results section of a report.

Rating scales have several distinct advantages. They offer economy of time and effort, compared to observing a child or interviewing a third party in person. They also tap into a larger data pool. While an evaluator can directly observe only a limited sample of behavior, ratings scales have informants summarize impressions formed over an extended period of weeks or months. Informants may have observed behaviors that are highly significant but infrequently seen, such as self-injurious behavior or cruelty to animals.

To get a full picture of a child's behavior, the evaluator may seek information from multiple informants. Rating scales are typically designed and normed for different informants: parents, teachers, or self-ratings by the assessed individual. Obtaining information from several sources can strengthen interpretations when findings are confirmatory or may complicate matters when findings are inconsistent.

Comprehensive rating scales are often employed when children are referred for social–emotional or behavioral concerns. *Broadband* measures, such as the Behavior Assessment System for Children (BASC), the Conners Comprehensive Behavioral Rating Scales, and the Achenbach System of Empirically Based Assessment (ASEBA), are composed of scales for rating several domains of externalizing behavior (e.g., hyperactivity, aggression, conduct problems) and of internalizing behavior (e.g., anxiety, depression, social withdrawal). These scales can identify clinically significant differences from the norm, signified by scores that are more than 1.5 or 2 standard deviations from the mean (i.e., *T* scores over 65 or 70, respectively). They also generate *ipsative* data—a profile in which an individual's norm-referenced ratings of behavior are compared across different areas (e.g., How atypical is the child's reported level of aggression compared to her levels of anxiety and depression?).

Narrow-band rating scales assess in depth a single aspect of behavior, such as executive functions, attention, adaptive behavior, social skills, or depression. Recently, rating measures have been developed to identify social and interpersonal strengths and assets (e.g., the Devereux Student Strengths Assessment and the Social Emotional Assets and Resilience Scales).

Rating scales must be interpreted with caution, since they convey the impressions of the informant and are subject to bias. An informant may be inaccurate, or even have reason to purposefully minimize, exaggerate, or distort. A parent may minimize misbehavior, feeling the need to convey that he is doing a good job (better than the ex!). A teacher may exaggerate learning problems to justify having made the referral or to ensure that help is on the way. High levels of parenting stress can have a negative effect on agreement among informants (van der Oord, Prins, Oosterlaan, & Emmelkamp, 2006). Raters may also differ in their reports on the same child because they see similar behavior through a different lens, or because they observe the child in different circumstances. Expectations and stressors may be different at school and at home, or the child may have reason to behave differently with her father than with her mother.

Testing

A defining characteristic of testing is the objectivity that ensues from standardized administration and scoring procedures. A child's scores on carefully standardized tasks can be meaningfully compared to the performance of other children the same age, grade, or gender (in the case of norm-referenced tests), or to some expected level of performance (in the case of criterion-referenced tests). Many facets of valid and responsible test use, such as evaluator qualifications and the selection of nondiscriminatory measures, are codified in federal special education regulations (see Box 3.3). Effective use of tests depends on a number of factors: strategic test selection, adherence to standardized procedures, adept interaction with the examinee, and skillful interpretation.

BOX 3.3. Evaluation Procedures Required Under Federal Special Education Regulations

SECTION 300.304 EVALUATION PROCEDURES

(b) Conduct of evaluation. In conducting the evaluation, the public agency must—

    (1) Use a variety of assessment tools and strategies to gather relevant functional, developmental, and academic information about the child, including information provided by the parent, that may assist in determining—

        (i) Whether the child is a child with a disability under Sec. 300.8; and

        (ii) The content of the child's IEP, including information related to enabling the child to be involved in and progress in the general education curriculum (or for a preschool child, to participate in appropriate activities);

    (2) Not use any single measure or assessment as the sole criterion for determining whether a child is a child with a disability and for determining an appropriate educational program for the child; and

    (3) Use technically sound instruments that may assess the relative contribution of cognitive and behavioral factors, in addition to physical or developmental factors.

(c) Other evaluation procedures. Each public agency must ensure that—

    (1) Assessments and other evaluation materials used to assess a child under this part—

        (i) Are selected and administered so as not to be discriminatory on a racial or cultural basis;

        (ii) Are provided and administered in the child's native language or other mode of communication and in the form most likely to yield accurate information on what the child knows and can do academically, developmentally, and functionally, unless it is clearly not feasible to so provide or administer;

        (iii) Are used for the purposes for which the assessments or measures are valid and reliable;

        (iv) Are administered by trained and knowledgeable personnel; and

        (v) Are administered in accordance with any instructions provided by the producer of the assessments.

    (2) Assessments and other evaluation materials include those tailored to assess specific areas of educational need and not merely those that are designed to provide a single general intelligence quotient.

    (3) Assessments are selected and administered so as best to ensure that if an assessment is administered to a child with impaired sensory, manual, or speaking skills, the assessment results accurately reflect the child's aptitude or achievement level or whatever other factors the test purports to measure, rather than reflecting the child's impaired sensory, manual, or speaking skills (unless those skills are the factors that the test purports to measure).

    (4) The child is assessed in all areas related to the suspected disability, including, if appropriate, health, vision, hearing, social and emotional status, general intelligence, academic performance, communicative status, and motor abilities.

    (5) Assessments of children with disabilities who transfer from one public agency to another public agency in the same school year are coordinated with those children's prior and subsequent schools, as necessary and as expeditiously as possible, consistent with Sec. 300.301(d)(2) and (e), to ensure prompt completion of full evaluations.

    (6) In evaluating each child with a disability under Sec. Sec. 300.304 through 300.306, the evaluation is sufficiently comprehensive to identify all of the child's special education and related services needs, whether or not commonly linked to the disability category in which the child has been classified.

    (7) Assessment tools and strategies that provide relevant information that directly assists persons in determining the educational needs of the child are provided.

Test Selection

Assessment measures should be selected to efficiently address the referral concerns and relevant areas of functioning for the given child. There may be child-specific reasons to favor certain tests over others, such as age and developmental level, language differences or limitations, sensory impairment, ability to sustain attention, or frustration tolerance. The extent to which an evaluation relies on tests versus other sources of assessment data will vary from case to case. Conventional psychological assessments tend to rely heavily on standardized tests. However, behavioral observations and third-party reports from interviews and rating scales will at times yield the most relevant information, for example, when attention or behavior is the primary concern. In some cases, little or no standardized testing may be warranted, such as for a procedurally required re-evaluation of a child who is receiving appropriate services and making good progress.

Some tests are simply better than others because they are adequately standardized and normed, and have strong evidence of reliability and validity. There are many published tests that fail to meet these standards, as Oscar Buros would lament in his preface to early volumes of the *Mental Measurements Yearbook* series. In addition to ensuring that test publishers have provided evidence of satisfactory psychometric properties, test users should ascertain whether the purpose for which a test was designed and the population on which it was normed are consistent with the intended use.

Having a repertoire of tests to choose from helps the evaluator individualize each assessment. There are advantages, however, to using the same measures regularly. With repeated use, the evaluator is able to administer a test accurately and fluently. Fluent administration enables the evaluator to attend closely to the child, resulting in more thorough observation and recording of relevant behaviors. Furthermore, the evaluator becomes increasingly familiar with the range of responses, and develops "clinical norms" to interpret the significance of qualitative findings and specific responses.

Attaching value to test scores relies on certain assumptions about how the scores were generated: that adequate rapport was established, that test conditions were satisfactory, and that standardized procedures were followed closely. These assumptions cannot be taken for granted.

Adherence to Standardized Procedures

Test results are interpreted with the assumption that the obtained scores reflect how the child performed under standardized conditions. However, examiner errors can negate this assumption, distorting test scores and compromising their value. Numerous studies have shown that deviation from prescribed administration and scoring procedures is all too common. A meta-analysis by Styck and Walsh (2016) examined 27 studies of examiner error on the Wechsler scales. On average, practicing psychologists made administration or scoring errors in 34% of test administrations, with an average of 7.7 errors per protocol; and graduate students made errors on 70% of test administrations, with an average of 3.4 errors per protocol. Apparently, examiner error does not desist with repeated use of a test. These findings suggest that, as evaluators become familiar with a measure, they rely more on memory and less on the test manual, resulting in drift from standardized procedures. Hence, experienced evaluators should periodically review the administration and scoring procedures of measures, especially those with complicated administration and scoring procedures. Of further concern, it should be noted that the Styck and Walsh (2016) meta-analysis underestimated examiner error rates, since most of the studies in their analysis investigated examiner errors by looking at protocols only. These studies could not determine whether examiners adhered to the full range of standardized administration requirements: verbatim wording, correct presentation of materials, complete recording of responses, correct use of prompts and queries, accurate timing, and so on.

Another noteworthy finding, reported in several studies (Belk, LoBello, Ray, & Zachar, 2002; Loe, Kadlubek, & Marks, 2007; Mrazik, Janzen, Dombrowski, Barford, & Krawchuk, 2012), is that graduate students do not make significant reductions in errors simply through multiple practice administrations. However, as Kuentzel, Hetterscheidt, and Barnett (2011) demonstrated, performance monitoring and feedback procedures can reduce scoring errors by 50% or more. The implications for training programs are clear. To ensure that students improve over time, instructors should use direct means of evaluating administration proficiency (i.e., observation or videotaping), and should closely check the test protocols of practice administrations, providing corrective feedback on each administration. A rubric for evaluating trainee administration and scoring skills, developed for an introductory level graduate course in psychoeducational assessment, is provided in Appendix B.

Rapport and Optimal Performance

A key objective in test administration is to elicit optimal performance within the bounds of standardized administration. This requires a delicate balance as the examiner (1) encourages the child's best effort without cueing right and wrong answers (e.g., with a smiling nod or expectant pause); (2) provides all required demonstrations, samples, and prompts, and only those that are permitted; and (3) delivers instructions verbatim, but with a conversational expression, rather than in a monotone. The evaluator notes when attention flags, motivation has tanked, or interfering factors (illness, anger, etc.) will yield invalid results, and responds accordingly—providing breaks in some situations and encouragement in others, and discontinuing testing when warranted.

Pacing is important. The evaluator should present tasks at a brisk pace to maintain attention and effort, but not so fast as to outpace the child's processing speed. Test materials should be presented without fumbling or uncertainty, minimizing delays and distractions. This not only helps keep the child engaged, but implicitly conveys that the evaluator is capable and in control of the situation.

Interpretation of Test Scores

Test results cannot be interpreted mechanically "by the numbers." There are many reasons why an obtained score may not be indicative of the ability or construct that was purportedly assessed. A child may be task avoidant and put forth little or no effort, may be unable to process verbal instructions because of language or dialect differences, or may be burdened by illness or trauma. Under such circumstances, it would be misleading to interpret the obtained score as a valid measure of the given construct.

Cognitive and academic test scores cannot be fully understood without considering the child's history and mindset. Practice effects and educational history are key influences. Virtually every kind of mental activity improves with exposure and practice. Has the child studied hard, read widely, or received extra tutoring? Does the child's family or culture value formal education? Has the child had the benefit of enriched language exposure and early learning experiences prior to school entry? As decisively demonstrated by Hart and Risley (1995, 2003), there are vast environmentally mediated differences in children's early language experiences, which have enduring effects on school performance.

When performance is compromised by an interfering factor, that factor may be the most noteworthy finding. For example, an examiner may conclude that the extreme anxiety or distractibility that interfered with test performance also explains why the child is not functioning successfully in the classroom. Various factors may account for underperformance: fatigue, motivation, persistence, attention, emotional distractions, hearing difficulties, language background, sensory impairment, and so on. Given the multiple determinants of cognitive test performance, obtained results are more appropriately characterized as "current functioning" than as ability or potential. This point is explicitly addressed in the *Standards for Educational and Psychological Tests* (American Educational Research Association [AERA], American Psychological Association [APA], National Council on Measurement in Education [NCME], 2014), the preeminent source of guidance on test development and use.

> Standard 10.12. In psychological assessment, the interpretation of test scores or patterns of test battery results should consider other factors that may influence a particular testing outcome. Where appropriate, a description of such factors and an analysis of the alternative hypotheses or explanations regarding what may have contributed to the pattern of results should be included in the report. (pp. 166–167)

The evaluator must also be cautious when interpreting and reporting composite scores that are derived from highly discrepant subtest or scale scores. It can be misleading to report an overall IQ score when there is a wide range of performance levels on the component scales. Similarly, it can be misleading to describe a child's functioning on a verbal comprehension or memory composite scale when the subtests contributing to the scale are nonunitary, that is, so discrepant that they are evidently not measuring the same underlying trait. On academic achievement measures, important information is lost when reporting composite scores that combine disparate skills, such as word level reading and reading comprehension or math calculations and math problem solving, rather than addressing each of these areas separately.

Measurement Error

Evaluators should take measurement error into account when reporting test scores, using language and qualifiers that are consistent with the level of reliability (Lichtenstein, 2013b). Just as we must keep in mind that time-limited observations and third-party rating scales are not perfectly reliable, so too are test scores only estimates of abilities, skills, and attributes, and therefore subject to variability with each measurement.

Many factors contribute to measurement error. We tend to focus on those associated with the examinee, as we recognize that a child's alertness, motivation, and even luck (when taking a best guess) can vary from day to day. Testing conditions and examiner behavior also account for measurement error. Less-than-optimal testing circumstances—a noisy room, frequent distractions, or a very long testing session—can detract from performance. Examiners vary in how they elicit best performance and adhere to administration and scoring rules. There is also measurement error associated with the test itself, as represented by internal consistency reliability: the specific items on a test are sampled from many possible choices, and different sets of items will yield different scores.

Given the many sources of error, the obtained test score must be recognized as an *estimate* of the construct to be measured, and not as a score that exactly and definitively quantifies the given ability or trait. This is certainly true for general intelligence, which should not be regarded as a fixed and enduring attribute, but rather a collection of skills and abilities that will vary with the specific measure used, with the child's day-to-day fluctuations in performance, and with long-term changes in learning, health, and mental attitude.

The evaluator should be aware of the degree of measurement error associated with a given test score and report findings accordingly. As indicated in the *Standards for Educational and Psychological Testing* (AERA, APA, & NCME, 2014, p. 43), "For each total score, subscore, or combination of scores that is to be interpreted, estimates of relevant indices of reliability/precision should be reported" (Standard 2.3).

An obtained score is an estimate of some hypothesized "true score" that falls within a specified range, or *confidence interval*. Test publishers routinely provide confidence intervals so that test users can appropriately qualify their reporting of a child's performance. By including confidence intervals in reports, the evaluator conveys that an obtained score is an estimate, and indicates how close that estimate is. This is readily understood by most readers, who are accustomed to having national poll results reported along with the "margin of error."

Despite their training in psychological measurement, evaluators often report exact test scores without qualifying them to reflect measurement error. Even when evaluators report confidence intervals, they may also describe performance using exact percentiles, thereby perpetuating the notion of an exactly pinpointed trait. For example, a child may be reported to have performed at the 36th percentile on a measure of word identification. In comparison, her reading comprehension score at the 41st percentile may appear to be higher, but the actual difference is neither statistically nor clinically significant, just as her word identification score at the 32nd percentile a year later would hardly represent a decline. Similarly, misinterpretation of results is often fostered by reporting subtest scaled scores in the body of a report (e.g., a Coding score of 9 and a Symbol Search score of 7), especially given the degree of measurement error associated with brief subtests.

Testing Limits

Evaluators can derive valuable clinical information by *testing limits*, that is, by presenting test items under alternative conditions to better understand the factors that interfere with performance. Some examples include extending time limits, giving instructions with alternative wording, or prompting the child to check his work for errors. More successful performance by the child under alternate conditions may have implications for classroom performance. Some standardized tests, such as the D-KEFS Trail Making Test and the Bender Visual–Motor Gestalt Test, employ a testing-limits approach by presenting variations of a task, with norms for each condition. The WISC–V Integrated consists entirely of alternative versions of subtests in which the influence of common interfering factors is reduced or eliminated.

Qualitative Findings

Standardized cognitive tests provide rich clinical information in the form of an extensive sample of behaviors and verbalizations as the examinee responds to a fixed set of tasks, interactions, and inquiries. What strategies does the child use to remember information? How does he deal with anxiety or frustration? Does she persevere in the face of difficulty or failure? Is he compliant? Avoidant? Talkative? As Alan Kaufman explained in *Portraits of the Children,* a National Association of School Psychologists (2003) video on culturally competent assessment.

> The clinician is always looking for *how*—how the child solves the problem, if they were anxious, if they were distractible, if they had a poor tolerance of frustration. All of that information goes into interpreting the scores. You can get the identical profile for ten different children and have ten different interpretations. . . .

Much of the value of cognitive testing arises from its applicability to interventions of a psychological nature. Qualitative findings about factors such as attitude, effort, self-image, and self-expectations have major implications for school performance. Box 3.4 provides some examples of how qualitative test findings can inform interventions.

INTERPRETATION AND USE OF ASSESSMENT FINDINGS

Collecting the right kind of data is essential, but what follows is even more important. The evaluator must put assessment findings to good use by interpreting them skillfully and formulating recommendations that reasonably follow from them.

Integration of Assessment Data

A thorough understanding of a child must consider personal and family history, characteristic behavior, environmental circumstances, and objective measures of performance. A comprehensive assessment draws from the multiple sources of information described in the previous section (i.e., review of records, observation, interviewing, rating scales, and testing). However, simply compiling assessment data from multiple sources does not ensure a useful assessment. Integration of assessment data is crucial to effective formulation and reporting. The skilled clinician weaves the data together to provide a clear, accurate, and

BOX 3.4. Qualitative Findings from Cognitive Testing Inform Psychological Interventions

Qualitative findings from cognitive testing are often the source of recommendations that have substantial bearing on behavior and learning goals. Here are some examples.

Qualitative findings	Interventions
Child has low frustration tolerance, will seek to discontinue a task when experiencing the first signs of failure.	• To reduce aversion to schoolwork, avoid frustration-level assignments; encourage child to request help when an assignment contains a high proportion of "unknowns." • Monitor difficulty level of assignments to ensure appropriately high rates of success for instructional and independent assignment. • Teach child ways of managing feelings of frustration, such as the use of brief relaxation and confidence-building self-statements. • Create incentives for guessing when uncertain, and for persisting in the face of incorrect responses.
Child is impulsive, often responds without fully understanding task demands or attending to all relevant details.	• Coach child to delay responding and engage in self-talk (e.g., "What I am being asked to do? What information do I need?"). • Instruct child to check work before submitting. • Encourage teacher to prompt child to double-check work before submitting it for grading.
Child has little interest in academics or intellectual pursuits, but will work for concrete reinforcers.	• Motivate child by establishing a token reinforcement or reward system for work completion. • Pair concrete reinforcers with task-related praise. • Design assignments to align with child's interests and culture, when possible. • Engage in ongoing conversations with child about his goals and how intellectual pursuits (e.g., reading, discussion, relevant practical experience) help him reach those goals.
Child intently seeks feedback about performance, asking repeatedly if answers are correct and trying to discern what the evaluator is recording.	• Have child maintain charts or records of performance to document progress toward key learning or behavior goals. • Introduce some assignments with no right answers (i.e., that require divergent thinking or reflection), and have child self-evaluate performance. • Engage child in conversations about performance, encouraging her to focus on successes more than shortcomings. • Discuss the concept of "good-enough" performance.
Adolescent is discouraged by "impossible-to-meet" parent expectations, makes little effort, and "has an attitude."	• Counsel parents to desist from conveying expectations critically or expressing dissatisfaction. • Encourage adults who influence the adolescent (parents, teachers, counselors, etc.) to accept the adolescent's goals, whatever they are, understanding that they are likely to change over time. • Arrange for adolescent to set personal goals for short-term achievement and long-term educational or career aspirations with a counselor or advisor.

relevant description of the child's functioning, circumstances, and needs. There is a world of difference between rote reporting of test results and integrating multiple data sources in a way that has valuable implications for the child in school and at home. Integrated interpretation of assessment data, a core principle of consumer-responsive assessment, is discussed further in Chapter 5.

Recommendations

The ultimate objective of an assessment is to bring about beneficial outcomes for its intended audience. Recommendations are the primary vehicle for promoting positive outcomes. The target audience for these recommendations may include family members, school personnel, service providers, the child, and others. With these various audiences in mind, recommendations must be carefully crafted to ensure understanding and to foster acceptance.

Recommendations in a report should be prominently featured, commensurate with their importance. They are usually listed in a Recommendations section at the end of a report, rather than scattered throughout a report or embedded in the narrative of a concluding section. Alternatively, in a report that uses a question-and-answer format, they might be set off by numbers or bullets at the end of each question-and-answer segment. Recommendations are best presented in full sentences, since telegraphic phrases (e.g., "Give attention selectively to reinforce prosocial behavior") often fail to convey who will implement the recommendation, under what conditions, or with what intent.

Evaluators may need to exercise caution and judgment when making recommendations that heavily tax the resources of a school system, agency, or family. A common dilemma is whether to propose optimal and generous services or to temper recommendations in light of equitable costs or available resources. Special education laws that obligate schools to meet children's needs irrespective of cost may encourage evaluators to recommend ideal, but unrealistic, programs and services. School psychologists may experience role conflict in balancing advocacy for children and the interests of the school system. This tension is exacerbated when school district policies discourage making recommendations that impose demands on system resources, or in the most extreme case, banning recommendations from reports altogether. One rationale for such restrictions is that the evaluator is just one contributing team member, and that IEP decisions are the shared responsibility of the entire IEP team. However, as we discuss in Chapter 5, recommendations can be formulated in ways that serve children and families with integrity, while respecting procedural requirements and institutional prerogatives.

Unfettered by school system policies, the independent evaluator has greater latitude when making recommendations and need consider only the best interests of the child. However, the independent evaluator should exercise caution as well, taking into account situational factors and procedural requirements. For example, the recommendation to provide a full-time classroom aide for a child may be complicated by the current assignment of aides in the child's classroom, or may result in excessive supports with this addition to existing services. Or, a recommendation may be at odds with the special education mandates that govern school policies and practices, such as the eligibility criteria for educational disabilities or the requirement to provide services in the least restrictive environment. Recommendations of independent evaluators can even be counterproductive, for example, when they fuel a preexisting adversarial relationship or lead parents to expect that the independent evaluator's recommendations will trump those of school personnel.

Above all, recommendations must be sound, meaning they must be practical, well suited to the individuals involved, and evidence based to the greatest extent possible. Recommendations also must be sensitive to the likely reactions of proposed implementers. A teacher or parent may be quick to interpret the evaluator's recommendations as critical of past efforts or as failing to recognize the limitations and stressors under which they labor.

PROFESSIONAL WRITING

Good writing is an advanced skill, the product of sound verbal skills, logical thinking, compulsive editing, and hard-wrought learning through practice and feedback. Professional writing skills are usually developed in graduate training programs, although, as already noted, there are drawbacks in terms of readability; writing for a course instructor with advanced technical knowledge must be approached differently than writing for a parent or teacher.

Sattler (2018) devotes a detailed chapter to report writing, offering recommendations on both clinical practice (e.g., integration of findings, citing of specific behaviors and sources) and effective writing style (e.g., concise wording, minimal use of technical terms and qualifiers). Braaten's (2007) report-writing handbook is a rich source of clinical considerations and wording to strengthen and individualize reports. Hass and Carriere (2014) and Schneider et al. (2018) provide excellent guidance on controlling the readability of reports to make them more accessible to consumers. Allyn (2012) devotes an entire book to the mechanics (style, tone, grammar, etc.) of writing to clients and referring professionals about psychological assessment results. Chapter 5 provides guidance on how to write consumer-responsive reports.

Simply put, we urge practitioners to present findings, both orally and in writing, with the unwavering objective of communicating effectively and pursuing positive outcomes. The goal is not to dazzle consumers or to impress other professionals, but to convey findings in a clear and direct manner that meets the needs of multiple audiences.

ASSESSMENT IN A MULTI-TIERED SYSTEM: THE NEW NORMAL?

Multitiered systems of support (MTSS), a service-delivery model designed to optimize outcomes for all students, has gained traction in the K–12 education world. MTSS is designed to reduce the rates of failure and reliance on special education, as well as to use existing resources most efficiently. Key aspects of MTSS have been espoused (e.g., with the Regular Education Initiative of the 1980s) and piloted (e.g., by the [Iowa] Heartland Area Education Agency's Problem Solving Model) in years past, but the MTSS model took a quantum leap forward with the endorsement of an RTI approach in the reauthorization of the Elementary and Secondary Education Act in 2002 and of the IDEA in 2004.[1] The MTSS model embodies the three major recommendations of the President's Commission on Excellence in Special Education (2002), which significantly shaped IDEA 2004: (1) focus on results—not on process; (2) embrace a model of prevention, not a model of failure; and (3) consider children with disabilities as general education children first.

MTSS employs a prevention-oriented public health model that matches students' academic and behavioral needs with an array of supports and services, irrespective of diagnostic labels and eligibility determinations. Core elements of MTSS include:

- Effective instruction and behavioral supports for all children as a feature of the general education program.
- Periodic and systematic data collection for timely identification of children who require heightened levels of service.
- A continuum of strategies, supports, and remedial services for students with academic and behavior needs, with progressively more intensive and specialized interventions at successive tiers.
- Implementation of proven (i.e., "scientifically-based") educational practices at all levels.
- Progress monitoring to determine whether interventions are effective.

The MTSS structure is typically represented as a three-tiered model, although some systems make finer distinctions to identify additional tiers or "sub-tiers." Tier 1 represents universal services and supports, providing all students with high-quality instruction and school environments that foster prosocial behavior. Also within general education, Tier 2 provides corrective supports and strategies for at-risk children in an effort to prevent mild and incipient difficulties from developing into full-fledged problems. When Tier 2 interventions are ineffective or insufficient, more intensive and individualized Tier 3 services and supports are delivered either in general education or special education. For students in general education, movement between the tiers is fluid, allowing for timely changes in a child's status and educational needs.

MTSS can effectively promote academic and social–emotional outcomes for students at all levels of need. Rather than respond initially to children's learning and behavioral difficulties with a referral to special education—a process that may take months to complete and may conclude with the child being found ineligible for special services—MTSS delivers remedial instruction and other supports without delay in general education.

In contrast, special education relies on a medical model, with specialized instruction and related services reserved for children who are deemed to have an educational disability. The comprehensive evaluation procedures prescribed by IDEA serve as the vehicle that informs the high-stakes determination of eligibility and provides input into educational planning. Consequently, the special education evaluation process has assumed considerable

---

[1]While often used synonymously, the term MTSS is preferred over RTI because it is understood to encompass both academic and behavioral goals, while RTI is generally associated with academic instruction. RTI also has the more specific meaning of describing an intervention-based method of LD identification.

weight and formality, and the assessments tend to emphasize findings that inform eligibility decisions.

Solution-Focused Assessments

In the MTSS model, assessments are conducted at each level, or tier, to determine (1) whether students are meeting standards or expectations, (2) whether additional supports or strategies are needed, and (3) whether services should be provided at some other tier—less intensive, if goals have been met and can be sustained without current levels of support, or more intensive if progress is unsatisfactory (see Box 3.5). Hence, MTSS requires assessments that are different from traditional psychological assessments.

Screening or benchmark assessment is employed at the universal level. Curriculum-based assessments (CBAs) are used to gauge levels of academic performance that indicate which children in a classroom or grade are meeting district, state, or Common Core standards, and may consist of stand-alone assessments or performance indicators that are embedded in curriculum materials. Progress monitoring is an essential feature of Tiers 2 and 3, as it provides objective data regarding whether interventions are effective and whether children are receiving services and supports at an appropriate level of intensity. CBA measures that are conducive to ongoing data collection and sensitive to short-term gains in performance track academic progress over time. Behavioral and social–emotional goals may be monitored by charting target behaviors or using goal-attainment scaling to assess changes over time on relevant measurable behaviors (e.g., attendance, rule adherence, work completion, staying on task).

Brown-Chidsey and Andren (2013) delineate two general types of psychoeducational reports: *comprehensive evaluation* associated with special education and mental health referrals and more narrowly purposed *solution-focused* reports of intervention planning and subsequent progress monitoring. Solution-focused reports "utilize continuous data to show how a student is responding to instruction" (Brown-Chidsey & Andren, 2013, p. 254), which may be conveyed in charts and graphs, as well as verbally. These reports tend to

BOX 3.5. Assessments in an MTSS Model

Tier	Service level	Target population	Assessments
1	Universal	General population, including those with special needs	• Screening • Benchmark assessment
2	Selective	At-risk children, those with elevated needs	• Progress monitoring • Comprehensive evaluation (if an educational disability is suspected)
3	Indicated	Children with serious or persistent needs	• Progress monitoring • Comprehensive evaluation (if an educational disability is suspected)

be brief and, as they document a child's performance over time, may involve a series of reports.

Progress monitoring is a key element of solution-focused assessment. However, the extent of progress monitoring required by MTSS poses a significant logistical challenge. It requires assessment procedures that are economical, accurate, and sensitive to short-term changes in performance. Curriculum-based measurement (CBM) serves this purpose especially well.

Curriculum-Based Measurement

CBM is a valuable tool that greatly facilitates the practical implementation of an MTSS model at all tiers. CBM is a specific type of CBA that uses brief, standardized assessment procedures to pinpoint academic skill levels. The rationale and methodology of CBA differ from that of traditional psychoeducational assessment tools. CBA relies on direct measurement of academic skills to inform decisions about instruction and intervention. While cognitive testing investigates a reading problem and diagnoses a learning disability by assessing processes that may interfere with a child's ability to read (e.g., naming speed, cognitive efficiency, symbol translation), CBA directly assesses functional reading skills, such as decoding, word identification, vocabulary, and passage comprehension. CBA establishes current levels of academic performance and monitors progress, rather than diagnosing underlying causes and identifying disabilities for eligibility purposes.

CBM originated with the work of Deno (1985, 2003), who demonstrated that very brief standardized assessments can accurately establish performance levels, predict future performance, and measure learning gains. CBM uses timed probes, administered under standardized procedures, to assess discrete academic skills. Because these probes are brief—each requiring from 1 to 3 minutes—CBM is highly suited to collecting the kind of data needed for MTSS.

CBM can be administered to an entire class or grade level, which makes it practical for conducting benchmark assessment to identify those children who need additional instructional supports within general education (i.e., Tier 2 services). Since CBM is practical for repeated measurement, it can be used for progress monitoring of individual children to determine whether Tier 2 services are effective or whether more intensive (i.e., Tier 3) services should be provided, either through general education or special education. CBM can also inform instruction, as it yields data for classroom teachers that determine whether the children in their class have adequately mastered the essential skills that were taught. The National Center on Intensive Intervention maintains a database of the characteristics and psychometric properties of specific CBM tools at *https://intensiveintervention.org/chart/ progress-monitoring-mm*.

CBM can also play a key role in special education evaluations when the determination of whether a child has a disability is confounded by lack of educational opportunity or appropriate instruction. Federal special education regulations (Sec. 300.306(b)) specify that a child must not be determined to have a disability if the determinant factor is lack of appropriate instruction in reading or math. If this possibility presents itself when a child is referred, one solution is to incorporate within the evaluation process a diagnostic period in which appropriate instruction is provided and the rate of progress is monitored using CBM.

Functional Behavioral Assessment

Functional behavioral assessment (FBA) is another type of solution-focused assessment. An FBA may be conducted under the auspices of either general or special education to inform problem analysis and intervention for serious or persistent behavior problems. By investigating the antecedents and consequences of the target behavior, FBA identifies the factors that reinforce the behavior (e.g., attention getting, task avoidance, or tangible gains). These findings have clear and direct implications, as behavior intervention plans guided by FBA findings predictably reduce problem behaviors through modification of contingencies and environmental triggers. FBAs and behavior intervention plans are explicitly cited in the IDEA as services to be considered for children with suspected or identified disabilities, but they can also be provided as general education services.

Implications for Assessment Reports

Reporting procedures for MTSS assessments in general education are discretionary and subject to varying practices. Federal regulations exempt "screening of a student by a teacher or specialist to determine appropriate instructions strategies for curriculum implementation" (Sec. 300.302). from the procedural requirements of special education. Such assessments fall within the realm of general education and do not necessitate formal reports, since they are considered an integral component of the education curriculum. However, parents should at least be notified of subpar performance on general education assessments that necessitate changes in a student's education program. This finding could be documented with the kind of solution-focused report described by Brown-Chidsey and Andren (2013). (See Chapter 7 for further discussion of such documentation and a report template.)

In the behavioral realm, mental health screening (typically by means of brief ratings scales completed by teachers) or disciplinary records may signal the need for selective interventions such as home–school communication or a behavior plan. It is often advisable to report such findings to parents, since the behavioral health interventions that follow may not be regarded as usual educational services. Correspondingly, the monitoring of a child's response to a behavior intervention plan may necessitate progress reporting that is more specific and frequent than standard reporting procedures in either general or special education.

Solution-focused assessment has distinct implications for traditional assessment reports. The implementation and monitoring of general education interventions generates highly relevant background information for a comprehensive evaluation. The particulars should be reported in great detail, including instructional procedures, implementing personnel, outcome measures, and performance levels. Progress monitoring provides key input for intervention planning, as it indicates what has been tried and with what level of success. This information is also critically important when using an RTI model for LD identification, since achievement levels and rates of improvement are the primary inputs for this method.

In conducting a comprehensive assessment, an evaluator might administer CBM assessment procedures in order to establish baseline data against which to gauge future progress. CBM procedures might also be used when another member of the evaluation team (e.g., a special education teacher or educational diagnostician) is administering a comprehensive achievement measure. The evaluator can add CBM to an assessment battery with relatively little increase in testing time to gain an independent indication of how the child reacts and contends with academic challenges.

Solution-focused assessments are philosophically aligned with consumer-responsive assessment. As discussed in Chapter 7, they provide information that is highly relevant to a child's daily school performance and can be presented in a manner that is readily understood by consumers.

CHAPTER 4

The Consumer-Responsive Approach

The ultimate goal of psychological assessment is to provide the greatest possible benefit for the child who is being assessed. As such, assessment is a process in which an evaluator communicates findings to consumers for the purpose of helping them understand the child and make decisions that will improve the child's life. Hence, this book focuses on the all-important aspect of communicating effectively with consumers.

In describing the consumer-responsive approach, we are guided by the writings of others—notably, Brenner (2003), Groth-Marnat and Horvath (2006), Harvey (2006, 2013), and Tallent (1993), by a small but consistent research literature on what consumers want from assessment (Hackett, Shaikh, & Theodosiou, 2009; Hilton, Turner, Krebs, Volz, & Heymann, 2012; Pelco, Ward, Coleman, & Young, 2009; Ward, 2008), and by our own combined 65 years of experience in practice and teaching.

The research studies strongly indicate that consumers want to feel listened to and understood. They want to be treated with respect and dignity and want their concerns to be taken seriously. They want to have ample time to ask questions. They want the evaluator to communicate directly, clearly, and simply in language that they, the consumers, can understand (Halpern, 1984; Hasnat & Graves, 2000; Hite, 2017; Moh & Magiati, 2012). They want recommendations that are specific and effective. They want to be partners in making treatment decisions (Moh & Magiati, 2012). And, they appreciate follow-up (Ho, Yi, Griffiths, Chan, & Murray, 2014; Nissenbaum, Tollefson, & Reese, 2002).

Broadly defined, the consumer-responsive approach is one in which assessment practices are designed and implemented both to serve the best interests of the child and to meet the needs of consumers (e.g., parents, teachers, and other service providers) who are in the best position to help.

CORE PRINCIPLES

As noted in Chapter 1, consumer-responsive assessment is guided by the following seven principles.

Collaborative Relationships

Like all clinical endeavors, the bedrock of consumer-responsive psychological assessment is the collaborative relationships that are established between the clinician (in this case, the evaluator) and others who are involved, typically the child, his family, his teachers, and other service providers. The collaborative nature of these relationships is initiated at first contact and sustained through reporting and follow-up.

Emphasize Process, Not Product

Consumer-responsive assessment is concerned with the overall process of understanding and planning for the child, from initial (prereferral) consultation and problem-solving efforts through follow-up activities. Relationships are forged even prior to a formal assessment referral. Through consulting with teachers and parents and in many cases participating in school-based problem-solving teams, the evaluator conveys that she is an ongoing helping presence. Further, she learns what has and has not worked in the past, often on a firsthand basis. When a referral is made, the process then involves further data collection and reporting of findings. While assessment content is the focus as the evaluator interacts with consumers to obtain background information and report results, these are important points of engagement as well. But the process does not stop there, as reporting is succeeded by follow-up activities. Only by following up can evaluators find out which recommendations were implemented and which were helpful. Also through follow-up, the evaluator demonstrates caring and concern for consumers in the most critical of ways: with efforts to ensure the optimal impact of the assessment.

Relevance

Assessment findings must be meaningful to consumers. For findings to be meaningful, they must be relevant to the assessment questions and to the child's daily life. A focus on intervention, past, present, and future is a key element of relevance, for intervention is what seeks to improve the child's day-to-day functioning. What interventions have been tried in the past, and what were their effects? What interventions should be planned for the future, and how should their impact be monitored?

Selectivity is another important aspect of assessment relevance. Procedures should be chosen on the basis of their relevance to assessment questions. Selectivity in reporting is especially important. Information that has no bearing on the assessment questions and concerns can distract, confuse, and soften the impact of the assessment, and is best left out. In deciding what meets the standard of relevance, the evaluator should have a sound answer to the question "So what?"

Importance of Oral Reporting

Oral reporting of assessment results is as important as written reporting. Evaluators spend a substantial amount of time creating elaborate written reports and relatively little time reporting their results orally. However, it is through the spoken interaction that consumers can ask questions, have results and recommendations clarified, and receive emotional support, greatly increasing the assessment's impact.

Accessibility

Assessment findings, whether presented orally or in writing, must be accessible to consumers. Accessibility calls for reporting in language that can be understood by consumers. Sentences should be short, vocabulary should be familiar, and the use of jargon and numbers should be minimized.

Multiple Sources of Assessment Data

Assessment findings emerge from a combination of sources—records, observations, interviews, and tests—which together create an integrated view of the child that is recognizable to consumers. Children function in contexts and with histories. A thorough assessment will explore the child's developmental, medical, family, social, school, and intervention history. Tests, while valuable, are limited in that they measure functioning at a particular time and in a single context. Convergent findings—those confirmed by multiple sources—are both more robust and more meaningful. Balancing test results with information from records, observations, and interviews broadens our understanding of the child and leads to recommendations that take into account a child's day-to-day life, and thus are likely to have greater impact.

Child Focus

Reporting of assessment findings should be child centered. This principle has bearing on the written report's organization (i.e., theme-based rather than test-based), as well as on the language and style, with the focus on the child rather than on the tests. It also calls for the integration of findings, such as in a Clinical Impressions or Conclusions section, and for recommendations that are individualized, powerful, and feasible.

The elaboration of the consumer-responsive approach in the remainder of this chapter revolves around the first of these core principles, the importance of collaborative relationships. We discuss the nature of consumer-responsive relationships, the establishment and maintenance of collaborative relationships during the course of an assessment, culture as an essential feature in those relationships, and bridging consumer and school needs.

COLLABORATIVE CONSUMER-RESPONSIVE RELATIONSHIPS

The sharing of information between evaluator and consumer is an essential part of conventional assessment (Smith, Wiggins, & Gorske, 2007). The evaluator engages with consumers as she hears about a child's perception of referral concerns, takes a developmental history from a parent, hears what a teacher has tried in the past, and learns about available resources from an administrator. Later, she reports her findings and recommendations to all involved. However, these encounters are both enriched and expanded in consumer-responsive assessment. Information is shared in a more open, trusting, collaborative, direct, and consistent manner. This approach facilitates the transfer of meaningful information, leaves the consumers feeling cared for, and improves adherence to assessment recommendations. As asserted by Finn and Tonsager (1977), "By treating clients as experts on themselves and engaging them as collaborators in each stage of the assessment, we demonstrate that we view them as valuable, capable individuals." (p. 381)

The Working Alliance in Assessment

Those who study the outcomes of psychotherapy write extensively about the importance of the "working alliance" (see, e.g., Norcross & Wampold, 2011; Shirk, Karver, & Brown, 2011). While definitions of the working alliance vary, there is general agreement that it comprises two major components: rapport (i.e., the empathic connection shared by client and therapist) and shared goals. The working alliance is seen as a common factor present in all types of psychotherapy, in contrast with an uncommon factor associated with a particular type of therapy, such as cognitive-behavioral, family/systemic, or psychoanalytic. The working alliance has been found to be the single strongest predictor of psychotherapy outcomes (Horvath, Del Re, Fluckiger, & Symonds, 2011; Shirk et al., 2011).

While psychological assessment is different from psychotherapy, there is an important similarity as well. A clinician, a client, and perhaps others are engaged in an activity that is intended to benefit the client. As such, it is reasonable to conclude that the concept of a working alliance is also applicable to psychoeducational assessment. Does the child, who is our client, feel that we are empathically connected to him or her? Does he sense that we can feel his embarrassment when he makes reading errors or his fear when he avoids school? Does she sense that we feel her emptiness when she struggles mightily to get out of bed due to depression or her utter confusion when beset by math anxiety? To what extent do parents feel that we share their anguish in having a child who cannot fulfill the activities of daily living or their embarrassment that their child disrupts a classroom? As for teachers, do they feel that we understand their sense of loss when a child fails to make progress or their desperation when confronted with a highly disruptive group of children? And do the child, the parents, and the teachers feel that we are on the same page, and that we are all working in the same direction? Are child, parent, and teacher all similarly committed to improving the child's reading? Are they working together to have the child learn to cope productively with taunts from others, to complete homework consistently, or to work hard, even when feeling defeated? When the answer to these questions is "yes," then the working alliance is strong. Children, parents, and teachers sense that the evaluator understands how they are feeling in a deep and compassionate way. Further, they all collaborate to reach the same goals. There is great power in forging these strong bonds. It is truly consumer responsive.

The concept of working alliance is not an explicit focus of conventional psychological assessment. In conventional assessment, the evaluator seeks to establish rapport, but usually with the goal of gaining compliance with the testing procedures. Each of the parties involved has goals, but they often differ. For example, the goal of an 8-year-old child with a reading disability might be to not feel dumb when reading, the parents' and teacher's goal might be to improve reading skills, and the administrator's goal might be to decide whether or not the child qualifies for special education. It is unlikely that the conventional process includes a discussion of goals. As a result, there is not a comparable emphasis on developing the kind of working alliance that facilitates the open transfer of information, sustains a caring relationship, and builds good agreement as to which recommendations will be implemented and how.

Elements of a Collaborative Working Relationship

A collaborative working alliance is clearly desirable. How are such relationships constructed? Various studies have identified important elements of a collaborative relationship: empathy, positive regard, genuineness, "present-ness," and trust (Norcross & Hill, 2004; Norcross & Wampold, 2011; Power, Eiraldi, Clarke, Mazzuca, & Krain, 2005). Norcross and Hill (2004) define empathy as the clinician's "sensitive ability and willingness to understand clients' thoughts, feelings, and struggles from their point of view" (p. 24). Positive regard is the clinician's warm acceptance of the client, family, and teacher, as well as all of their struggles. Genuineness calls on the clinician to be real and to give freely, while maintaining proper professional boundaries. Present-ness means allowing oneself to be fully engaged with the child, family member, or teacher; being attentive to what they say, feel, and do in the moment; and responding accordingly.

Trust is a broader concept that connotes a two-way relationship. The evaluator needs to trust that the child will attend assessment sessions, share information during interviews, and cooperate at least minimally with assessment tasks. The evaluator further needs to trust that parents and teachers will be reasonably open in providing background information and then later in giving serious consideration to recommendations.

In turn, consumers need to trust that the evaluator is competent, has compassion, and is ethical (Power et al., 2005). Competence means that the evaluator has the technical skills to administer and interpret assessment measures and the requisite psychological and educational knowledge to analyze and address the child's problems. Competence also involves skill in relating with others and communicating clearly. Compassion requires that the evaluator empathize with the struggles of all consumers and convey deep caring. It necessitates a degree of acceptance and understanding that sometimes runs counter to instinctive reactions, calling for empathy even when consumers are critical of the evaluator, reject team recommendations, or fail to attend school meetings. To be ethical means that the evaluator acts in the best interests of the child and does so in a way that is professional and well bounded.

Putting the Collaborative Relationship into Practice

Establishing a collaborative working alliance is essential in the consumer-responsive approach. The alliance is manifested in concrete actions and specific behaviors, which are often initiated even before the assessment referral is placed. These interactions occur as the evaluator collaborates with teachers and parents in a problem-solving process. Alliance-building actions continue with preparatory interviews in which the evaluator listens attentively, takes consumers' concerns seriously, and develops referral questions collaboratively. Consumer-responsive actions further involve writing and speaking clearly in terms that all parties can understand. They include both feedback and follow-up sessions with parents, children, and teachers separate from formal group meetings. Throughout, these actions involve the allocation of sufficient time for as many questions and answers as are needed to understand and plan well. They also involve the building of bridges between the cultures of the school, the evaluator, and the consumers.

The objectives of a consumer-responsive collaborative approach are realized through a constellation of specific behaviors that convey warmth, interest, reciprocity, curiosity, emotional responsiveness, and humility. Warmth is expressed throughout the assessment both formally and informally—formally, through questions that attend to the child's and consumers' concerns, comments that are emotionally supportive, and invitations for the child and other consumers to ask any questions of their own; and informally, through a warm handshake, a knowing glance, and a supportive gesture. The expression of warmth begins with the initial welcome. Asking about travel issues (e.g., "Did you have trouble finding the office?") or commenting on an interest implied by an article of clothing (e.g., when a Boston client wears a baseball cap, "Oh, do you like the Red Sox?") are good starts. These queries can be followed by attention to the child's or parents' physical comforts ("Is that chair comfortable enough for you?"; "Is the temperature OK?").

Listening skills are of paramount importance in conveying interest. Simply listening goes a long way. (As a former supervisor of ours once advised, "The less you say, the smarter they think you are.") The full repertoire of listening skills includes nonverbal attention, use of door openers and rephrasing, and reflecting thoughts and feelings. *People Skills* (Bolton, 1979) is a timeless guide to these essential and widely applicable clinical skills. Effective listening skills not only help the evaluator obtain background information, but also set the stage for collaboration with a teacher, parent, or child in planning and monitoring interventions. Interested and attentive listening can be conveyed from the start of the initial interview with a simple question: "How can I be of help?" This question can be followed with repeated invitations for the child, parents, or teachers to ask any questions of their own. If the child, parents, or teachers challenge the evaluator's approach, an appreciative and nondefensive response is best. Statements such as "I'm glad you brought that up," "What concerns you about that," or "What didn't you like about that" convey a willingness to listen and understand.

The next group of behaviors concern reciprocity—the back-and-forth exchanges that facilitate effective conversation. The evaluator should be fully attentive to what is said rather than being absorbed in a prearranged agenda. She should maintain eye contact, with the manner and extent best modulated with consideration of cultural differences. Eye contact contributes to expressive delivery and also enables the evaluator to gauge how information is being received. Furthermore, and perhaps most important, reciprocity involves an awareness of what is said, followed by a relevant response and an invitation to an additional response in a kind of repeated serve-and-return that continues until the topic is finished. Such give-and-take requires time, which is reason to schedule a sufficiently long meeting and to give the consumer necessary seconds or minutes to share reactions when presented assessment findings (Smith, Wiggins, & Gorske, 2007).

Curiosity is also a valuable aspect of collaborative behavior. To be curious involves asking questions and being actively interested in their answers. In the words of the author and humanitarian Elie Wiesel (2000), "Questions unite us; answers divide us." By asking questions we convey our interest in both the answer and in the person who answered. "What part of reading is hard for you?"; "What do you think is causing Mary's very low feelings?"; "Is there anything you have done that seems to help John behave better in the classroom?"; "When did this problem start?"; "What questions do you have that I might try to answer with this assessment?" These questions and thousands of others both elicit important information and help someone feel heard. By asking questions, we let consumers know that we value their expertise as well as our own. The evaluator's receptivity to additional information is conveyed by open-ended questions that should be asked at the end of nearly every interview: "Is there anything I left out?"; "Is there something I should have asked you but didn't?"; "Is there anything else you would like me to know?"

Next in this group of collaboration-facilitating behaviors are those that relate to emotional responsiveness. To be emotionally responsive means that we are open to emotions—those of our consumers as well as our own. By accepting emotions, we remain attentive and are not overwhelmed, fearful, demoralized, or angry. When an adolescent tells about the pain of sexual abuse, can we continue to comfort her without dissuading her narrative? When a child describes his fury at being humiliated by a teacher whom we respect, can we accept his angry protests without defensiveness and try to understand more? When a parent talks about being unable to get out of bed or prepare breakfast or check her second grader's homework because of debilitating depression, can we empathize with her?

Emotional responsiveness also involves responding in ways that support, contain, and explore further. When a child shuts down for fear of losing control, do we wait patiently, note that he seems upset, and then ask if there is anything more he can tell? When we see a tear in a parent's eye, do we notice this, ask if it was elicited by something we said, and then follow the parent's lead in proceeding? When a parent cries uncontrollably upon hearing that her son has a debilitating disorder, do we wait, then offer a tissue, then ask if there's anything we can do to help? When we see a teacher wring her hands when describing how difficult it is to get a 10th grader to pay attention in class, do we empathize with her frustration, and then ask what she has tried? In all cases, we acknowledge the emotion expressed, try and keep its expression within limits that we can manage in the interview, and then learn more about their experience.

The final set of collaboration-facilitating behaviors relates to humility. While we can take pride in our knowledge, skills, compassion and dedication, we must also remain humble. Being humble, we must acknowledge the expertise of parents and teachers. We must strive to understand events from the consumers' perspective. We must be receptive to the consumer's questions and concerns as they arise throughout the assessment process. We must actively seek and then value their opinions. We must learn how consumers understand both their struggles and their successes. When devising recommendations, we must ask our consumers what is feasible, what they think will work, and what other ideas they may have. Being humble does not mean shortchanging our own knowledge, skills, and expertise. Rather, being humble allows us to enter into a consumer-responsive dialogue between partners that fosters a strong working alliance.

CONSUMER-RESPONSIVE PRACTICES OVER THE COURSE OF THE ASSESSMENT

The qualities of empathy, trust, positive regard, genuineness, and present-ness contribute to collaborative working alliances with consumers. These consumer-responsive qualities should be fostered over the course of the assessment.

Activities That Precede the Referral

While assessment begins formally at the time of referral, its foundation is formed earlier through relationships that convey the evaluator's competence, trustworthiness, openness, and commitment to furthering the best interests of the child. For school-based providers, these relationships begin in day-to-day interactions with parents and teachers in classrooms, in the school's hallways, at drop-off and pick-up times, and on parent nights. They are strengthened in more formal contacts, for example, when the evaluator consults with teachers, meets freely with family members, and participates in problem-solving processes. Evaluators based outside of the school build important connections through their willingness to come into the school to observe in classrooms, to contribute to school activities, such as staff in-service workshops and presentations to parents, and to participate in problem-solving meetings. Relationships are established and important information is exchanged. In all cases, an appreciation that the assessment is but one phase in an ongoing process and that evaluators must consider the effects of what has been tried before is key in fulfilling the assessment's ultimate goal, which is to promote beneficial outcomes.

In all cases, friendly contact, respect for the perspectives of others, and an appreciation for what has been tried in the past solidifies relationships, making it more likely that assessment will be a collaborative process and that recommendations, once developed, will be implemented.

Initial Interviewing

Consumer-responsive relationships proceed with an initial interview of parents, teachers and, as relevant, other service providers. Best-practice guidelines recommend that interviewing be a part of the assessment process (Mazza, 2014), but this practice is not done consistently. In a national study of school psychologists, Shapiro and Heick (2004) found that only 55% of providers evaluating students for social, emotional, or behavioral problems conducted a parent interview of any type in the majority of their cases. Similarly, only 57% routinely interviewed teachers.

The purposes of a consumer-responsive initial interview go beyond the collection of background information and clarification of referral concerns, which are the typical objectives in conventional assessment. The consumer-responsive purposes include forging a working alliance founded on sturdy rapport and shared goals, deriving and discussing referral questions cooperatively, and explaining assessment procedures.

What questions do the parents and teachers have that the assessment might answer? What does the teacher believe the child needs? What are the child's assets? What has been tried in the past, and what has and has not worked? Of similar importance, what should the parent and teacher expect from the assessment?

Parents are the single most important consumers of a child's assessment. Parents not only influence, but are also affected by, a child's development and well-being on a daily basis. The child's capabilities and behavior implicitly reflect on the parents, who may react in a highly personal way to questions and requests for information about their child. This calls for a rare blend of sensitivity, diplomacy, clarity, and honesty on the part of the evaluator. What is helpful in guiding these efforts is to consider that, except in very rare situations, parents care about their children, have positive hopes and aspirations for them, and have been doing the best they can. A sample introduction to the assessment process for parents is presented in Box 4.1.

BOX 4.1. Sample Explanation to Parents about a Psychoeducational Assessment

ESSENTIAL ELEMENTS

- Explain your role and function.
- Explain the assessment process.
  - o Describe assessment procedures
  - o Describe benefit to the child
  - o Be accurate and honest
- Allow opportunity for questions and discussion.

EXPLANATION

"Thank you for taking the time to meet with me. We will talk for about 45 minutes, and I will ask you many questions about Johnny—about his life both in school and at home, about how he has been in the past, and about your wishes for him for the future. In the coming weeks, with your permission, I will observe Johnny in his classroom and will meet with him two or three times to talk with him and give him some tests that will better help me understand how he is doing and what might be helpful for him. The good part of this is that, if needed, we will be able to give Johnny help that benefits him a great deal. The bad part is he might find the testing a bit stressful. This happens only with some children; for most children, the stress goes away shortly after we begin. Do you have any questions so far?

"Also, please know that I will share the results only with you and with people at school who work directly with Johnny."

In addition to describing upcoming assessment procedures, the content of the initial parent interview includes an exploration of their concerns, their perception of school functioning, and their knowledge in many areas in which they are the experts: the family, the child's medical and developmental histories and the child's functioning at home and in the community. A list of possible topics to inquire about in an initial parent interview is presented in Box 4.2.

As with parents, rapport with teachers is critical for obtaining the valuable information they can contribute. Teachers are occupied with countless responsibilities and demands in the course of a school day. It is essential to respect their time (e.g., ask when they are available to talk, or if it is okay to catch them in passing) and to be sensitive to their state of mind (not putting your own business first when they are distracted, agitated, exhausted, etc.). To establish credibility, the evaluator must exhibit a practical understanding of what goes on in classrooms and of what resources, such as time, personnel, and materials, are available to support recommendations and interventions. Most important, the evaluator must acknowledge and respect teachers' expertise, appreciating their unique and valuable input, noting uncritically their past efforts, and interacting in an egalitarian manner as a collaborator, rather than as an "all-knowing consultant." Trust built with teachers in these early stages of assessment amplifies the trust formed prior to assessment, through consultation and other prereferral activities. A list of areas of inquiry to be included in an initial teacher interview is presented in Box 4.3.

By taking ample time and exercising sensitivity in interviewing parents and teachers at the outset of an assessment, the evaluator conveys caring and competence, obtains critical information, and continues a process that will increase the consumer's engagement through all phases of the assessment. Recommendations—the most important part of the assessment—implicitly ask parents, teachers, special educators, other service providers, and often the child herself, to change. Change is most likely to occur under conditions of ongoing trust and confidence.

Relating to the Child

Establishing a productive working relationship with the child is the foundation for what follows in the course of an assessment. It involves a skillful balance between engaging the child in a friendly, supportive, reassuring, and flexible fashion and presenting tests, tasks, and interview questions in a standardized and professional manner. The child should be engaged from the outset as a partner in the process. In particular, the date and time of testing appointments are discussed with the child ahead of time. Too often, children are simply informed of appointments, and sometimes even pulled out of a classroom with no advance notice. Parents also may be unaware of the specific date of testing. Few adults would stand for being called into an office while at work, then told that they were to begin psychological testing. Children need at least the same degree of preparation.

The evaluator's objective is to elicit optimal effort within the bounds of standardized procedures, while establishing a positive environment and being responsive to the child's personality and needs. Most children join in a collaborative spirit. However, some are fearful or distrustful, regardless of the evaluator's efforts to establish rapport. This is meaning-

BOX 4.2. Scope of an Initial Parent Interview

The questions included here pertain to a comprehensive interview; in practice, questions should be asked selectively, as relevant to the reasons for referral and both the parent's and evaluator's concerns.

INTRODUCTION AND OPENING

- Explanation of the purpose of the assessment, likely assessment procedures, duration and scope of the initial interview, and review of consent.
- Opening question: "How can the assessment be of help?"
- Review of child's identifying information: age, grade, race, ethnicity, etc.
- Open-ended description of the child: "Please, tell me about _____."
- Parents' perception of the child's problems.
- Parents' perception of the child's strengths.

SCHOOL FUNCTIONING

- Current school functioning: academic, social, behavioral, extracurricular.
- Past school functioning: academic, social, behavioral, extracurricular.
- Special services and other school interventions.
- Parents' opinion of the child's current school program.
- Parents' perception of home–school relations.
- Parents' own experiences in school; impact on expectations for the child's experience.

DEVELOPMENTAL AND MEDICAL HISTORIES

- Child's developmental history.
- Child's current health and medical history.
- Child's history of psychiatric disorders.
- Child's history of medical and psychiatric treatment.

FAMILY FUNCTIONING

- Family composition: "Who lives at home?"; "Is there anyone else in the family?"
- "Is there anyone else like a family member, anyone else important to _____."
- Child's current home functioning: social, academic-related (attitude toward school, homework, etc.)
- Family history: births of siblings, changes in family composition, significant changes in family experiences (e.g., losses, household moves, financial changes)
- Current stresses at home (e.g., finances, changes in family composition, household moves, illness, emotional struggles, traumatic experience, military deployments)

(continued)

- Family values: What is important to the family in terms of education, the child's experiences in life, religion, community connections, for example?
- Family culture: racial, ethnic, religious, sexual orientation, disability status, etc.
- Family resources: Who, in the nuclear or extended family, might be able to help the child?

COMMUNITY FUNCTIONING

- Description of the community in which the family lives.
- Community resources: recreational, child care, medical, mental health.
- Community stresses, if any.

CONCLUSION

- Recap referral questions and invite parent to add or elaborate (e.g., "Any additional thoughts now on how assessment could be of help?"; "Any questions about your child you would like me to answer?")
- Last questions: "Are there any questions I missed?"; "Is there anything else you would like to tell me?"
- Description of upcoming assessment procedures, including testing, reporting, and follow-up.

ful information in and of itself. For example, a child who has been exposed to severe trauma may perceive the one-to-one interaction with an unfamiliar adult as threatening, and revert to self-protective fight or flight behaviors. A child who feels embarrassed and anxious about weak reading skills might ask to go to the bathroom several times during reading subtests. While these behaviors may interfere with efforts to accurately assess mental capabilities, they are highly relevant in revealing what is interfering with learning or social development.

The first task in meeting with the child is to explain the purpose of the assessment, the likely procedures, and the intended benefits. The purpose should be specific (e.g., "to understand more about how you read so that we can help you read better," "to understand the reasons why you get into fights so that we can help keep you out of trouble"). The evaluator describes the expected amount of time required and the kind of assessment measures that will be used. He invites and addresses the child's questions and concerns, and ascertains that the child is amenable to being a participant in the process. All of this is conveyed in developmentally appropriate terms that the child can understand. The child's willingness to proceed should not be assumed but rather confirmed, with a brief question such as "Can we go on?" Any reservations voiced by the child then can be the basis for additional discussion. If the child flatly refuses to cooperate despite reasonable attempts at explaining the procedures, the session should be stopped and teacher and parent should be consulted to plan the next steps. Sample explanations of an assessment for children of varying ages are presented in Box 4.4.

In an interview, the child is asked to provide input about referral concerns, as well as general information about his views, preferences, and circumstances (e.g., "How is school for you?"; "Is there anything in school that is hard for you, or getting in your way?"; "How

BOX 4.3. Scope of an Initial Teacher Interview

As with the parent interview (Box 4.2), these questions should be asked selectively, as relevant to the reasons for referral and both the teacher's and evaluator's concerns.

INTRODUCTION AND OPENING

- Explanation of the purpose of the assessment, likely assessment procedures, duration and scope of the initial interview.
- Child's identifying information: grade/subject taught, age, race, amount of contact, ethnicity, etc.
- Teacher's description of school context: classroom, academic demands, other students in classroom, etc.
- Opening question: "How can the assessment be of help?"
- Open-ended description of the child: "Please, tell me about _____."
- Teacher's perception of the child's problems.
- Teacher's perception of the child's strengths.

SCHOOL FUNCTIONING

- Current school functioning: academic, social, behavioral, extracurricular.
- Past school functioning: academic, social, behavioral, extracurricular.
- Special services and other school interventions.
- Teacher's educational values: What is important to the teacher in his or her teaching, interaction with children, classroom climate, and on other issues?
- Teacher's perception of the match between school culture and the child's culture.
- Teacher's opinion of the child's current school program.

FAMILY AND COMMUNITY FUNCTIONING

- Teacher's perception of the family, its strengths, and its impact on the child's problems.
- Teacher's perception of home–school relations.
- Teacher's perception of community resources: recreational, child care, medical, mental health.
- Teacher's perception of community stresses, if any.

PROBLEMS AND SOLUTIONS

- Teacher's perceptions of the causes of the child's problems as related to the child herself, the school, the home, family culture, and the community.
- Teacher's reports on the effects of interventions that have been tried in the past.
- Teacher's perception of needed services, if any, in and out of school.

(continued)

CONCLUSION

- Recap referral questions and invite teacher to add or elaborate (e.g., "Any additional thoughts now on how assessment could be of help?")
- Last questions: "Are there any questions I missed?"; "Is there anything else you would like to tell me?"
- Description of upcoming assessment procedures, including testing, reporting, and follow-up.

BOX 4.4. Sample Explanations to Children about a Psychoeducational Assessment

FOR A PRIMARY GRADE OR INTELLECTUALLY DEFICIENT CHILD

"Thank you for working with me today. We're going to spend some time together, and I'll ask you to do a lot of different things. This will help me get to know you better, . . . to find out what you know, what you're good at, and what things you need to work on at school. This will help teachers to teach you better. You won't know all the answers. Try your best. Do you have any questions?"

FOR AN UPPER ELEMENTARY/MIDDLE SCHOOL-AGE CHILD

"Thank you for working with me today. We're going to meet probably two or three times so that I can find out more about you—what you know, how you solve problems, how you think about things, what you're good at. . . . The reason is to help teachers figure out the best way to teach you, and whether we can make any changes that help you do better in school. I'll be asking you to do a lot of different things. Some will be easy for you, some will be hard. Usually, the questions or problems will get harder and harder until they're too hard for you. You're not expected to know all the answers. Just try your best. Any questions?"

- Indicate the amount of time you plan to meet with the student now and over time
- Discuss the best times to meet with the student.

FOR A MIDDLE SCHOOL/HIGH SCHOOL-AGE CHILD

"Thank you for working with me today. Has anyone—your teacher or parent—mentioned this to you? [What did they tell you? What are you expecting?] We're going to meet a few times, starting today, so that I can find out more about you—what you have learned, how you solve problems, how you think about things—to help things go better for you in school. It's my understanding that [general explanation of referral concerns, e.g., poor grades, completing work on time, following teachers' instructions.]. After we finish, we'll talk about what I find out and how it might be helpful."

- Indicate the amount of time you plan to meet with the student now and over time
- Discuss the best times to meet with the student

do you like to spend your time?"; "Who do you live with?"; "How do you get along with others?"; "How do others treat you?"). McConaughy (2013) and Braaten (2007) provide extensive guidance about conducting such interviews. The child is asked about his perspective on referral questions and concerns.

The testing that is conducted is responsive to the needs of the individual child. Explanations are provided in language that is easily understood. Conditions are monitored to ensure his physical comfort. Session length is adjusted as needed to accommodate his ability to pay attention.

Assessment Reporting

A collaborative relationship plays a critical role in consumer-responsive assessment reporting. Communication must flow openly in both directions, from evaluator to consumer and vice versa. The purposes of this communication are to help the consumers feel cared for, to provide answers to assessment questions, and to propose a plan of intervention that is in the best interests of the child. Recommendations that emerge from the user's own words and ideas have the greatest likelihood of being implemented with integrity and investment (Kratochwill, Altschaefl, & Bice-Urbach, 2014).

As noted previously, it is critical that written reports be both meaningful and accessible to consumers. Oral reporting should facilitate a dialogue in which the evaluator speaks directly to the concerns of consumers and provides emotional support. Consumer-responsive written and oral reporting are discussed at length in Chapters 5 and 6, respectively.

Follow-Up Contacts

The needs of consumers don't stop with written or oral reporting; neither do the responsibilities of the evaluator. A key step for the evaluator in consumer-responsive assessment is for the evaluator to check in with both the consumers and the agents of intervention at a reasonable interval, approximately 1 to 3 months following reporting, to find out what recommendations have been implemented and what the response has been. The timing and frequency of follow-up should be determined by the needs of the case; in exceptional circumstances, such as high-risk needs or complex interventions, recurrent follow-up might be called for.

Follow-up contacts are invaluable for several reasons. First, following up conveys an ongoing sense of caring to the consumers. Second, the follow-up contact allows the evaluator to provide brief consultation, thereby exploring whether recommendations have been implemented or disregarded, what questions have arisen, and what results have ensued. This consultation also gives consumers an opportunity to ask for clarification about the assessment findings or to inquire about resources or referrals. Third, follow-up information provides important feedback to the evaluator about the value of the recommendations made. Which interventions were feasible? Which were easily accepted by the child, school staff, parents, and other professionals? Which appear to have been effective? This type of information contributes to the evaluator's clinical expertise and benefits future consumers of the evaluator's assessment services. Follow-up interviews are best done face-to-face, but they can also be done over the phone or by email. Sample follow-up questions are listed in Box 4.5.

BOX 4.5. Sample Follow-Up Interview Questions for Parents or Teachers

After the reorienting introduction (i.e., warm greeting, brief summary of assessment findings, recap of the earlier feedback meeting), questions like the following are asked.

- "How have things gone for [child's name] since the time I shared feedback with you [or, . . . since the last time we spoke]?"
- "I am going to read the recommendations from the assessment report I shared with you; for each one, please let me know if the recommendation was implemented and, if so, whether or not it is showing signs of effectiveness."
- "Is there any new information about school or home that might impact the child's functioning?"
- *"For parents:* Is there anything you would like me to pass on to [child's] teacher or guidance counselor?"
- *"For the teacher:* Is there anything you would like me to pass on to [child's] parents?"

Consumer Evaluation

Finally, it is advisable to determine whether the assessment, in the eyes of the consumer, fulfilled its intended purposes. For this purpose, we recommend distributing a brief evaluation questionnaire for each assessment. Consumer evaluation provides the opportunity to clarify any misconceptions and to return to any areas that were neglected, misunderstood, or inadequately addressed.

Appendix C describes an assessment clinic protocol for conducting follow-up procedures, including a prearranged follow-up contact and an online consumer satisfaction survey.

RESPECTING CULTURE

To be consumer-responsive involves being aware and responsive to many characteristics of consumers, including culture. As defined in the American Psychological Association (2002) guidelines, culture is not only as a set of specific practices related to one's race or ethnicity, but rather "the embodiment of a worldview through learned and transmitted beliefs, values, and practices." Culture defines how we think, feel, and behave, and also how we construct our own identities and how we perceive others. Culture is determined to a great extent by race and ethnicity, but also by gender, age, geographic location, socioeconomic resources, military service, religion, immigration status, sexual orientation, and gender identity.

If evaluators are to relate well and communicate clearly, the two pillars of consumer-responsive assessment, they must take culture into account—their own as well as that of consumers. What does a Black child make of a White examiner who asks personal questions? What is the impact on rapport when we ask a gay male teen if he has a girlfriend, and not simply if he has someone special? What do we miss when we fail to ask a family with strong evangelical beliefs about the importance of their faith? When evaluating a child for school refusal, do we understand the closeness of a Dominican family? How do we convey the mainstream concept of intelligence to an Iraqi family for whom intelligence is associated more with day-to-day resourcefulness and survival than with academic potential? What will the Salvadoran immigrant parents who barely speak English make of our reports written in English? In providing oral feedback to a Chinese family, how will they understand our asking for their thoughts about their child's problems when what they expect is an authoritative account of his difficulties and a specific plan of action?

Conventional assessments adhere to culture-responsive guidelines prescribed by legal mandates and professional standards. Federal special education regulations require that assessment materials

(i) Are selected and administered so as not to be discriminatory on a racial or cultural basis;

(ii) Are provided and administered in the child's native language or other mode of communication and in the form most likely to yield accurate information on what the child knows and can do academically, developmentally, and functionally, unless it is clearly not feasible to so provide or administer; (Sec. 300.304(c)(1))

The *Standards for Educational and Psychological Testing* (AERA, APA, & NCME, 2014) call for cultural fairness in various aspects of test development and interpretation of tests, and specifically address language issues as follows:

Standard 3.13. A test should be administered in the language that is most relevant and appropriate to the test purpose.

Standard 3.14. When testing requires the use of an interpreter, the interpreter should follow standardized procedures and, to the extent feasible, be sufficiently fluent in the language and content of the test and the examinee's native language and culture to translate the test and related testing materials and to explain the examinee's test responses, as necessary. (p. 69)

Furthermore, tests must be valid for the populations with which they are used. The issue of validity here concerns both content that is relevant to the decisions that are to be made and standardization procedures that are appropriately inclusive. Appropriately inclusive here means that the child's cultural group was included in the normative sample at a frequency proportional to the general population or, even better, that separate norms have been produced for that cultural group in addition to the general population norms.

While consumer-responsive assessment, with its emphasis on trusting relationships and clear communication, is responsive to these standards, it calls for evaluators to do more. Consumer-responsive assessment is consistent with the ethical guidelines promulgated by the American Psychological Association (2017).

Psychologists are aware of and respect cultural, individual, and role differences, including those based on age, gender, gender identity, race, ethnicity, culture, national origin, religion, sexual orientation, disability, language, and socioeconomic status and consider these factors when working with members of such groups.

Geva and Wiener (2015) have written an excellent guide to the assessment of culturally and linguistically diverse groups of children. In addition to covering key dimensions of cultural differences, such as perspectives on individualism, collectivism, short- and long-term orientation, and language and acculturation, they suggest important ways for working with a diversity of children and families. Furthermore, they offer suggestions for culturally-responsive reporting that emphasize an appreciation for cultural beliefs, as well as clear and understandable communication. Jones (2018) describes the central role of culture in every aspect of assessment, from gathering background information through test selection, interpretation of results, and recommendations. She values family contributions throughout the assessment process and stresses the importance of focusing on a child's and family's strengths.

Culture and Trust

Trust in a relationship, even the relatively brief relationship between evaluator and consumers, is reciprocal. The evaluator trusts that the consumers will expend some effort and be reasonably open, forthcoming, and honest. The consumers trust that the evaluator has the requisite knowledge and skills, and will work hard, strive to understand them, treat them fairly, and put their interests before his own. However, there is a long history of mistrust between individuals of different economic, ethnic, and racial backgrounds in the United States. Does the working-class White single mother, with three kids, two jobs, and no husband, trust that the upper-middle-class evaluator, dressed in a well-tailored suit, can understand what she is going through? To what extent does a Black mother, disadvantaged in housing and income and confronted by discrimination in many spheres of her life, trust that a White evaluator will provide equal treatment for her Black child? To what extent does a Guatemalan immigrant teenager, fearing maltreatment or even deportation, trust that an evaluator is truly interested in helping, rather than condemning, him when he responds to questions about his family and friends? What of the girl in the hijab? Can she trust that the evaluator will strive to understand her perspective and help her rather than reject her as an alien other?

Consumer-responsive evaluators need to take specific actions to build bridges of trust across cultural divides. These bridges facilitate understanding and respect, and consist of three types. The first bridge is constructed of kind, compassionate, and competent interviewing skills that convey to all consumers, children and adults alike, that the evaluator is interested in them and cares. Is the evaluator warm? Is she inquisitive? Is she welcoming and respectful? Is she empathic, realizing what the consumers she interviews are feeling, and allowing herself to feel some of the same emotions, and then respond, based on those emotions? Does she take the time to listen? Does she strive to see the situation from the others' perspective?

The second bridge is constructed of the evaluator's awareness of the perceptions, expectations, and interactive behaviors determined by his or her own culture. How does the evaluator's culture influence her concepts of childhood, education, proper behavior, the role of parents, what is and is not considered a disorder, and how disorders are to be treated? Similarly, how does the evaluator expect to be perceived by a child or a parent? What expectations does he have for how consumers will relate to him and for how they will respond to his explanations and recommendations? Similarly, how does the evaluator interact with others? How warm is he? Does he laugh or smile? Does he shake hands or pat others on the back? How loudly does he speak, and with what degree of eye contact? How open is he about personal matters? All of these are culturally determined. If the evaluator is aware of them, then he or she can modulate them based on the culture of the consumers.

The third bridge consists of questions and comments that indicate that culture is something that can be discussed. We must feel free both to ask and comment about culture. Culturally sensitive interviewing begins in the earliest stage of the encounter, when we ask parents who their child is. In addition to asking about age and grade, we may routinely ask about both the child's and family's identity, considering questions about race, ethnicity, religion, sexual orientation (from the early teenage years), disability status, veteran's status (for parents), and where the child or family has lived previously. Many teens now want to be asked what pronouns we should use in addressing them (e.g., he, she, or they). We must also ask what languages are spoken in the home and, if we believe it to be the case, from what country the family emigrated and how long ago. In the current political climate, we need to be sensitive about this last question, as some family members fear that their answers might prompt our reporting them to Immigration and Customs Enforcement. These initial questions about race, ethnicity, and other aspects of culture, are essential in forming the foundation for the remainder of the interview. Suggested culturally sensitive interview questions are listed in Box 4.6.

Furthermore, we must be very cautious about cultural assumptions, as they can be misleading. For example, we shouldn't assume that a person's ethnicity matches his or her appearance. Further, our assumptions, even if correct, tell us little about the degree of acculturation or the strength of cultural identification. Are there other aspects of culture, aside from our assumptions about race or class, that are equally important?

I [B. E.] am reminded of a colleague who is African American, lesbian, and a highly respected mental health practitioner and advocate. As for which is "primary," she relates that the most important aspect of her identity is that she was raised as an Army brat.

Much has been written about culturally responsive care. Sue and Sue (2016) provide an excellent foundation, and the American Psychiatric Association's *Cultural Formulation Interview* (Lewis-Fernandez, Aggarwal, Hinton, Hinton, & Kirmayer, 2016) is a useful guide for diagnostic interviews.

Culture and Communication

Communication requires clear understanding and open expression between parties. Does the evaluator strive to understand the cultural meanings of parents' statements? Does the evaluator speak in everyday language, avoiding jargon, that she believes any non-psychologist will understand? Are reports written in everyday language, minimizing the use of technical terms? Does the evaluator clarify terms she feels might be misunderstood? At a basic and essential level, does the evaluator speak the primary language of the child and of the parents?

Language differences can present challenges for effective communication. According to 2011 U.S. census data, 21% of Americans over the age of 5 (60.6 million people!) speak

BOX 4.6. Culturally Sensitive Interview Questions

An important goal of all interviews is for the interviewer to understand the interviewee's perceptions, that is, to see the world through the interviewee's eyes. Those perceptions are determined, in part, by culture. Questions about culture should be asked selectively, with the content and timing decided with sensitivity on an individual basis. Consider the following types of questions.

IDENTIFYING QUESTIONS

- "When you think of who you are, and what your identity is, what is important to you?"
- "Do you feel part of a community? What is your racial background? Your ethnic background? Where did your ancestors come from?"
- "What languages do you speak? What languages does your child speak? How well?"
- "Is faith important to you? Are you a part of a religious community? Do you often go to a church, mosque, synagogue, or temple? What beliefs guide you in your life?"
- *For parents:* "Who is in the family? Who lives at home with you? Whom are you close with?"
- *For teens:* "Is there anyone who is special to you? Are you romantically involved with anyone? Who? Do you feel strongly male or strongly female?"

QUESTIONS ABOUT THE PROBLEM(S)

- "What do you think are the causes of your child's problems? What do people in your community think causes these types of problems?"
- *There are more specific alternatives:* "What do other [African Americans, Chinese, or people in your Irish neighborhood] think about this? Is it a problem? If so, what causes it?"
- *Or, with even greater specificity:* "Do you think that being Asian has anything to do with how the teacher treated your son?"
- *For a child:* "How does it feel to be the only [Black kid or White kid] in your class?"
- *For a gay teen who has acknowledged this with the evaluator:* "Do you think they're picking on you because you're gay?"

QUESTIONS ABOUT INTERVENTIONS

- "Do you have thoughts about what we might do to help? How about people in your community? What do they think would be helpful? Is there anyone in your community that could help with this? What do people in your community usually do when people have this kind of problem? What kinds of healers do they go to?"
- *Alternatively, one could ask more specific questions such as:* "You told me you have a large Italian family [where relatives are very important]. What do your relatives think would help with this? Do you agree?"

QUESTIONS ABOUT THE EVALUATOR–PARENT RELATIONSHIP

- "How is it for you to work with someone who is [Black, White, Asian, etc.]?"
- "Do you think I get it? Would it be different if I were [same race or ethnicity as child or parent]?"

a language other than English at home (Ryan, 2013). For the majority of these Americans (37.6 million), that language is Spanish. Conventional assessment standards call for a child to be assessed in her strongest language. In many cases, however, the preferred course is for a bilingual evaluator to conduct the assessment in two languages. Similarly, consumer-responsive assessment practice calls for interviewing parents or teachers in the language in which they can express themselves best. This means that even when a child speaks English but his parents do not, a bilingual evaluator who can communicate directly with all parties should be sought. Furthermore, since many bilingual children and adults switch back and forth between two languages, it is best if they can be interviewed by evaluators who can do the same. Interpreters can be used when no bilingual evaluators are available; however, all possible attempts should be made to secure them.

A similar standard holds for reporting assessment results. Important assessment findings and recommendations should be reported in a language that consumers can understand. Sometimes, the ideal course is to write reports in two languages; bilingual evaluators should be given ample time to do so by their employers. When resources don't allow, bilingual evaluators could write a summary of the report in the second language. Oral reporting also needs to be done in the languages that consumers comprehend. The extra time and effort involved in reporting in two languages is well worth the gain in increased consumer understanding, engagement, and collaboration.

BRIDGING SCHOOL REQUIREMENTS AND PARENT NEEDS

Local school districts are tasked with determining whether students have a disability that qualifies for special education services and with designing IEPs that provide children with disabilities with a free and appropriate public education. Decisions regarding special education eligibility and program planning are made by the school-based IEP team, which consists of administrators, teachers, special educators, related service providers (i.e., school psychologists and other specialists), parents, and older students. The special education administrator is ultimately responsible both for the appropriateness of the program that is planned and for its funding.

Although IEP decisions are often made collaboratively by team members, parent involvement is not universal. Of a large national sample of parents who attended their 11- to 19-year-old child's initial IEP team meetings, 70% believed that they were involved "the right amount," and 29% wanted to be involved more (Wagner, Newman, Cameto, Javitz, & Valdes, 2012). Parents of older students, African American and Latino parents, and parents with lower household incomes tended to report feeling less satisfied than parents of younger students, White students, and those with higher household incomes. Parents who were unsatisfied with the team process reported feeling confused, lost, or disregarded. In some cases, they believed that schools act more to protect their budgets than to provide needed services.

Consumer-responsive psychological assessments can play a vital role in bridging the school–family divide. Built on the foundation of collaborative relationships and clear communication, consumer-responsive assessment brings parents, students, and teachers into the process from the beginning. Such collaboration forms the basis for a successful IEP team process, as all members become active participants who feel heard and valued.

School administrators may fear that consumer-responsive assessment creates an unhelpful alliance between the evaluator and parents, students, or teachers, amplifying their voices over those of the other members of the IEP team and adding to divisions and conflict. We strongly disagree. Consumer-responsive evaluators can build strong and collaborative relationships with consumers, while still valuing the expertise of all others on the team and maintaining realistic expectations for the IEP process. The consumer-responsive evaluator joins with a family, but does not become its champion. The evaluator must be an independent agent who is attuned to the interests of the child, the family, and the school. There is ample evidence that children are served best when their parents and their schools work together (Christenson & Reschly, 2010; Ferguson, 2008; Hattie, 2009). Students whose parents are involved and engaged with their school achieve more, interact better with others, and are more likely to graduate and obtain further education (Henderson & Mapp, 2002). Such collaboration is beneficial for all students, including those who receive special education services (Turnbull, Turnbull, Erwin, Soodak, & Shogren, 2015).

Collaborative consumer-responsive relationships work to serve the ultimate goal of assessment as described herein, that is, to provide the greatest possible benefit to the child who is assessed.

CHAPTER 5

Consumer-Responsive Report Writing

An informative assessment report is built on a foundation of standard good practice. Essential elements of standard good practice, as discussed in Chapter 3, include the following:

- The choice of assessment procedures is individualized to address referral questions and concerns.
- The evaluator considers multiple sources of data: records, interviews, observations, and testing.
- Tests are selected based on their relevance to referral questions and the soundness of their psychometric properties.
- Measurement error is recognized when interpreting scores.
- Interpretation of data emphasizes convergent findings from multiple sources.
- Recommendations are specific, practical, and responsive to referral concerns.

While assessment reports that apply these practices have merit, a consumer-responsive approach augments standard good practice in ways that enhance the likelihood of producing positive outcomes. As discussed in Chapter 4, greater benefit results from a purposeful process of responsive and productive personal relationships. The written report plays a unique and valuable role in this process. In addition to fulfilling the basic functions of conveying essential information and informing interventions, the written report (1) serves as formal documentation for procedural purposes, (2) ensures that all parties have a common understanding of assessment findings and recommendations, and (3) helps consumers to recollect key findings and renew their efforts to support the child.

The core principles of consumer-responsive assessment have major implications for written reports. If the ultimate goal of assessment is to promote positive outcomes, report writing should be guided by the objective of effectively communicating relevant information to key consumers. Given that most consumers do not have formal training in psychological measurement, the written report should be responsive to their needs with respect to organization, content, and language. And while the target audience may also include professionals with expertise in assessment and measurement, clear and focused writing will be of value to them as well.

Some authors of report-writing guides propose that the style and structure of reports should vary with the intended purpose and audience (Braaten, 2007; Goldfinger & Pomerantz, 2014; Ownby, 1997). They describe various types of report, such as a brief narrative, neuropsychological evaluation, forensic report, and psychiatric evaluation, some of which are discussed in Chapter 7. This chapter, however, proceeds on the assumption that the great majority of child assessment reports are of a similar nature. They are comprehensive in coverage and intended for a broad audience that includes parents. Whether generated by a school psychologist, mental health clinic psychologist, or an independently practicing evaluator, these assessments contain much the same kind of information and employ a similar outline. Given these similarities, the guidance that follows is widely applicable.

CHARACTERISTICS OF CONSUMER-RESPONSIVE REPORTS

Consumer-responsive reports promote effective communication in a number of ways: selectivity of content, theme-based organization, focus on the child (rather than tests), effective presentation of data, and comprehensible language.

Selectivity

To maximize relevance and value, the evaluator should be selective about what to include in a report. As Braaten (2007) advises, "Be succinct in your writing. If information does not contribute to an understanding of the referral question or to the observed difficulties, the information is irrelevant and does not need to be included" (p. 10).

We refer to this litmus test as the *"So what?"* principle, a shorthand for the criterion evaluators should apply in deciding what to include or emphasize in a report. Content that does not contribute to a better understanding of the student, the student's circumstances, or the student's needs should be omitted for failing to meet this standard. By ensuring that all content serves a purpose and by eliminating material of little or no value, the evaluator clarifies for the reader what is important and makes the report more readable and useful.

The "So what?" principle highlights a common shortcoming of traditional reports: indiscriminate and overly technical reporting of test performance. Too often, extraneous or uninterpretable standardized testing results are included in a report simply because the evaluator generated the data. If the referral concern is a suspected language-based reading disability and the child demonstrates average performance on the Visual–Spatial factor of the Stanford–Binet, why devote a paragraph to analysis of visual–spatial skills? If a child is evaluated for concerns about depression or anxiety and the Processing Speed Index on the WISC-V is higher than the Verbal Comprehension Index, why does this test result merit a comment? If findings have no bearing on the evaluator's conceptualization of a case and have no impact on recommendations, their exclusion will not detract from the report. The evaluator might reason that such information does no harm, but there is indeed a cost: the report loses focus, and relies on the reader, rather than the evaluator, to distinguish what is important from what is not. Lack of selectivity makes a report longer, less accessible, and less likely to be read with care.

How, then, does one apply the "So what?" principle? One way to operationalize the principle is to consider whether the assessment finding will have any bearing on referral concerns, key interpretations, or recommendations. A coherent consumer-responsive report highlights significant findings that run through the report in a consistent thread, from assessment findings to conclusions to recommendations, clearly framing what is meaningful and relevant. Questions and concerns are addressed, irrelevant material is discarded, and the reader is enlightened.

It is no small irony that the more the evaluator writes, the less a reader is likely to read. Applying the "So what?" principle will reduce report length when warranted and, in contrast to reports with a fixed template, allows report length to vary on a case-by-case basis. There is nothing inherently wrong with a long report. It is justified in certain circumstances, for example, in a complex case with referral concerns in multiple areas—cognitive, social–emotional, and physical—for which a great deal of assessment data is relevant. However, that is the exception rather than the rule. By distinguishing between what is essential and what is inconsequential, the evaluator will produce reports of varying lengths that correspond to assessment purpose and case complexity.

Theme-Based Organization

Organizing findings by theme (i.e., area of functioning, hypothesis, or referral question), rather than by test, is a common recommendation in the literature on report writing (Groth-Marnat, 2009; Hass & Carriere, 2014; Harvey, 2013; Jones, 2018; Lichtenstein, 2013a; Schneider et al., 2018; Wiener & Kohler, 1986). Theme-based organization involves grouping findings of a similar nature from different tests or from different sources of assessment data (i.e., records, interviews, rating scales, observations, tests). Hence, a theme-based approach directs the reader's attention where it belongs: on the child, rather than on assessment measures.

A theme-based approach emphasizes the integration of multiple sources of assessment data. Confirmatory evidence across data sources provides strong assurance that findings are robust, relevant, and valid. It is highly instructive to connect the teacher's report of slow and halting reading in the classroom with standardized test results of deficient oral reading fluency and naming speed, or to relate teacher and parent reports of impulsivity with observations of impulsive behavior during testing that interferes with cognitive and academic performance. These are highly valid findings that the evaluator does well to highlight.

Most evaluators report findings on a test-by-test basis, leaving the reader to identify themes and connect related information. This method can result in contradictory or inconsistent results appearing in different parts of a report, without any comment or reconciling explanation. With theme-based organization, the evaluator is inclined to give heightened emphasis to confirmatory evidence and to acknowledge and perhaps explain inconsistent findings (e.g., that the apparent discrepancy reflects the influence of some other factor, such as attention, motivation, or fatigue).

Test-by-test reporting can have other undesirable side effects. It encourages pointless descriptions of subtests and technical elaboration of test characteristics. The explanation that the Information subtest was administered even though it does not contribute to the Verbal Comprehension and Full Scale scores is of little value in understanding the child. Likewise, the lay reader gains little from the explanation that Block Design "involves arranging two-color blocks to construct a design that matches a pictured model within a specified time limit." Expounding on each administered subtest, rather than limiting descriptions and interpretations to a select and meaningful few, makes for a longer report of lesser value.

Evaluators may recognize the advantages of presenting results and organizing findings by theme but find it difficult to do so. Lichtenstein (2014) raised the topic of theme-based reports as part of an online discussion with school psychologists. Participants heartily endorsed theme-based organization, but acknowledged that test-by-test reporting is the norm and that transitioning to a theme-based approach will not come easy.

Child Focus (vs. Test Focus)

In conventional reports, the presentation and interpretation of data largely revolves around norm-referenced tests and rating scales. Evaluators may report assessment data from records, interviews, and observations as well, but only as a prelude to the "real" assessment findings. Interpretation of findings takes place in the section where test results are presented (e.g., Test Results and Interpretations), whereas the contribution of other data sources to the conclusions and recommendations goes unacknowledged. This report structure gives the impression that all noteworthy findings were derived from testing, rather than reflecting the integrative nature of skilled clinical interpretation. Assessment reports would be highly speculative and of limited value if standardized testing alone were relied on to understand a child's functioning and to inform recommendations. Background information, behavioral observations, and interviews contribute critically important findings that are indicative of everyday functioning. A test-centric approach also reinforces the notion that a DSM-5 diagnosis or a special education disability category can be determined entirely from test scores, thus perpetuating the mystique of the psychologist's proprietary toolkit.

Recognizing that records, interviews, observations, and tests all contribute significantly to conclusions and recommendations has major implications for report structure and organization. For starters, all sources of assessment data, not just standardized tests, should be recognized when assessment inputs are identified at the beginning of a report. The list of data sources should be labeled "Assessment Procedures," rather than "Tests Administered." Similarly, the report structure and wording should reflect that "assessment findings" refer to *all* data collected by the evaluator, not just test results. Since all four "RIOT" elements (records, interviews, observations, and tests) contribute valuable assessment data, this can be made explicit with a report structure that gives equal billing to each source, for example, by including all sources under the superordinate heading Assessment Findings.

Report structure greatly influences the extent to which the evaluator emphasizes, or overemphasizes, test results. Most notably, it is common practice for evaluators to include tables of test scores in the body of the report. Doing so not only expands the Test Results section of the report, but predisposes the evaluator to dwell on the findings. Having included tables of test scores, the evaluator may feel obliged to explain, or at least make reference to, every score, irrespective of its importance or relevance to referral concerns. This is inconsistent with the selectivity an evaluator employs when reporting only the meaningful historical information and observed behavior, while dispensing with trivial or uninformative data. Furthermore, with the inclusion of all test results in the body of a report, the evaluator is likely to attempt tenuous or convoluted explanations that are insufficiently supported by psychometric rigor, convergent data, or research. Thus, the evaluator may venture an explanation of why one subtest score in a scale is higher than another (e.g., that a rehearsal strategy can facilitate Recall of Digits Forward, whereas Recall of Digits Backward requires more active mental manipulation of data), even though the difference in scores is relatively small and there is no other support for this pattern. Typically, these tenuous interpretations do not carry over into the Discussion, Summary, or Recommendations sections of the report, where the evaluator highlights and applies key findings. They serve no function other than to perplex readers and discourage paying attention to this section of the report, although arguably, one function may be to convey that the evaluator possesses advanced assessment skills and technical knowledge that are beyond the scope of the reader.

As an alternative approach, we strongly recommend relegating tables of test scores to a report appendix that comprehensively documents test results and related psychometric data. This *Data Summary* frees up the evaluator to report test results selectively in the body of a report. In deciding what test results to emphasize in the report, the evaluator distinguishes between findings that are noteworthy and meaningful and those that are trivial and irrelevant. It is the evaluator's job to make these distinctions explicit, rather than reporting test results exhaustively and leaving the reader to figure out what actually matters.

One reason often cited for embedding tables and technical explanations of test scores in a report is that it is of interest to assessment-savvy professional readers. However, by providing a Data Summary, the evaluator makes the test data available for the discerning professional, while presenting findings in a focused and accessible way in the body of the report for the benefit of all readers. The Data Summary section is described in greater detail later in this chapter.

Presentation of Data

Given the goal of clear communication with consumers, there is much to be said about how data are presented. Numbers can either obscure or facilitate understanding. A score of 90 on a Wechsler scale of intelligence may be regarded as average range functioning, whereas a score of 90 on the Achenbach System of Empirically Based Assessment (ASEBA) Child Behavior Checklist suggests a severe problem. How is the average reader to make sense of psychometric information that evaluators learn only through extended exposure in graduate school?

In deciding how to present test results, the evaluator should consider (1) whether the reader will understand the information provided and (2) whether the manner of presentation will avert misinterpretation of findings and misconceptions about the traits being assessed. The first point concerns what format to use in conveying quantitative results. The second point involves the recognition that measurements of human traits and behavior are subject to error and to change over time.

Measurement Error

The concept of measurement error, or *reliability,* is well known to psychologists. It is incumbent upon an evaluator to take measurement error into account when presenting and interpreting test results, using language and formats that are consistent with the reliability of a measure. Measurement error is a major topic in courses on testing and measurement, and is emphasized in the *Standards for Educational and Psychological Testing* (AERA, APA, & NCME, 2014).

> Standard 12.18. In educational settings, score reports should be accompanied by a clear presentation of information on how to interpret the scores, including the degree of measurement error associated with each score or classification level. (p. 200)

Accordingly, test publishers provide the confidence intervals associated with test scores, and textbook authors propose scripts for reporting confidence intervals. For example, Sattler (2018) uses the following format:

> [Gregory obtained] a Full Scale IQ of 92 ± 6 (30th percentile rank). The chances that his true IQ is between 86 and 98 are about 95 out of 100 (p. 746)

Nevertheless, evaluators routinely report exact scores without reference to measurement error (e.g., "Philbert earned a score of 96 on the General Cognitive Ability scale of the DAS-II"), perhaps with the justification that citing the obtained score forthrightly conveys the child's actual performance. This presumes that the reader will know that scores are inexact measures of a construct.

The score obtained on a given test on a given day is only an estimate of a person's skill, ability, or characteristic functioning.[1] It may or may not be a good estimate of the hypothesized "true score" and, in all probability, will not match the score obtained by another form of the same test, or the score that might have been obtained on the same test on some other occasion. The reasons for variation are many: testing conditions; the examiner's administration and scoring accuracy; the examinee's attention, effort, and mood; lucky and unlucky guessing when uncertain; and the specific test items selected, to name a few. Thus, it is misleading for the score obtained on a given occasion to be regarded as an exact measure of the ability or trait it is intended to measure. If a score is off the mark, failing to recognize the range of possible scores may compound the error. Similarly, when scores from different points in time are compared, differences due to chance may be misinterpreted as gains or losses.

Evaluators who lose sight of measurement error may interpret differences between scores that are actually baseless (i.e., not statistically significant). To guard against this, some test publishers provide data on score differences needed to reach statistical significance and

---

[1] Walrath, Willis, and Dumont (2014) suggest reporting test scores in the past tense (e.g., "Iris earned a score of 92") "to emphasize the fact that they are the scores the student happened to earn that day" (p. 440).

on base rates of differences between scores. Even in the absence of an explicit interpretation, drawing attention to small differences (e.g., "Winston earned a score of 9 on immediate recall and a score of 7 on delayed recall") may lead to unwarranted conclusions. Just because one score is higher than another does not mean that it should be described as such in the report narrative. If two scores have overlapping confidence intervals, it is entirely possible that the difference is due to chance.

A measure's confidence interval and standard error of measurement are derived from reliability estimates. Test publishers typically provide users with a choice of confidence intervals, such as the 68%, 90%, or 95% level. The 68% confidence level has inherent meaning (i.e., the range of scores within one standard error of measurement of the obtained score), but is not advisable for clinical use, as it leaves the hypothesized "true score" outside of the confidence interval about one-third of the time. The wider 90% and 95% confidence intervals are better options.

One might reason that "being right" about 90% of the time is quite respectable and does justice to the psychometric properties of carefully developed norm-referenced measures. However, there is good reason to favor the more conservative 95% confidence interval. Evaluators should be circumspect in their use of confidence intervals for the simple reason that test publishers routinely provide low estimates of measurement error (Lichtenstein, 2013b). In most cases (i.e., other than on timed measures), test publishers derive the standard error of measurement from internal consistency reliability, typically using the split-half method. Unlike test–retest reliability, internal consistency reflects the measurement error associated with the score obtained *on that occasion only,* meaning that the confidence interval reflects the likelihood that the score obtained on that particular day was on the mark. This is inconsistent with the way most psychologists explain confidence intervals, that is, as the range in which scores would expectedly fall if the test were administered repeatedly, without practice or memory effects. Internal consistency reliability disregards the many reasons that scores vary from day to day, such as fluctuations in a child's alertness or effort, or examiners' differences in how they administer tests and score responses. Tables 5.1A and 5.1B show how split-half and test–retest reliability compare on two major cognitive ability tests—the WISC-V and the KABC-II [the Kaufman Assessment Battery for Children—Second Edition]—with split-half reliability yielding the higher reliability figures in most cases. (Interestingly, the pattern does not hold true for verbal comprehension measures.) The more conservative 95% confidence interval has the added advantage of being easily calculated if it is not provided by the publisher; it is almost exactly two times the standard error of measurement, and therefore can be estimated by doubling the 68% confidence interval.

Issues of validity further complicate interpretation, and they are often disregarded as well. Evaluators tend to accept at face value that a scale is a valid measure of the construct indicated by its name. The discerning clinician, however, will be cautious about referring to the broad construct that a composite score purportedly measures when the contributing subtests do not widely sample the domain. As examples, (1) the Reading Composite score of the Wide Range Achievement Test–4 (WRAT–4) is derived from subtests that assess reading single words and comprehension of isolated sentences, which should not be equated with reading ability; and (2) the Fluid Reasoning scale of the WISC-V consists of only two subtests (Matrix Reasoning and Figure Weights) and is limited to nonverbal reasoning.

TABLE 5.1A. Comparison of Internal Consistency and Test–Retest Reliability for the WISC-V

WISC-V subtests	Split-half reliability	Test–retest reliability[a]	Corrected test–retest[b]
Similarities	.87	.82	.88
Vocabulary	.87	.89	.90
Information	.86	.85	.88
Comprehension	.83	.81	.83
Block Design	.84	.79	.81
Visual Puzzles	.89	.78	.80
Matrix Reasoning	.87	.65	.78
Figure Weights	.94	.76	.82
Picture Concepts	.83	.63	.71
Arithmetic	.90	.75	.84
Digit Span	.91	.79	.82
Picture Span	.85	.72	.80
Letter–Number Sequencing	.86	.77	.82
Coding[c]		.79	.81
Symbol Search[c]		.76	.80
Cancellation[c]		.79	.82

Note. All coefficients are averaged across age ranges using Fisher's *z* transformation.
[a]From test publisher's study with *n* = 218; test–retest intervals ranged from 9 to 82 days, with a mean interval of 26 days.
[b]Corrected for the variability of the normative sample.
[c]Split-half reliability is not appropriate for tests of processing speed.

TABLE 5.1B. Comparison of Internal Consistency and Test–Retest Reliability for the KABC-II

KABC-II subtests	Split-half reliability, ages 7–18[a]	Test–retest reliability, ages 7–12[b]	Corrected test–retest, ages 7–12[c]	Test–retest reliability, ages 13–18[b]	Corrected test–retest, ages 13–18[c]
Number Recall	.79	.76	.81	.78	.82
Word Order	.87	.72	.69	.69	.74
Hand Movements	.78	.59	.60	.56	.60
Block Counting	.87	.57	.53	.68	.72
Rover	.80	.64	.59	.71	.69
Triangles	.87	.81	.85	.79	.80
Gestalt Closure	.74	.68	.70	.89	.92
Atlantis	.86	.71	.65	.66	.74
Rebus	.93	.81	.76	.84	.81
Delayed Recall	.90	.81	.79	.81	.80
Pattern Reasoning	.90	.73	.74	.73	.74
Story Completion	.77	.74	.74	.69	.70
Expressive Vocabulary	.86	.89	.88	.87	.90
Riddles	.86	.86	.87	.90	.91
Verbal Knowledge	.89	.78	.77	.88	.89

[a]Mean reliabilities averaged across age ranges using Fisher's *z* transformation.
[b]From test publisher's study; *n* = 82 for ages 7–12, *n* = 61 for ages 13–18; test–retest intervals ranged from 12 to 56 days.
[c]Corrected for the variability of the normative sample.

Formats for Describing Performance Level

Interpretation of norm-referenced scores is complicated by the use of various scales to signify the position of a given value relative to a distribution of scores. These include IQ-format scores with a mean of 100 and standard deviation of 15, T scores with a mean of 50 and a standard deviation of 10, and scaled scores with a mean of 10 and a standard deviation of 3. While these different ways of conveying performance levels are familiar and meaningful to the evaluator and other trained professionals, they are not readily understood by parents, teachers, and other consumers. Hence, a consumer-responsive report should not rely exclusively on scores, and might minimize or eliminate their use altogether in the report narrative.

Range Descriptors

A reasonable alternative is to use descriptors such as "Average," "Below Average," and "Extremely High" to convey in familiar language how an individual performed. These descriptors may be paired with quantitative scores (percentiles, standard scores, T scores, etc.) or used on their own. Relying primarily on descriptors will result in little, if any, loss in meaning or effect on interpretations. Furthermore, by providing scores and related psychometric data in a Data Summary, the evaluator enables professional readers to ponder the implications of finer distinctions.

Every method of reporting performances has both advantages and shortcomings, and descriptors are no exception. There is some degree of variability within each descriptive range. This is especially true for the "Average" range, which is usually associated with standardized scores of 90–109. There are noteworthy differences in level of performance from the bottom to the top of "Average" range, and they may (or may not) have implications for understanding and making decisions about a child. Furthermore, scores near the bottom or top of a range are only minimally different from scores in the adjoining range, to which a different descriptor is assigned. For example, an "Average" score of 90 is virtually the same as a "Low Average" score of 89. Accordingly, these scores might be qualified as being "at the lower end of the Average range" or "the upper end of the Low Average range." However, such descriptors can be confusing, especially when the normal curve is divided into many ranges, some with barely distinguishable descriptors (e.g., "Superior" vs. "Very Superior"). To make sense of these finer distinctions, the reader may need to see the full set of descriptors, with their corresponding standard scores and percentile ranges, as an entry in a Data Summary.

A related issue is that test publishers use different sets of descriptors to describe scores that are based on the exact same normal-curve-derived scales. For example, rating scales typically use T scores and assign descriptors to bands that are one standard deviation in width (i.e., 10 points), with scores within 1 standard deviation of the mean described as the "Average" range, 60–69 as the "At-Risk" range, and 70 and above as the "Elevated" or "Clinically Significant" range. However, the ASEBA extends the "Normal" range to T scores of 64, and describes 65–69 as the "Borderline Clinical" range. The range descriptors supplied by publishers are not only inconsistent, but may change over time. As examples, (1) "Borderline" has been widely discontinued as a descriptor; (2) the term "Superior" has been discontinued by the Stanford–Binet (SB-5) and the Differential Ability Scales (DAS-II), but retained by the Woodcock–Johnson (WJ-IV) tests; and (3) the Wechsler Individual Achievement Test—Third Edition (WIAT-III) now describes the "Average" range as standard scores of 85 to 115. To illustrate the inconsistencies, an "Average" range standard score of 115 on the WIAT-III is not far off from a "Superior" score of 121 on the WJ-IV Tests of Achievement. Willis (2015) documented these inconsistencies and weighed options for improving clarity and consistency for readers, and concluded, "There is no known way to present test results without confusing someone" (p. 1).

One way to deal with the diverse sets of descriptors is to include in the Data Summary, as an accompaniment to a table of scores, an interpretive guide listing the descriptors and corresponding test score ranges that the test publisher has specified for each test. By referring to the Data Summary, the reader might sort out the different descriptors used. This approach will explain, but not resolve, the inconsistent use of descriptors from one test to the next.

Lichtenstein (2013b) advocated for the adoption of a uniform set of descriptors, and invited NASP members to participate in an online discussion about the general proposal and to consider a specific set of standard descriptors. Over a dozen NASP members participated in the discussion, all of whom endorsed the idea of uniform descriptors. Furthermore, the participants reached consensus on a uniform set of descriptors, refining the initially proposed set to arrive at the descriptive ranges shown in the top part of Table 5.2. One

TABLE 5.2. Universal Descriptors Proposed by Lichtenstein (Top) and by Kranzler and Floyd (Bottom)

Standard score	Percentile rank	T score	Descriptor
> 130	> 98	>70	Extremely High
116–130	85–98	61–70	High
110–115	75–84	57–60	High Average
91–109	27–73	44–56	Average
85–90	16–25	40–43	Low Average
70–84	2–15	30–39	Low
< 70	< 2	<30	Extremely Low

Note. Adapted from Lichtenstein (2014). Copyright © 2014 National Association of School Psychologists. Bethesda, MD. Reprinted with permission of the publisher. *www.nasponline.org.*

Standard score		T score	Descriptor
≥ 140		≥ 77	Extremely High
130–139		70–76	Very High
120–129		64–69	High
110–119		57–63	High Average
91–109		44–56	Average
81–90		37–43	Low Average
71–80		31–36	Low
61–70		24–30	Very Low
≤ 60		≤ 23	Extremely Low

Note. Adapted from Kranzler and Floyd (2013).

modification that ensued from this discussion was that, while Lichtenstein (2014) proposed applying the term *Average* to scores within 1 standard deviation of the mean, participants in the online discussion opined that scores in the 85–90 and the 110–115 ranges have clinical implications that should be distinguished from Average. Hence, the consensus version identifies these ranges as "Low Average" and "High Average."

It should be noted that this proposed scheme for reporting test performance uses broad descriptive ranges, and these ranges are based on an objective standard—standard deviation units. There is inherent logic in defining the "Average" range as being within 1 standard deviation of the mean. As the name implies, a standard derivation is a statistical estimate of the average distance from the mean of all values in a normal distribution. In contrast, the customary 10-point ranges (intervals of two-thirds of a standard deviation) are of happenstance origin and not derived from any psychometric construct.[2] For comparison purposes, the bottom part of Table 5.2 also includes the set of descriptors proposed by Kranzler and Floyd (2013), which uses the 10-point range convention.

Broad ranges serve well for practical purposes. They are readily understood and are sufficiently informative about a child's functioning to guide recommendations and decisions. Fewer categories, anchored by percentiles or a normal curve illustration, will be less confusing to consumers than trying to fathom the distinctions between High Average, High, Very High, and Extremely High, which are only meaningful to regular test users. The broad-range descriptors characterize performance as falling within typical range, a moderate distance away, or very far from the mean. Consider how a patient makes sense of the results of a medical test, such as a blood test. The patient receives a report with numbers indicating levels of cholesterol, triglycerides, liver functions, and the like. These numbers alone would be meaningless to most patients. They are readily interpretable, however, when the test report includes a key that specifies ranges that correspond to at-risk and elevated levels. The physician may further clarify the significance of the test findings with explanations about the reliability of the test or the influence of other contributing factors (e.g., fatigue, body mass, emotional distress, caffeine intake), thereby enhancing the patient's understanding of the results and the implications for treatment. The physician might summarize this information in a brief written report that references noteworthy scores and the additional considerations for understanding them. A psychologist would do well to use descriptive ranges in a similarly effective way.

Similar logic is applicable to reporting performance on subtests that use scaled scores (i.e., mean of 10, standard deviation of 3). Consistent with their relatively high measurement error, scaled scores have been rounded off in the conversion from raw scores, with each 1-point interval representing one-third of a standard deviation. Thus, it is inappropriate to apply overly fine distinctions when providing verbal descriptions of subtest performance. Table 5.3 displays broader ranges, based on standard deviation units, that might be used in a report to characterize levels of performance, and includes several options for wording descriptors associated with each range.

---

[2]The 10-point width of standard score ranges is the result of arbitrary decisions. Terman and Merrill (1937) initially relied on a quotient (i.e., mental age/chronological age × 100) to derive an overall score on the Stanford–Binet, the long-reigning industry standard, which yielded a 16-point standard deviation in the standardization sample. In moving to a deviation IQ (i.e., based on a normal curve distribution), Wechsler (1939) rounded off the standard deviation to 15 points to better correspond with our base-10 numbering system.

TABLE 5.3. Qualitative Descriptors for Subtests

Scaled score	*T* score	Percentile range	Descriptors
19 18 17 16	≥ 70	> 95th	Exceptional Strength *or* Far Above Average *or* Very Advanced
15 14 13	58–69	80th–95th	Strength *or* Above Average *or* Well Developed
12 11 10 9 8	43–57	25th–75th	Average
7 6 5	31–42	5th–20th	Weakness *or* Below Average *or* Poorly Developed
4 3 2 1	≤ 30	< 5th	Exceptional Weakness *or* Far Below Average *or* Very Deficient

Percentiles

Reporting normative performance with percentiles (or percentile ranks) is useful because they can be readily understood by consumers. Their meaning may already be familiar to readers, but the evaluator can assure that the concept is understood by explaining percentiles when first used in a report. Walrath, Willis, and Dumont (2014) propose the follow formulation:

> Percentile ranks tell what percentage of other same-age students scored the same as or lower than Keesha. For example, a percentile rank of 36 would mean that Keesha scored as high as or higher than 36% of students her age and lower than the other 64%. (p. 441)

But percentile rank can be misleading since it is not an interval scale. Because scores cluster in the middle of the normal curve, small differences in scores near the mean translate into large differences in percentiles. For example, an IQ score of 96—just 4 points below the mean of 100—corresponds to the 39th percentile, which seems a fair distance from the mean. By contrast, the difference between scores of 73 and 77 is just two percentiles (4th vs. 6th).

Evaluators routinely report percentiles as exact numbers, thereby disregarding measurement error. In doing so, they perpetuate the notion that the obtained score precisely describes an ability level or trait. One way to reflect measurement error is to round off percentiles to the nearest multiple of five and describe them as approximations. For example, a percentile score of 72 would be described as performing "at approximately the 70th percentile," and a percentile score of 14 as "approximately the 15th percentile." Scores very close to the mean, say from the 45th to 55th percentile (corresponding to standard scores of 98 to 102), could be appropriately characterized as "near the 50th percentile." Extremely high or low scores might be conveyed with a range, for example, "below the 5th percentile" or "above the 99th percentile." These approximations will not distort the interpretation of the findings, and misconceptions about exact scores will be averted. The interested reader can find exact percentiles in the Data Summary.

Including percentile ranks in tables of subtest scaled scores (i.e., scores with a mean of 10 and a standard deviation of 3) is a highly questionable practice. Although it is possible to specify the percentile rank for a given scaled score (e.g., 8 = 25th percentile, 9 = 37th percentile, 10 = 50th percentile), these scale scores have already been rounded off in the raw score to scale score conversion. Hence, the difference of a single raw score point, which may hinge on the scoring of a marginal response to a Vocabulary item or the precise timing of a Block Design item, can translate into the difference between the 37th percentile and the 50th percentile. Test publishers do not provide tables that translate cognitive subtest raw scores into percentiles for a reason. These individual subtests have considerable measurement error and are intended to be combined with other subtests to form more reliable and valid composite scores. As an example, most Wechsler scale subtests have a standard error of measurement of about 1.0—approximately one-third of a standard deviation. Therefore, the 68% confidence interval (i.e., plus or minus 1 standard error of measurement) for a subtest score of 9 would encompass a range from about the 25th to the 50th percentile, and the 95% confidence interval would span a range from about the 16th to the 63rd percentile.[3] This is a far different picture than what might be understood when an evaluator reports a result suggesting that the performance can be pinpointed at the 37th percentile.

Grade and Age Equivalents

Grade-equivalent and age-equivalent scores can be misleading and should *not* be used to report performance on norm-referenced tests. While they may appeal to consumers because of their seemingly clear meaning, they are subject to misinterpretation. A grade-equivalent or age-equivalent score is the median (50th percentile) score for individuals at that grade or age level. Since growth occurs at different rates for different skills and abilities, the functional implications of a below-grade-level score will vary greatly depending on the grade level of the child and the skill or ability being measured (Reynolds, 1981). Depending on

---

[3]These are not exact mathematical computations, but are conceptually sound and should serve to illustrate the point.

the particulars, the statement "Amelie is reading 1 year below grade level" may be inconsequential or may be cause for concern. To illustrate, the difference between grade 1.5 and grade 2.5 performance on the WIAT-III Word Reading subtest is substantial (raw scores of 15 vs. 30 words read), whereas the difference in performance between grade 10.5 and grade 12.5 is trivial (raw scores of 61 vs. 63). In the former case, the "1 year behind" second grader earns a standard score of 82, whereas in the latter case the "2 years behind" twelfth grader earns a standard score of 97. Furthermore, one cannot draw conclusions about educational implications from grade-equivalent or age-equivalent scores. Since academic expectations vary from school to school, there is no regular correspondence between a grade-level score and the instructional level in the classroom. A useful reference to share with colleagues or consumers is the online advisory from test publisher Pearson (n.d.), "Interpretation Problems of Age and Grade Equivalents."

Uninterpretable Scores

Many evaluators report overall scores (e.g., Full Scale IQ, General Cognitive Ability) when there are wide differences between the scores on major composite scales, or report composite scores that are derived from highly discrepant contributing subtests. The evaluator may have addressed the differences by advising caution in interpreting the scores, but this advice will not suffice to prevent confusion or misinterpretation. Why report a score at all if it lacks validity and can lead to errors in case conceptualization and decision making? The recommended course of action is to omit an uninterpretable score from the report narrative, and explain why it is excluded (see Box 5.1). To be transparent for professional readers, the evaluator might still include the obtained score in the Data Summary.

Invalid Scores

A related situation occurs when an evaluator generates a test result that is clearly not interpretable as an indicator of what the test is intended to measure. Common examples include (1) a test administered in English to a child with limited English proficiency, (2) test per-

---

BOX 5.1. Conveying Uninterpretable and Invalid Findings

- "Given his wide variability in performance on the Primary Index scales, Fred's overall cognitive functioning cannot be meaningfully represented by a Full Scale IQ score."
- "Wilma obtained highly inconsistent scores on the subtests that contribute to the Nonverbal Reasoning Ability scale; therefore, her reasoning ability cannot be meaningfully estimated from her score on this scale."
- "Barney's extremely low performance on the Symbol Search subtest was the result of his losing track of the instructions, and should not be interpreted as a measure of his processing speed."
- "Betty resisted making up stories in response to the situations pictured by the Roberts–2 cards, and would only name the apparent roles of the characters shown (e.g., father, daughter, friend). Therefore, no scores were computed for Social Perception—how well she understands social situations."

formance that has been substantially compromised by a child's sensory impairment, and (3) the testing of a child who is clearly uncooperative or intentionally not making an effort. This is not to say that standardized testing in these situations is inappropriate or irresponsible. Invalid scores can reveal useful information about a child's capabilities or the extent to which a child's status or condition interferes with performance, but the findings must be interpreted clinically rather than statistically. In these situations, the obtained score should not be reported in a way that suggests it is a valid estimate of the intended construct and is best excluded rather than reported with a caveat. The evaluator might go so far as to say, for example, "Alfie's performance suggests that his nonverbal reasoning ability is at least average for his age, and possibly well above."

The evaluator faces a more difficult situation when tests scores are not clearly invalid, but test performance appears to have been compromised by extraneous variables, such as distractibility, impulsivity, anxiety, or low motivation. This kind of moderating influence of test behaviors is common and often illuminates factors that interfere with everyday functioning. Parsing out the effect of interfering factors requires insightful clinical judgment. When the interpretation of such test results requires clinical judgment, the evaluator should provide a rich explanation of how the interfering factor manifested itself during test performance.

In Summary

To summarize, we recommend reporting performance levels in the body of a report using a uniform set of descriptors. Descriptors may be effectively paired with percentiles that are rounded off to reflect measurement error. If standard scores are used in the body of the report to convey performance on major scales, they should be accompanied by, or presented as, confidence intervals. Evaluators should be cautious about reporting performance on subtests of cognitive measures, taking care not to imply that small differences are statistically or clinically significant and not supplying percentile ranks associated with scaled scores. Box 5.2 contains examples of how test performance might be expressed in a consumer-responsive report.

Most important, test results should be included selectively in the report narrative, applying the "So what?" test to eliminate clutter and confusion. The evaluator should report only meaningful and relevant results in the body of the report and include a comprehensive presentation of scores and related data in an appended Data Summary.

Language and Writing Style

As emphasized throughout this book, reports should be written in language that consumers can clearly understand. Evaluators should use simple declarative sentences and familiar vocabulary to the greatest extent possible. The active voice is clearer and simpler than the passive voice. Sentences are best kept short. The evaluator should resist the temptation to use a long or fancy word when a short or common one will do: "spoke" instead of "verbalized," "use" instead of "utilize," and so on.

BOX 5.2. Describing Test Performance in the Report Narrative

The sample formats below describe test performance in a way that can be readily understood by nonprofessional readers and that effectively serves to inform conclusions and recommendations. The information in the report narrative is supplemented by a full account of test scores and related technical information in the Data Summary.

- "On the WISC-V, a measure of general cognitive functioning, Miriam obtained a Full Scale score in the Below Average range, at approximately the 10th percentile." [Note: the first reference to percentiles may be accompanied by an explanatory footnote.]
- "On the Working Memory scale, Miriam scored within the Average range, near the 50th percentile for children her age. This represents a relative strength compared to her performance on other cognitive scales."
- "On the Knowledge factor of the SB-5, Joseph earned a score in the High Average range, at approximately the 80th percentile for his age."
- "On the Depression scale of the BASC-3 Teacher Rating Scales, the ratings placed Daniel within the Clinically Significant range, at approximately the 95th percentile; that is, only about 5% of children obtain scores that are this indicative of a serious problem."

Harvey (1997) offered the following guidance to increase the readability of assessment reports:

- Shorten sentence length.
- Minimize the use of difficult words.
- Reduce the use of jargon and acronyms.
- Avoid passive verbs.
- Make use of subheadings.

Hass and Carriere (2014, p. 50) offer many suggestions and examples for improving the readability of assessment reports. They cite an essay by George Orwell, from which they adapted the following rules for writing:

- Never use a long word when you can use a short one instead.
- If it is possible to cut a word out, cut it out.
- Never use the passive voice where you can use the active voice;
- Never use a scientific word or jargon if you can think of an everyday English equivalent.

Evaluators can determine the difficulty level of their reports by using the "readability statistics" feature of Microsoft Word or a website that calculates text readability. They should aspire to writing at a Flesch–Kincaid reading difficulty level of grade 11 or lower (see Appendix A). This is no easy matter for evaluators who are accustomed to academic writing or to communicating with other professionals. Granted, it takes ingenuity and effort to produce simple wording that clearly conveys a psychological or psychometric concept.

The use of technical terms should be limited to those that are important for understanding the child, and that the parent or teacher is likely to encounter again (e.g., phonological awareness, executive functioning). The evaluator should accompany these terms with a definition or explanation in "plain English." Walrath et al. (2014) provide some examples of how routinely used psychometric terms might be explained to consumers, such as adding a footnote like the following when first referring to confidence intervals:

> Even on the very best tests, score can never be perfectly reliable. This interval shows how much scores are likely to vary randomly 95% of the time. (p. 441)

Box 5.3 lists examples of "plain English" wording for some terms that appear in reports. However, we advise against substituting these phrases on a rote "find-and-replace" basis. Evaluators should customize language to best fit the situation. For example, an explanation of executive functioning might emphasize planning and organization for one child and monitoring and adapting strategies for another.

One reason evaluators may prefer to use technical terms is because they convey the intended meaning precisely, while everyday language may fail to fully capture the meaning of a concept (Hammond & Allen, 1953). "Speed and accuracy in recognizing and applying familiar information" doesn't quite say the same thing as "processing speed." There appears to be a cost to translating technical terms into plain language, sacrificing meaning to make a report more accessible to consumers. However, it is questionable whether practitioners have a clear sense, let alone a consensus, about the exact meaning of the technical terms they use (Harvey, 2006; Ownby & Wallbrown, 1986). When evaluators fail to explain terms, this predicament is conveniently circumvented—at the expense of the reader.

Seemingly minor word choices can affect the tone of a report. Evaluators often use the word "presented" (as in, "The child presented as shy and unresponsive"), sometimes correctly and sometimes not. The word may come in handy, but it is stilted "medical-speak" and best avoided. Referring to oneself in the third person (e.g., "the examiner cautioned Jeff . . .") may be preferable to using the passive voice ("Jeff was cautioned . . ."), but use of the first person ("I cautioned Jeff . . .") is acceptable, clear, and personal. Another way to personalize a report is to identify informants and other parties by name, rather than by role, after the initial identifying reference—as Mr. Escalante, rather than "the teacher," and as Ms. Turnblad, rather than "the mother." However, it may be advisable to specify roles in a report that refers to many individuals (current and former teacher, parent, grandparent, school counselor, physician, therapist, etc.) so the reader can keep the players straight.

REPORT STRUCTURE

Various structures have been proposed for psychological reports (Braaten, 2007; Goldfinger & Pomerantz, 2014; Groth-Marnat & Wright, 2016; Hass & Carriere, 2014; Ownby, 1997; Sattler, 2018). The report structures proposed by most authors differ only in minor respects, with pretty much the same sections in pretty much the same order. Only Hass and Carriere (2014) diverge significantly from a familiar format, proposing a report structure that relies

BOX 5.3. Plain English Alternatives to Jargon and Academic Language

Technical terms and jargon	Plain English
Aphasia	A problem in understanding or expressing language
Apraxia	A problem in coordinating movements
Auditory and visual stimuli	Bits of information that are heard and seen
Cognitive proficiency	Ability to conduct simple mental operations (matching, copying, remembering bits of information, etc.) easily and accurately
Decoding (reading)	Reading accuracy
Dyscalculia	Difficulty with math
Dysregulation	Lack of self-control
Emotional regulation	Ability to control feelings
Executive functioning	Mental abilities used to carry out new and complex tasks, such as planning, organizing, shifting attention, and adjusting strategies
Family dynamics	How family members interact with each other
Fluid intelligence	Reasoning and problem solving
Memory consolidation	Storage of memories
Memory encoding	Taking new information into memory
Adequate recognition memory, with deficits in free recall	Unable to pull up information from memory, but can demonstrate that it was remembered by recognizing it when seen or heard again, such as in a multiple-choice format
Neurocognitive profile	Pattern of results in the areas tested (e.g., thinking and performance)
Oral reading fluency	Ability to identify words in a written passage quickly and accurately
Orthographic processing	Ability to recognize letters and words from the way they look
Perseveration	Repeating an action over and over again
Personality disorder	Serious and enduring mental problem that makes it very difficult to get along with others or to meet the demands of daily life
Pharmacology	Use of medication
Premorbid functioning	Functioning before the problem started
Quantitative	Using numbers and math
Rigid behavior	Stiff, inflexible, unable to adjust behavior to fit different situations
Semantics	Use of words
Sound segmentation	Able to hear the separate sounds in words
Spatial manipulation	Hands-on activity
Syntax	Grammar; combining words correctly in phrases and sentences
Underlying etiology	Cause(s)
Within normal limits	Normal; within typical range (for age)

(continued)

Academic language	Plain English
Apparent	Clear, noticeable
Apprehensive	Uneasy or fearful
Artifact	Misleading finding
Attributed to	Result of
Decrement	Drop; reduction
Deficient	Lacking; weak
Demeanor	Appearance
Exemplify	Show; serve as an example
Impede	Get in the way of; interfere with
Latent	Hidden
Manifested	Seen in
Modulate	Adjust; vary
Proficiency	Skill
Secondary to	As a result of
Subjective	Based on personal judgment
Subsequently	Afterward; later on
Unintelligible	Could not be understood
Verbatim	Word-for-word

on a question-and-answer format (e.g., Does Ross have an emotional disturbance as defined by special education regulations? What supports will help Rachel behave more appropriately and improve her academic performance?).

The way a report is organized reflects the evaluator's approach to assessment, even with seemingly minor variations in the basic format. For example, a test-focused approach may list sources under the heading Tests Administered, rather than Assessment Procedures, and may confine interpretations to a Test Results and Interpretations section, rather than integrate multiple data sources in a Conclusions or Clinical Impressions section.

Consumer-responsive assessment has no standard or ideal report structure, but some structures are more conducive to this type of assessment than others. The subsequent discussion of report sections uses the following prototypical outline, while also allowing for certain variations.

- Identifying Information
- Reason for Referral
- Assessment Procedures
- Background Information
  o Intervention History
  o Interviews

- Behavioral Observations
- Assessment Results (*or* Test Results)
- Clinical Impressions
- Summary
- Recommendations
- Data Summary

Appendix D contains sample reports that demonstrate consumer-responsive principles. A sample consumer-responsive report by Lichtenstein and Axelrod (2016) is included in *Intelligent Testing with the WISC-V* (Kaufman et al., 2016), and an annotated sample report by Lichtenstein and Chalukian appears in *Essentials of Assessment Report Writing* (Schneider et al., 2018). Readers may note some variation in the structure of these reports, which is to be expected; a consumer-responsive approach relies on goal-driven principles, rather than on any fixed format.

Identifying Information

An assessment report begins with identifying information: the child's name, age, grade, school or program, and dates when the assessment took place. By custom, the dates include those on which the evaluator met directly with the child for purposes of data collection, either through testing or interviewing. Evaluators typically do not include the date or dates when they observed the child in a naturalistic setting, even though it would be appropriate to do so, especially in cases in which observations provide critically important data (e.g., in assessing a preschool child or a child with a severe behavioral disorder). The evaluator's name and credentials may optionally be included here, even though this information will appear with the evaluator's signature at the end of the report.

Reason for Referral

The Reason for Referral section identifies the referral source and states the purpose(s) of the assessment. The referral questions and concerns of the referring party are clearly identified, and significant concerns of other key parties may be cited as well. Referral concerns are conveyed in clear and concise terms (e.g., "to determine why Joey has difficulty understanding what he reads"), reserving further details for the Background Information section. Although stated briefly, (e.g., "to determine the need for special education services . . ."), referral concerns benefit from sufficient specificity to clarify the focus of the assessment (e.g., " . . . because of suspected language impairment"). Some evaluators include stock phrases that can apply to almost any assessment (e.g., "to identify areas of strength and weakness" or "to inform recommendations and team decisions"). Such verbiage, although innocuous, is uninformative and may be omitted without detracting from the report. However, if the evaluator has little else to go on, such generic statements signal the need to confer with the referring parties to ensure that the purpose of the assessment is clear and agreed upon.

Assessment Procedures

A list of assessment procedures follows the Reason for Referral, thus identifying the assessment measures that were purposefully selected to answer the referral questions and to test hypotheses relating to them. The list should include all sources of assessment data that the evaluator relied on to address referral questions and concerns. In addition to tests and rating scales, the list should include observations in naturalistic settings (e.g., classroom observation, home observation) and the types of interviews conducted (e.g., parent interview, teacher interview). The list should be inclusive, but not overly detailed or technical. The use of existing documents, such as school records and prior evaluations, may be subsumed under a general reference to "review of records." The full title of all administered tests should be specified, including the edition number. If a test is adapted in some way or administered only in part, this should be noted accordingly (e.g., "Universal Test of Executive Functions—selected subtests"). For ratings scales with versions for different informants, the evaluator should specify which versions were used (e.g., "Mania Rating Scale—Parent Report, Self-Report").

The list of procedures should include only the evaluator's own data collection activities. A report may be enhanced by secondhand sources, such as a previous psychological assessment or a teacher-administered academic measure. If these sources were documented elsewhere, they fall under the category of "review of records"; if not, the source should be qualified (e.g., "administered by . . .").

Background Information

The Background Information section provides detailed elaboration of the Reason for Referral, as well as essential information about the child's history, status, and circumstances. The elaboration of referral information may include how concerns have evolved over time; under what conditions they have been more and less problematic; what interventions have been tried and with what results; and how referring and nonreferring parties regard the situation. Box 5.4 illustrates this correspondence between the Reason for Referral and Background Information material.

The Background Information section is ideally organized by theme or topic. Appendix E identifies common themes and a logical sequence in which to present them, along with an example of a Background Information section for an involved case.

Assessment data from secondary sources—that is, other than the evaluator's direct contact with, or observation of, the child—belong in Background Information.[4] Secondary sources include school and agency records (e.g., service reports, attendance records), special education documentation (e.g., referral forms, the child's IEP), general education progress monitoring data, intake questionnaires, interviews with key informants, and prior evaluations. An assessment report may benefit greatly from incorporating assessment data from other members of the evaluation team, such as academic achievement test results from a special education teacher.

---

[4]As discussed in the Assessment Results section that follows, rating scales completed by a third party, such as a parent or teacher, are an exception to this rule.

BOX 5.4. Correspondence between Reason for Referral and Background Information

The Reason for Referral section should state questions and concerns specifically, but concisely. Further elaboration and details should be reserved for the Background Information section. Examples of what might appear in each section are provided below.

Reason for referral	Background information
"Louise's teacher, Mr. Gehrig, reports that Louise rarely completes in-class seatwork or homework."	• Does this apply to any particular type of assignment? • What are the consequences of not submitting work? • Has Mr. Gehrig tried to address the problem in any way? What was the result of these efforts? • Are Louise's parents aware that she has homework that isn't getting done?
"Tyrone's mother, Ms. Cobb, is concerned that Tyrone dislikes school and pleads to stay home."	• How many absences has he had this year and in past years? • How often does he ask to stay home? • What reasons does he give? • How does Mrs. Cobb respond to Tyrone's requests to stay home? What then occurs? • What is her understanding about why Tyrone is avoiding school?
"Christy has made little progress in reading since first grade."	• What specific areas of reading are lagging (e.g., word identification, fluency)? • How has reading progress been assessed, and what are the specific findings? • What strategies or remedial services have been implemented? What has helped, and what has not?
"Ruth has frequent verbal and physical altercations with peers."	• Description(s) of typical altercations. • What precipitates these altercations? • Under what conditions do these incidents occur and not occur? • What consequences or disciplinary actions follow (e.g., office visits, detentions, suspensions)? Have occurrences increased or decreased as a result?

In relying on secondary sources, the evaluator cannot verify the accuracy of background information. Therefore, the information should be attributed to its source, rather than presented as fact. To avoid sentence-by-sentence identifying of sources, the evaluator might devote an entire paragraph or subsection to a given individual or source. This organizing scheme works especially well when one source contributes a substantial amount of information on a given topic, which might be afforded a subsection heading of its own (e.g., "Parent Interview" or "Prior Evaluations"). However, information about a given topic that is informed by multiple sources is best organized by theme, for example, the discussion of educational history might include input from parent and teacher reports, school records, and prior evaluations. Placing same-topic information from multiple sources in the same paragraph or section brings into focus whether the sources complement one another or offer different perspectives.

How much background information to include in a report should be guided by the purposes of the assessment and may be far less than what the evaluator has collected. The evaluator should be selective in reporting information that has been documented in other reports or in records that are otherwise available to consumers. Alternatively, the evaluator may determine that circumstances call for a comprehensive documentation of information that will be of value to current or future readers. Regardless, the evaluator should apply the "So what?" principle, rather than include material simply because it was obtained in conducting the assessment.

Intervention History

The documentation of what interventions have been tried, and with what results, is a key element of background information. This is critically important input for weighing the merits and particulars of potential interventions. Although many conclusions and recommendations that emerge from the assessment of a child's cognitive, academic, and social–emotional development are well-educated guesses, findings that are informed by actual experience—how a child responded to specific strategies and supports—are truly evidence based. Instructional methods, specific curricula, environmental supports, motivational techniques, behavior plans, and other items that have proven to be effective should be documented in fine detail. In qualitative research, this is called "thick description." What personnel were required, and what did they do? How frequently was the intervention provided? Was it immediately effective, or did it take hold after some delay? Was the plan productively modified over time? It is also important to include details of what has not worked as well, rather than simply naming the method, since specific aspects of implementation may have compromised the effectiveness of a potentially valuable intervention. Thus, intervention history should be a major focus of interviews with parents, teachers, and service providers. It is also advisable to ask the child about interventions: What was helpful? How did she experience these supports? What does he think would be helpful going forward? Information about intervention history not only informs the current set of recommendations, but may prove useful to service providers or caretakers at a later time.

Progress monitoring data is a key source of intervention particulars. The documentation of CBM performance, response to a behavior plan, or goal attainment scale outcomes provide valuable information about performance levels and rates of improvement. The examiner might productively supplement these data by talking with the individuals who implemented interventions or collected the data to learn how the interventions were conducted and what factors affected outcomes favorably or unfavorably.

When there is a substantial amount of data available about past services and interventions and how the child responded to them, it is advisable to present this in a separate Intervention History section, or a separate subsection of Background Information. Data on prior supports and interventions should be routinely available when an RTI model is used for LD identification, since federal special education regulations explicitly call for documentation of "the instructional strategies used and the student-centered data collected" (Sec. 300.311(a)(7)). A good deal of information about services provided and performance levels should be available when a child who receives special education services is reevaluated—in fact, this information should be core material for the assessment and the ensuing report.

Interviews

The evaluator may choose to integrate interview findings with other data in a theme-organized Background Information section. Alternatively, these findings could appear in a separate Interviews section, possibly with subheadings for the types of informants (e.g., Parent Interview, Teacher Interview). This approach may be well suited for capturing the extended input of an interviewee whose perspective and insights are of distinct importance. For example, an Interview section might feature the historical account and explanations of a parent who initiated a referral because of disagreements over how the school has managed the child's behavior problems.

Some information that the evaluated child provides (e.g., regarding educational history or family structure) clearly belongs in Background Information (e.g., regarding educational history or family structure). However, this section is not necessarily the place to report the child's responses to clinical interview questions. A clinical interview delves into the child's attitudes, beliefs, view of self and others, social-emotional status, and the like (see sample questions and topics in Box 5.5). This material has more in common with personality testing (sentence completion measures, in particular) and may be best included in the Assessment Results section.

BOX 5.5. Sample Clinical Interview Questions

- "What are you good at?"
- "What do you like to do in your spare time?"
- "What do you think is going on with [referral concern]? Has anything made the situation better? Is there anything you think might be helpful?"
- "Who are you closest to at school?"
- "If you had a serious problem, what adult would you talk to?"
- "What makes you mad? sad? glad? scared?"
- "If you could have any three wishes, what would you wish for?"
- "If you could be any animal for a day, what animal would you be and what would you do?"
- "What do you see yourself doing after you finish with school?"

SCREENING FOR DEPRESSION OR SUICIDALITY:

- "How are you sleeping? eating?"
- "How you have been feeling lately?"
- "On a scale of 1 to 10, how would you rate your mood?"
- "Do you ever feel so bad that you think about hurting yourself?"

Behavioral Observations

The evaluator's direct observations of behavior convey vital information about the child's capabilities, personality, attitudes, and self-image. Furthermore, by citing a child's telling characteristics in a report, the evaluator provides a vivid sense of the child and conveys to a parent or teacher that she came to know the child well.

The Behavioral Observations section *may* include observations of the child in one or more naturalistic settings, which should be presented in a separate paragraph or subsection. It should *always* include observations of the child in the assessment sessions and related interactions with the evaluator (e.g., during initial introductions or negotiations, in a waiting room, en route from classroom to testing room, or during breaks).

Since naturalistic observations convey critical information about how the child responds to environmental demands and interacts with others, the context in which the behavior occurs should be described. For example, classroom observations might be framed by noting the nature and size of the peer group, what adults are present, the kind of lesson or activity, and what student responses are expected. The date or dates when the child was observed and the time of day may also be significant.

A cardinal rule, as noted in Chapter 3, is to report specific behaviors without making inferences. Taken to the extreme, a narrative observation can take the form of a "play-by-play" account, in which many discrete behaviors are described in order of occurrence. Although such reporting is objective and "low-inference," it can be tedious and self-defeating. Imagine a dense paragraph with three separate descriptions of help-seeking behavior, interspersed with other detailed accounts of less-relevant behaviors. The reader may be "unable to see the forest for the trees." Instead, the evaluator might synthesize key observational data (reporting, for example, that "Monica asked the teacher for help three times during the half-hour independent work period") and illustrate the pattern with a detailed description of one characteristic incident.

In describing the child's behavior during the assessment, the evaluator makes note of the child's general presentation (mood, social skills, energy level, interpersonal behavior, distinctive speech patterns, etc.) and how the child responds to testing and interviewing (cooperative, curious, engaged, persistent, anxious, distractible, defensive, etc.). The interaction with the evaluator may be telling, so it may be necessary to describe the evaluator's role in the interaction, for example, in offering breaks, setting limits, or providing unscripted task instructions. It is common for an evaluator to describe her role in the third person (e.g., "The examiner grabbed the small blocks before Chandler could swallow them, which caused him to cry") or using the passive voice (e.g., "The blocks were removed abruptly before Chandler could . . ."). However, a first-person reference ("I grabbed the blocks . . .") is genuine and clear, and quite acceptable.

There is some difference of opinion as to whether to provide a physical description of the child. It is informative and meaningful to describe salient and distinctive aspects of the child's physical characteristics (e.g., petite, overweight, crossed eyes), attire (e.g., unkempt, fashionable, untied shoes), or accessories (e.g., backward baseball cap, heavy backpack). Such features affect how others respond to the child, and may also provide clues about the child's behavior, attitudes, or home environment. Physical descriptions should inform the reader, rather than be an obligatory entry in a report. Generic descriptors that are uninformative or applicable to most children (e.g., "attractive," "pleasant," "age-appropriate") are best omitted, as they suggest that the evaluator has made little effort to know the child as an individual.

Assessment Results

The Assessment Results section contains noteworthy findings from standardized measures. The section could be called Test Results if it is limited to tests. This would be a misnomer, however, if the section also includes the findings from rating scales or a clinical interview of the child.

Ratings scales administered to a parent, teacher, or child have much in common with interviews. The informant responds to carefully scripted questions about areas of functioning that are typically addressed in interviews. However, the responses are quantified and subjected to norm-referenced interpretation, much like tests. Including rating scales in this section avoids possible confusion about what a parent, teacher, or child has "reported," since the informant has actually responded to individual items that describe specific behaviors, rather than reporting that a child is inattentive, anxious, or aggressive. The diagnostic labels derive from the scores on scales. Even then, it is advisable to use language that accurately captures the type of data provided, saying, for example, "The classroom teacher's ratings of his behavior indicated a clinically significant level of aggressive behavior," instead of "The classroom teacher reported a clinically significant level of aggressive behavior."

Whether to report the child's responses to interview questions in the Assessment Results section, rather than in the Background Information or Interviews sections, is a matter of judgment. Our inclination, in favoring a theme-based report structure, is to organize assessment data according to content. Thus, the child's reporting of factual material (e.g., family composition, school history, services received, use of eyeglasses or hearing aids) should be part of Background Information; while more clinically oriented information (e.g., concerning attitudes, impressions, preferences, motivation, self-expectations, hopes, and fears) is a good fit with Assessment Results, as it complements the findings from social–emotional assessment measures. The placement of child interview responses may also depend on whether the report includes a critical mass of social-emotional assessment data. If social–emotional functioning is not a substantial aspect of the assessment, it may be best to relegate the child interview responses to Background Information or Interviews.

The Assessment Results section should be organized and labeled by broad functional areas, such as *cognitive* (including neuropsychological), *academic*, and *social–emotional* functioning. *Adaptive behavior* is an essential area to include when a child has, or is suspected of having, an intellectual disability. There may be overlap between the broad categories, such as when problem behaviors interfere with performance on cognitive tasks. It may be advisable to report cognitive and academic functioning together, as these two areas often interact, such as when impaired language functions (e.g., in phonological processing or syntax) contribute to reading difficulties.

The broad areas are organized into subsections by theme or topic, each of which is addressed in one or several paragraphs. It is helpful to label these topics with subordinate headings such as *language*, *memory*, and *emotional regulation* (see Box 5.6). Selectivity is

BOX 5.6. Topics for Organizing Assessment Results

In organizing assessment findings, the evaluator selects from among possible themes or topics. Addressing all topics is impractical; addressing the same topics in each report undermines the focus. Priority should be given to topics that yield interpretable findings and are relevant for understanding the child. (Note: CHC theory offers an alternative organizing scheme for cognitive and academic functioning.)

Cognitive Functioning

General intelligence; broad cognitive functioning
Language
    Receptive; verbal comprehension
    Expressive (morphology, syntax, semantics)
    Vocabulary; word knowledge
    Pragmatic language
    Phonological processing
Acquired knowledge; information
Fluid reasoning (or Reasoning and problem solving)
    Verbal
    Nonverbal
    Pattern recognition
Memory
    Working memory/short-term
    Long-term
    Verbal memory
    Visual memory
    Retrieval
    Use of strategies
Information processing
    Fluency; rapid naming
    Processing speed
    Visual scanning
Spatial ability
Attention
    Arousal
    Selective attention
    Sustained attention
    Shifting attention
Executive functions
    Planning
    Organization
    Shifting; flexibility
    Monitoring; updating
    Inhibiting of responses
Sensorimotor
    Auditory
    Visual
    Fine motor
Visual–motor integration

Academic Skills

Reading/literacy
    Word identification
    Reading fluency
    Comprehension
Math/quantitative skills
    Calculation
    Reasoning; problem solving
Writing
    Composition
    Spelling
    Handwriting

Adaptive Behavior

Daily living skills; self-care
Socialization
Community living skills
Communication
Motor skills

Social–Emotional Functioning

Resources/coping skills
Vulnerabilities/risk factors
Resilience; ego strength
Social relations
Social cognition
    Social perception (e.g., intent of others)
    Problem solving
Social responsiveness, engagement
Mood
Emotional regulation
Externalizing behavior
    Aggression
    Conduct problems; noncompliance
    Hyperactivity
Internalizing behavior
    Anxiety
    Depression
    Social withdrawal
Need for control
Need for approval
Need for attention

critical. Only those areas of functioning that are relevant to the assessment questions should be included, and they will vary from case to case. Although it requires insightful clinical analysis to customize the topic structure of each report, it is highly preferable to organize cognitive findings according to the relevant characteristics of the individual child rather than on the basis of the scales of the tests that were administered. Test-based organization makes the illogical assumption that a child's functioning corresponds to the choice of tests, such that the child will be understood one way if the WISC-V is administered and some other way if the child is given the DAS-II or the SB-5. The organizing scheme, however, may be influenced by the evaluator's preferred theoretical model. For example, proponents of a neuropsychological model might organize findings by cortical functions: language, spatial abilities, attention and executive functions, memory, and sensorimotor skills. Alternatively, proponents of a cross-battery assessment approach will organize findings according to Cattell–Horn–Carroll (CHC) theory abilities.

Test-based organization can lead to a fragmented presentation of findings, as related findings appear in different parts of the report. For example, an evaluator might discuss memory at three different points: when reporting on the Working Memory scale of a general intelligence test, when reporting on a diagnostic memory test (e.g., Wide Range Assessment of Memory and Learning–Second Edition, Children's Memory Scale, or the California Verbal Learning Test–Children's Version), and again when reporting on the recall condition of a Bender–Gestalt II or the Rey–Osterrieth test. In doing so, the evaluator may fail to identify convergent findings or, conversely, may report inconsistent findings without attempting to resolve or explain them. Furthermore, extenuating factors that widely influence test performance but don't correspond with the structure of administered tests may not be adequately highlighted. For example, severe distractibility may have affected the child's performance on several different tests, resulting in scrambled findings with no clearly interpretable pattern. Organizing findings according to the scales of the tests administered would then be of little value, whereas an Attention subsection would be very meaningful.

Another issue in reporting test results is how to convey to the reader what a test, scale, or subtest measures. The name of a scale may or may not accurately reflect what is relevant about the child's performance. For example, if severe impairment in language output is the cause of poor performance on a Verbal Comprehension scale, the evaluator should explain that the score is indicative of the child's *expressive language,* and might label the subsection as such, rather than as verbal comprehension.

Arriving at the most apt interpretation of assessment findings may still leave the reader perplexed if the evaluator relies heavily on technical language that is unfamiliar or confusing to nonprofessional readers. It is important for the evaluator to define key terms using everyday language, especially those that the consumer is likely to come across again (e.g., phonological processing, executive functioning, emotional regulation, dyslexia, intellectual disability).

Although it requires insightful clinical judgment, evaluators might report findings strategically by taking advantage of the different ways subtests are combined into scales. This has long been a feature of the Woodcock–Johnson scales. Similarly, the WISC-V, with the recent addition of Ancillary Index scales (i.e., Quantitative Reasoning, Auditory Working Memory, Nonverbal, General Ability, and Cognitive Proficiency), now includes alternative ways of combining subtests into scales. Thus, in the case of a child with generalized information processing deficits, an evaluator could report deficient performance on the WISC-V Working Memory and Processing Speed scales in separate subsections, but might more productively combine these findings in a Cognitive Proficiency or Information Processing subsection.

What is *not* helpful is to use a rote description of a scale or subtest, citing all the skills, abilities, and influences associated with the measure, regardless of the child's performance. For example, Sattler (2018) describes the Nonverbal Fluid Reasoning subtest of the SB-5 as measuring "induction, general sequential reasoning, deductive reasoning, visualization, cognitive flexibility, and concentration" (p. 573). To routinely list all of these elements in a report is uninformative. It leaves the reader guessing as to which, if any, are relevant in understanding the child's functioning. It is the job of the professionally trained evaluator, not the reader, to make this determination. If the evaluator is unable to determine whether any of the contributing skills and abilities are particularly applicable, it is best not to introduce these elements.

Insightful reporting of the child's functioning requires the melding of quantitative and qualitative findings. Qualitative findings, such as a child's approach to tasks, use of strategies, persistence, motivation, response to uncertainty and frustration, and extraneous behaviors and verbalizations greatly enhance the interpretation of test scores. To adequately explain a child's capabilities and characteristic functioning, the evaluator may need to supplement the recording of scores with descriptions of test behaviors or verbatim samples of responses and comments. Similarly, noteworthy behavior that is unique to, or more pronounced during, a particular task should accompany the reporting of performance in this section. However, when a child's approach (e.g., impulsive, avoidant) or verbalizations (e.g., self-critical, seeking help or feedback) occur throughout the testing session, this should also be described in the Behavioral Observations section.

As noted earlier in this chapter, exhaustive reporting of test results regardless of what is relevant to the individual child is not meaningful and discourages a close reading of the Assessment Results. How, then, is the evaluator to determine what assessment findings to report and what findings to leave out? Perhaps the most helpful advice is to consider what findings will contribute to the key sections that follow: Clinical Impressions, Summary, and Recommendations. Findings that have no bearing on these sections will not pass the "So what?" test and should receive little or no attention in Assessment Results.

The ability to identify which of several possible ways to organize and interpret assessment results is the mark of a skilled clinician. This kind of expertise requires clinical experience, evidence-based professional knowledge, and flexible thinking, among other attributes. The novice evaluator is likely to rely on formula-driven organizing and reporting of assessment findings, while devoting most report-writing time and effort to presentation of data and scripting of sentences. To develop advanced clinical skills, an evaluator must resist the kind of shortcuts that enable the economic production of "acceptable" reports, but serve as obstacles to sustained improvement.

Clinical Impressions

The Clinical Impressions section is the heart of the report. Assessment data from multiple sources are integrated to convey a rich understanding of the child and to address referral questions and concerns. The practical implications of assessment findings are presented in straightforward language. In the process, the evaluator cites the contributing assessment data that establish that these interpretations are evidence based and make her reasoning transparent to other professionals. Whereas in previous sections findings were presented in a factual manner, the evaluator now makes inferences and interpretations. The title of the section—which might alternately be called Diagnostic Impressions, Interpretations, or Conclusions—communicates that this section is the product of the evaluator's clinical expertise.

The first paragraph should frame the situation or problem(s) that led to the referral, recapping relevant history and circumstances. How long has the problem been evident? What important contextual factors (e.g., school or family changes) have contributed to the problem? Are there significant medical or developmental issues? Are there relevant cultural or linguistic factors? We suggest that this opening section include a brief description of the child, citing important strengths or assets. This introductory paragraph is intended to orient and engage the reader.

As the section proceeds, referral questions and any other major findings that emerged in the course of the assessment are addressed in turn. Data from records, observations, interviews, and standardized measures are interwoven to answer each question or explain each point. Does the child have a learning disability? Is the child depressed? Are attentional or executive deficits interfering with day-to-day functioning? What is the nature of the aggressive behavior; how serious is it and what affects it? The questions are organized from most to least important. Sufficient evidence is included to document the reasoning behind these impressions and conclusions.

As is the case throughout the report, the evaluator reports findings selectively. Only information that addresses referral questions or that meaningfully contributes to understanding the child and his circumstances is included. Answers, explanations, and implications are presented in straightforward language that ensures they will be similarly understood by all readers. If the evaluator cannot provide a clear answer to a referral question, this is best stated directly rather than muddying the waters with oblique or technical language or failing to address it.

The Clinical Impressions section is also the place to provide a psychiatric diagnosis or to inform a special education disability determination. How to present diagnostic conclusions depends on the evaluator's status and the nature of the assessment. A DSM-5 or ICD-9 diagnosis may be central to the referral question, and may be required by a third-party payer or expected by the agency that is the primary recipient of the report. In such cases, the diagnosis should be clearly identified in a separate paragraph labeled Diagnostic Conclusion at the end of the Clinical Impressions section.

An evaluation conducted by a school psychologist as part of a school district's educational evaluation calls for a different approach, since the determination of an educational disability involves a process that considers the input of all team members. Federal special education regulations explicitly state, "A group of qualified professionals and the parent of the child determines [sic] whether the child is a child with a disability" (Sec. 300.306(a)(1)). Nevertheless, the school psychologist's assessment may yield findings that clearly support a particular disability. How can this dilemma be resolved in a way that respects both the weight of the school psychologist's findings and the legal authority of the team? The school psychologist's report can provide compelling evidence to support the warranted conclusion by explicitly addressing the key criteria that form the basis of the eligibility decision, while not making a definitive statement about the disability category. For example, she might signify that a child has an intellectual disability by reporting that he demonstrates significantly subaverage intellectual functioning and delays in adaptive behavior, and that these deficits have persisted over time and are not secondary to sensory impairment or environmental circumstances.

Summary

The Summary section recaps the key points that appeared earlier in the report, including a brief restatement of core referral questions and concerns, and a description of the child's salient qualities and strengths. As the name implies, no new information is introduced. The Summary concisely restates the most pertinent information and findings without the elaboration or the reference to supporting evidence that was provided in Clinical Impressions. Thus, the Summary provides a synopsis of the Clinical Impressions section, highlighting the findings that address the referral concerns and the implications of those findings for the child's day-to-day functioning.

One way to conceptualize the distinction between the two sections is to note that each major finding that merits a paragraph in Clinical Impressions is recapped with a sentence or two in the Summary. Samples of such statements are provided in Box 5.7. If a diagnosis or disability category is included in Clinical Impressions, it should be included in the Summary section as well. The Summary section may be a single paragraph and is typically no longer than a half page.

Cash (2017) proposed that reports not include a Summary, lest the reader rely on this synopsis and forgo reading the full report. The reality, however, is that a busy principal or

---

BOX 5.7. Sample Summary Section Statements

- "Scarlett has weak reading skills that make it hard for her to progress in all areas of language arts."
- "Denzel suffers from depression that interferes with his ability to focus on a task for any length of time and to complete an acceptable amount of schoolwork."
- "Rosie's recent concussion is the likely source of her problems with paying attention, remembering directions, and planning and organizing school assignments."
- "Kal has above-average cognitive ability, but has significant difficulty expressing his ideas orally or in writing."
- "Dwayne can do grade-level schoolwork, but is not invested in his academic performance and makes little effort. He is far more interested in socializing and in participating in organized sports."

pediatrician may have limited time or opportunity to read a report, and a Summary will serve their needs better than a cursory gleaning of the entire document. Also, the Summary helps orient readers to the report's key findings (hence, some opt to read it first) and can serve to refresh the memory of a person who previously read the full report.

Another function of the Summary section is to preface, and provide the rationale for, the recommendations that follow. There is no justification for "gratuitous" recommendations that appear out of the blue, with no connection to the findings that were discussed in the Clinical Impressions (or Conclusions) section and cited in the Summary. The link between the Summary and the recommendations that follow should be strong and direct, which can be made clear by labeling the final section "Summary and Recommendations," and by transitioning between the two sections with a sentence like "Given these findings, recommendations are as follows."

In reports with a brief Clinical Impressions section—say, less than a single-spaced half page—a Summary section may seem redundant, as it will likely reiterate what was stated in the previous section. An option in this case is to combine the two sections. This section would recap referral and background information, state key findings with reference to supporting evidence, and address practical implications. Given the inclusion of new information, this section would more aptly be called Conclusions, rather than Summary.

Recommendations

If the Clinical Impressions section is the heart of the report, the Recommendations section is the voice, arms, and legs—the part dedicated to accomplishing results. Consumer-responsive recommendations must be relevant, specific, evidence-based (to the extent possible), individualized, and feasible.

Relevance is key to the consumer-responsive approach. The evaluator must refrain from adding recommendations that are unrelated to referral questions or to significant findings that emerge. Although well-intentioned, a long list of recommendations may result in a loss of focus and diffusion of priorities, making it less likely that the recommendations will be implemented. A report with five relevant recommendations that directly respond to referral concerns is more likely to generate constructive action than a report with 15 or more recommendations, some of which are vaguely related.

For similar reasons, recommendations must be specific. Recommendations are written to influence the behavior of teachers, parents, special educators, mental health providers, and the child himself. Specific recommendations offer clear guidance for action; they can be understood, discussed, agreed upon, and implemented. If they lack specificity, recommendations may be misunderstood or implemented in ways other than what was intended by the evaluator. However, this guideline must be applied judiciously, taking care not to preclude acceptable options. The evaluator may be inclined to recommend a specific curriculum, program, or intervention by name. However, there might be an alternative curriculum, program, or intervention that is just as likely to help the child and that the child's school or agency is better prepared to implement. Hence, it is advisable for the evaluator to describe the *type* of intervention that will meet the child's needs, identifying key elements of the proposed approach without naming a specific curriculum or placement (see examples in Box 5.8). Recommending an intervention by name might constrict a parent's or advocate's expectations, setting the stage for disappointment or conflict. The specific intervention may be inappropriate, unavailable, or unfeasible for reasons unknown to the evaluator.

Recommendations should also be individualized. Generic recommendations lack the kind of individual attention that sharpens their relevance and leaves the consumers feeling understood and cared about. No two children with a reading problem are the same. No two adolescents with depression can be helped the exact same way. The evaluator might make use of a bank of recommendations that can be individualized and adapted for different children. However, copying complete recommendations from lists stored on a computer is unlikely to achieve the individual focus that is essential to consumer-responsive reporting.

Recommendations should, to the extent possible, be evidence based. The American Psychological Association Presidential Task Force on Evidence-Based Practice (2006) defines evidence-based practice as "the integration of the best available research with clinical expertise in the context of patient characteristics, culture, and preferences" (p. 273). Thus, practitioners are directed to meld scientific knowledge with the needs of the particular client, using informed judgment to factor in situational variables. It is important for evaluators to keep up with the current literature, but research findings should not be applied indiscriminately. Even when research informs us about evidence-based practice, the findings apply to groups of subjects; individuals in a study respond in various ways, some improving, others not.

BOX 5.8. Sample Recommendations That Inform Interventions without Usurping the IEP Team's Authority

- "Ernest will benefit from a highly structured classroom environment that has clear rules that are consistently enforced."
- "Pearl's instructional level in reading and language arts should be monitored closely, with new material (vocabulary words, math problems, etc.) introduced only after she has fully mastered the previous material in the curriculum. Her independent assignments should include less than 10% new material to reinforce prior learning and to sustain her motivation by enabling her to experience success."
- "Scott will benefit from increased opportunities, both in school and in the community, to interact with supportive nondisabled peers—ideally, those who share and encourage his interests in art and photography."
- "Rudyard should be introduced to strategies that will help him regain his composure and self-control. He may initially need prompting by adults to use these strategies, but should be taught, allowed, and encouraged to apply these strategies on his own."
- "Virginia will benefit from a therapeutic relationship with a mental health professional who can help her reflect on, and effectively cope with, anxiety-producing situations."
- "Teachers and aides should respond selectively to Vladimir's attention-seeking behavior, giving little or no attention to negative behaviors and offering praise when he behaves in a socially appropriate or constructive manner."

Often, there is no clear evidence-based intervention that promises to address the needs of the individual child. Hence, the evaluator's clinical judgment comes into play. The use of clinical judgment, however, should not be regarded as random or subjective. As expressed by Kurt Lewin's oft-repeated and oft-quoted maxim (McCain, 2015), "There is nothing so practical as a good theory." The well-trained evaluator relies on a substantial body of knowledge that spans child development, behavioral principles, psychopathology, intervention research, interpersonal dynamics, and other areas.

Faced with the uncertainty of formulating recommendations, the evaluator can do better than simply make a well-informed best guess. The evaluator can apply data-based decision making on an individual case basis by systematically following up with consumers to determine whether recommended interventions have been successful, require some adjustment, or need to be reconsidered. As noted by Sattler (2018, p. 19):

> Assessment recommendations are not the final step in helping to resolve a child's difficulties. Recommendations are starting points for the clinician and for those who implement the interventions. Assessment is an ongoing process that includes modifications to the interventions . . . Effective consultation requires monitoring the child's progress with both short-term and long-term follow-ups.

The evaluator's ultimate concern is whether an intervention works for the individual who was assessed. Thus, following up on the effectiveness of recommendations is the epitome of evidence-based practice.

Finally, recommendations must be feasible. Feasible recommendations are acceptable to and within the capacity of the teachers, parents, school districts, mental health providers, and others who are expected to implement them. As Harvey (2006) advised, "Recommendations and interventions should be described in such a way that the reader is convinced not only that they are appropriate, but also that they can be implemented without undue duress" (p. 14). A recommendation that is not implemented provides no benefit. Furthermore, recommendations that prove to be unfeasible lead to frustration and conflict among those who care for the child. A parent may perceive that a school district is failing to address her child's needs. Teachers may feel burdened when advised to do what they don't know how to do. School administrators may feel boxed in when asked to provide resources that they do not think will be helpful or that are prohibitively expensive. The evaluator must balance the role of advocate with that of problem solver, pressing school districts to meet their obligations by writing recommendations that are necessary for the child's progress, while optimizing the likelihood of successful outcomes.

A school psychologist or other school-based evaluator may face challenges in seeking this balance. In accordance with federal and state special education mandates, no one member of the school team should make unilateral decisions about a child's educational disability, eligibility for special education, or the specific programs and services to include in the child's IEP. These decisions are the responsibility of the IEP team, which includes the child's parent, and are based on input from multiple parties. Understandably, a school district would not want written recommendations on record that contradict the decisions made by the team. The solution is to make recommendations that identify the child's needs and describe the type of supports or services that will be helpful, while allowing the team to consider what specific options are consistent with these recommendations. (This is illustrated by the sample recommendations Box 5.8.) This approach allows the team flexibility in selecting programs, services, and strategies, while making use of the evaluator's guidance about the essential conditions or characteristics that should be met.

Data Summary

The Data Summary is an appendix to the report that provides detailed documentation of the test scores and related psychometric data (confidence intervals, percentile ranks, etc.). It follows the Summary and Recommendations and evaluator's signature, starting on a new page. Excluding data tables from the body of the report helps the evaluator report findings selectively, as it reduces the inclination to discuss every test finding. (This might be put to a test, as described by Research Idea 5.1.) However, the full documentation of test results in the Data Summary allows psychometrically inclined readers to inspect and weigh the evidence that contributed to the evaluator's interpretations and impressions. It also provides a handy archive of test results that may prove valuable for comparisons with subsequent assessment data.

A Data Summary template with suggested formats for various measures is provided in Appendix F. Case examples of Data Summaries can be found in the sample reports in Appendix D.

RESEARCH IDEA 5.1. The Impact of Test Score Tables on Assessment Report Narratives

Research question: Does the inclusion of test score tables in the body of a report (i.e., interspersed within a Test Results section) result in longer and more detailed narrative reporting of test findings?

A causal–comparative study is proposed that compares two types of reports by practitioners: those with test score tables inserted in the Test Results section and those that provide such tables in a separate Data Summary. These reports might be compared on variables such as (1) the amount and percentage of total text devoted to description and interpretation of test findings and (2) the proportion of test descriptions and interpretations in the body of the report with little or no relevance (operationally defined as having no bearing on report recommendations). This study would investigate the hypothesis that, by including test score tables in the body of a report, evaluators are inclined to discuss test results at greater length, regardless of their relevance.

Support for this hypothesis would encourage evaluators to provide complete test data in the Data Summary only and to be more selective in reporting and interpreting test results.

CONCLUDING COMMENTS

The time has come for practitioners to rethink the nature and value of conventional psychological reports. Many evaluators feel that the quality of their work is largely represented by their reports. They spend vast amounts of time writing long reports that are replete with technical language and extensive analysis of test scores. These reports may impress consumers and convey a sense of the evaluator's expertise, but fall short with respect to their most important purpose: to benefit children and those who support them. Conventional reports have value, but could be far more responsive to the needs of consumers.

The proposed features of a consumer-responsive report follow from the bedrock principle that the parents, teachers, and other consumers who read psychological reports can provide greater benefits to the child when the report is relevant, understandable, and child focused. This philosophy has implications for report structure, content, and style. The structure of a consumer-responsive report reflects the reality that multiple sources of information (i.e., records, interviews, observations, and standardized tests and measures) contribute significantly to the findings. Content should be selective, favoring information that is relevant to referral questions and concerns, and enhances the reader's understanding of the child and her circumstances. The evaluator applies the "So what?" principle to distinguish between what is relevant and what is dispensable or trivial. The child, rather than the administered tests, is the focus of the report. Assessment findings are organized thematically, and interpretations integrate the findings from all sources of assessment data. Everyday language is used throughout the report, while technical terms and statistical concepts are included sparingly and purposefully.

Psychologists of all stripes have endorsed these principles and strategies, yet assessment practices have been impervious to change. For current evaluators, making the transition will require a significant investment of time and effort, and the support of colleagues and supervisors. For future practitioners, adopting consumer-responsive practices will depend on a shift in the focus of graduate training experiences and exposure to consumer-responsive models in textbooks and in the field. Appendix G contains a rubric that can be used to provide feedback for trainees or self-evaluation for practitioners as they aspire to write consumer-responsive reports.

CHAPTER 6

Straight Talk
Oral Communication of Findings

Report writing claims a large proportion of the time devoted to psychological assessment—so much that evaluators may equate the quality of the report with the value of the assessment. It is indeed the case that the report serves as a permanent record of the assessment, and that the findings and recommendations may be consulted by future users. However, it is the oral presentation of findings at a team meeting or individual conference that has the greatest potential impact on consumers. The personal interaction with parents, teachers, and administrators greatly determines the extent to which they understand and accept key findings and feel inclined to follow the evaluator's recommendations. Given that benefit to consumers is the ultimate goal of an assessment, it is of paramount importance that evaluators become skilled at presenting their findings in person.

Effective oral communication of assessment findings calls for many of the same advanced skills as report writing: sound organization, clear presentation, insightful integration of data, strategic emphasis, and sensitive use of language. Relational skills, however, are every bit as important. Establishing positive connections with consumers is a critical aspect of assessment, as it fosters receptivity to assessment findings and recommendations.

INTERPERSONAL AND COMMUNICATION SKILLS

The effectiveness of an oral presentation relies heavily on interpersonal and communication skills. Quine and Rutter (1994) found that consumer satisfaction with an evaluation is influenced more by process variables—the perception that an evaluator is a good communicator and is approachable and direct—than by the content of the evaluation. As discussed in Chapter 4, personal characteristics, such as empathy, sensitivity, nonjudgmental attitude, and listening skills, are keys to establishing rapport and gaining the trust of parents and teachers. For optimal effect, these characteristics are complemented by oral communication skills that inspire confidence and make it easier for consumers to process the material and become engaged in discussion.

Much of the material in this chapter may seem like common sense or basic good manners—and to a large extent, it is. That does not make it any less important. Relating to consumers in an attentive and respectful manner goes a long way toward creating a positive impression. When busy practitioners focus narrowly on conveying assessment findings and lose sight of consumers' needs, interpersonal considerations may fall by the wayside. All too often, the oral presentation involves technical information and one-way communication, thus squandering the opportunity to provide value above and beyond the written report. This kind of presentation is especially likely to occur when the evaluator has the written report in hand and follows it closely as a guide to the oral presentation.

Approaching an oral presentation from the perspective of the consumer results in a different kind of interaction, with different results. Evaluators must keep in mind that assessment feedback meetings are not routine events for parents and teachers. They have limited understanding of, and use for, test scores and psychological jargon. Their concerns are straightforward and practical: to better understand the child and address her needs. The evaluator earns their trust and confidence by being responsive to these concerns.

Tone and delivery are critical aspects of oral communication. The evaluator should speak clearly at an appropriate pace and in a relaxed and confident manner. Making eye contact is essential, although the manner and extent should be modulated in consideration of cultural differences. Eye contact contributes to expressive delivery and also enables the evaluator to gauge how information is being received. Reading from a report or a prepared script negates the potential value of an in-person meeting. It interferes with eye contact, discourages interaction, and conveys a lack of confidence in one's ability to impart information.

Relationship skills should be an instructional focus from the very beginning stages of professional training, and should continue to be refined through reflective practice. These skills should be explicitly taught at the preservice level and further addressed through clinical supervision and performance evaluation at the in-service level. Audio and video recordings can be especially valuable for training and supervision purposes. Oral communication and rapport-building skills are a major focus of the training activity in Appendix H—an assessment-case feedback simulation for a graduate-level assessment course.

FEEDBACK MEETINGS

Assessment findings are typically conveyed in person to parents, teachers, and other consumers, sometimes as a group (e.g., in a team meeting at school or a feedback conference at a clinic) and sometimes as individuals.

Team Meetings

Team meetings to consider assessment findings are routinely convened in schools and are sometimes held in mental health clinics and private practice settings. When evaluations or re-evaluations are conducted for special education purposes, the assessment findings are presented at a meeting of the IEP team. Federal special education regulations require that an IEP team include specified school personnel (i.e., regular and special education teachers, and educators who are knowledgeable about curriculum and instruction, system resources, and evaluation results), as well as parents. The team may also include advocates, consultants, outside evaluators, and the assessed child himself. Students must be invited to attend team meetings at which postsecondary plans and related transition services are discussed.

While special education teachers and specialized instructional support personnel (e.g., school psychologists, speech and language pathologists) attend IEP meetings regularly, classroom teachers participate less often and parents do so only occasionally. Hence, a cardinal rule in conducting team meetings is to be sensitive and responsive to the perspectives and feelings of the infrequent participants—parents, teachers, and students. Occasional participants should be made to feel like equal members of the team whose contributions and questions are welcome. The evaluator should direct her presentation to the parent or parents and to the student, if he is in attendance, to encourage their active participation and to monitor their understanding and receptivity.

The tone of a team meeting begins to develop before participants even sit down. Informal greetings can promote rapport with parents, teachers, and other nonregular attendees and can set them at ease. ("Idle conversation" *does* serves a purpose.) Before turning to the business at hand, it may be necessary to attend to participants' situational needs and issues. Is the teacher pressed for time? Did the parent have difficulty making it to the meeting?

Subtle issues can be meaningful in setting the right tone. Seating arrangements matter, especially in meetings with many participants. When school personnel sit together on one side of the table and parents and their invitees (e.g., advocate, consultant, therapist) sit on the other side, it creates a sense of opposing teams with competing interests. Seating is best interspersed to counteract this effect. The tenor of a meeting is shaped by other factors as well, such as school personnel responding to interruptions or leaving midmeeting, or participants partaking of snacks or beverages. These elements can carry implicit messages, such as that the meeting is casual and friendly or that it is of secondary importance. It is important to avoid circumstances that suggest an uneven playing field that favors the "home team" over the "visiting team." For example, if school personnel arrive with coffee mugs in hand, parents and other visitors should be offered a hot beverage as well.

When the meeting is formally convened, opening messages are critical for establishing a productive tone. A team meeting should begin with introductions or reintroductions. Adult team members should all use either first names or last names; doing otherwise is awkward and conveys the wrong message. Addressing participants by titles (Mr., Mrs., or Dr.) adds a tone of formality and heightens attention to differences in status and education.

After introductions, it is advisable for the meeting facilitator to preview what is to be accomplished and in what time frame. This orients nonregular participants to the meeting structure, establishes a common understanding of the process, and promotes a shared intention to use the time well. This preview also helps the facilitator play timekeeper in a diplomatic manner, fending off unproductive digressions and redundant verbalizations with a reminder of what needs to be accomplished. Keeping to the agenda is of no small importance, as it helps ensure that ample time is allotted for questions, concerns, and a discussion of recommendations.

Active parent participation greatly enhances feedback conferences. The meeting facilitator's opening remarks should include an explicit invitation to parents to offer information and ask questions. A welcoming message alone, however, is insufficient. Formal meetings can be intimidating to parents, as they are in an unfamiliar situation, among highly educated professionals who are in their own element. To reduce parents' reluctance to participate, it is advisable to elicit their input early on in a meeting. The evaluator might prompt them to provide valuable information by tapping their unique knowledge of the child. This establishes their realm of expertise, since parents have extensive knowledge of their children's history, behavior, and personality. This input is also useful as a validity check for determining whether parents have observed the same kind of behavior that the evaluator determined to be noteworthy. It is helpful to provide multiple opportunities for a parent's comments or questions, either verbally (e.g., "Is that what you have observed?"; "Any questions about that?"; "Anything to add?") or nonverbally (e.g., with an expectant look or an encouraging nod). These methods of encouraging parent participation are also useful for engaging inexperienced or reticent teachers.

It is a reality of the school day that team meetings are scheduled for a fixed period of time—perhaps scheduled back to back for 60–90 minutes each—and that classroom teachers are available on a limited basis. However, some meetings will require more time if disagreements arise or if new information needs to be processed. The decision to prolong a meeting can be problematic. Professional staff may be under pressure to keep to a tight schedule. Ending the meeting at the scheduled time may result in important topics being addressed hurriedly or not at all. Extending the meeting time may result in team members being on edge or under duress. Continuing at a later date can pose problems as well, as it may be difficult for parents, interpreters, or advocates to make time for another meeting. It is highly problematic to conclude a meeting with important issues left hanging or having spent little time on interactive problem solving. An unsatisfactory conclusion is a loss for all involved, and leads to discouragement and ill feelings that can undermine collaboration and optimism.

Given these complications and pitfalls, there are enormous benefits to conducting an efficient and productive meeting in which key agenda items are adequately addressed. The importance of reporting assessment findings in a clear, concise, selective, and engaging manner cannot be overemphasized. A lengthy and overly technical presentation of findings comes at a great cost. Many feedback conferences suffer from the same shortcomings as traditional assessments, in that they emphasize identifying problems rather than making inroads to solve them. Sufficient time should be devoted to recommendations and to consumers' reactions to recommendations. (Are they clearly understood? Are they practical? Has anything similar been tried before?). All too often, a feedback meeting involves professional evaluators reporting their findings in turn, using language geared to other professionals—talking about standard scores, relative weaknesses, base rates, and the like. Thus the time devoted to discussions about eligibility, recommendations, and available services and programs is reduced, which has the further effect of communicating to parents and classroom teachers that their input is of little consequence.

An interactive meeting requires a skillful facilitator—one who can keep a meeting from getting stuck or sidetracked. A parent, teacher, or other participant who feels misunderstood may persist or escalate in making a point. A helpful strategy is to restate and acknowledge the validity of the message (e.g., "You believe your child needs more individual help. You're discouraged by the lack of progress he has been making"). This strategy allows the individual to feel heard and move on.

The structure of team meetings influences the content and impact of findings. The familiar format of having each professional report in turn—teacher, educational diagnostician, school psychologist, speech and language pathologist—can result in a presentation that is fragmented and redundant, in which the focus is on separate evaluations rather than on the whole child. In contrast, a child-centered meeting structure might have participants discuss each of several issues in turn: the child's strengths, her levels of performance in important functional areas, and proposed supports and strategies. Thus, input from parents, teachers, the child, and other occasional participants is solicited on each key topic. A child-centered structure can also contribute to more efficient meetings, as the presentation of nonessential assessment results may be minimized.

Individual Meetings

A separate meeting with one or more parents or with a teacher is a prime opportunity to provide feedback and discuss assessment results. Meeting separately with parents, possibly accompanied by the child, is common practice in a clinical setting or independent practice, but less so in schools.

Individual feedback meetings allow for an open and extended conversation between the evaluator and consumer (Smith et al., 2007), which can be of mutual benefit. Individual meetings offer an important opportunity to strengthen relationships with consumers and ensure their understanding of assessment results. They also encourage an exchange of information. The evaluator, however skillful, still has an imperfect or incomplete understanding of the child, and will benefit from feedback about the accuracy of clinical impressions. An individual meeting also allows the evaluator to gauge the consumer's reaction to findings and receptivity to recommendations, which can influence what to emphasize in the report or at a subsequent team meeting. It is especially important to discuss with teachers, parents, or students whether any recommendations of the sort that the evaluator is considering have already been tried, and with what results.

Individual meetings tend to be more conducive than team meetings to in-depth discussion of assessment findings. A school-based evaluator may find it difficult to arrange separate feedback sessions with parents and teachers on a regular basis, but dispensing with individual meetings can come at a substantial cost. By forgoing this opportunity, the assessment may be compromised by incomplete or inaccurate information, misguided interpretations, or unacceptable recommendations. A prior individual meeting is especially valuable when state regulations or school district policies require the evaluator to produce a final report at or before the IEP team meeting at which the assessment is formally reviewed. Under these circumstances, a separate prior meeting not only enables the evaluator to discuss findings at length with the consumer, but also affords the only opportunity to get feedback about tentative interpretations and recommendations and to revise the assessment report accordingly.

CONVEYING FINDINGS

When discussing assessment results, the focus should be on the child, rather than on tests and assessment measures. A good starting point is to establish that you have come to know the child well, and that you appreciate the child's positive qualities and strengths (Glazer, 2014). Personal knowledge of the child may be conveyed by citing one or more of the child's essential winning characteristics (e.g., generous, determined, helpful, curious) and sharing an illustrative anecdote or observation from the assessment. Highlighting the child's strengths up front helps to foster an alliance with parents and to set a positive tone for the meeting.

A well-organized presentation of findings uses time well and conveys information effectively. It is more productive to focus on relatively few key points—perhaps two or three, and no more than four—than to try to recap every assessment finding. Only a few main points from the meeting are likely to be remembered, so the evaluator should purposefully identify which ones to emphasize. To ensure that major findings are fully understood and remembered, the evaluator should touch on them at multiple points during the meeting, including a brief preview that precedes the full explanation and a closing statement that recaps key points (see Box 6.1 for examples). As the saying goes, "Tell them what you're going to tell them, then tell them, then tell them what you just told them."

While it is good practice to describe the assessment procedures that informed the evaluation, this explanation can be covered in just a few short sentences (see Box 6.2). A detailed description of each assessment procedure is unnecessary and a dubious use of meeting time. For similar reasons, assessment results should be reported selectively, as needed to illustrate key major findings. In highlighting these findings, the evaluator might describe a telling observation or test performance in detail, and explain how it is relevant to school performance or other referral concerns. By limiting such elaboration to the most significant findings, the evaluator uses meeting time well and sets the stage for the discussion of recommendations.

Recommendations from earlier chapters about using "plain English," minimizing jargon, explaining key technical terms as needed, and presenting test results in an understandable format are especially applicable to oral presentations. The evaluator should take note of how the presentation is being received—with attentive nods and astute questions or with puzzled looks—to determine whether the presentation is clear and useful to consumers.

Postal and Armstrong (2013) offer suggestions on how to present complex cognitive findings in an effective manner that "sticks." Most of all, they stress the importance of speaking simply. They also elaborate on the following principles, adapted from the organizational psychology literature:

- Concreteness—Explain the meaning of scores for everyday life.
- Credibility—Demonstrate your knowledge and establish your authority.
- Unexpectedness—What is stated in a novel manner is remembered well.
- Emotions—Stimulate the client's emotions to help the information stick.
- Stories—Offer metaphors or stories to illustrate findings and make them memorable.

COMMUNICATING WITH DIFFERENT CONSUMERS

Even though most guidance for reporting assessment results is applicable to all consumers, some advice is particularly applicable to one group or another. Evaluators should be attuned to issues and considerations that relate specifically to communicating with parents, with children, and with teachers.

Communicating with Parents

The relationship with parents is all-important. As discussed in Chapter 4, this relationship should be fostered throughout the assessment process and especially when presenting oral feedback. There is no substitute for working with parents respectfully and empathically,

---

BOX 6.1. Preview and Summary Statements

The following are examples of preview statements that set the stage for key findings that will follow, and of summary statements that return to key points in closing.

Preview	Assessment finding	Summary
"I learned some important things about why Fred doesn't follow instructions in class and seems confused at times."	"Fred has difficulty processing spoken language. When complex, or academic, language is presented at a rapid pace, he is likely to miss key information. It takes a lot of concentration for him to follow a lecture presentation, and he will get tired and tune out if it continues for a long time."	"We talked about how Fred doesn't take in spoken information as easily and as quickly as other children his age. We came up with some promising ideas about how he can get the information in other ways and keep up with classmates."
"After talking with Ethel and observing her in class, I now understand why she is having trouble getting along with classmates, even though she gets along fine with family members and friends in the neighborhood."	"Ethel is very bright and takes pride in her achievements. At school, she is totally focused on the business of learning. She is less interested in and comfortable with socializing. She gets impatient with classmates, who enjoy breaks and like to play, which she sees as a distraction from learning. As a result, peers see her as aloof and a know-it-all, which can lead to her being excluded and teased."	"We would like to see Ethel have more positive interactions with her classmates. It would help for her to learn some new social skills. We also had some ideas about how she could take on advanced material, without it causing tension with classmates."

BOX 6.2. Sample Explanation of Assessment Procedures

Assessment procedure	Brief description (recommended)	Detailed and technical description (not recommended)
Preface	"For this assessment, I relied upon several different sources of information."	"In conducting this assessment, I obtained data from various sources: a review of records, systematic observation in multiple settings, ratings scales, and standardized tests."
Background information	"For background information, I reviewed Ricky's school records, including a previous psychological evaluation, talked with his teacher, and met with his parents."	"The review of records provided me with background information. This included a review of the school cumulative file, which has attendance records and comments by previous teachers, and of the special education file, which included his current IEP, records of previous meetings, and prior evaluation reports."
Observations	"I also had the chance to observe him in his regular classroom and with the art teacher."	"I observed Ricky for 45 minutes of a Reading and Language Arts period and for 30 minutes of an arts lesson, using time-interval recording to get an estimate of his on-task and off-task behavior."
Rating scales	"The rating scales that the teacher and parents completed told me about Ricky's typical behavior as seen by adults."	"I had the teacher and parents complete the BASC-3—the Behavioral Assessment System for Children—rating scales. These provide information about problem behaviors, such as aggression or inattention, as well as adaptive or positive behaviors, such as adaptability, leadership, and social skills."
Tests	"And I administered tests to assess his mental abilities and academic achievement."	"I administered several different tests. I used the Stanford–Binet Intelligence Scale to assess verbal and nonverbal cognitive abilities. I also administered the TOMAL-3, a separate measure of memory and learning, and the attention and executive functioning subtests from the NEPSY-II. For academics, I administered the WIAT-III—the Wechsler Individual Achievement Test—to assess reading, writing, and math skills."

and responding nonjudgmentally to their questions and concerns. Key findings should be presented in plain language, free of irrelevant and technical information, with the emphasis on meaningful information and its everyday implications.

Professional team members should recognize that parents experience feedback meetings in highly personal ways that evoke strong feelings. While the evaluator reports on the child's performance and behavior in a matter-of-fact fashion, the parent may be experiencing shame or resentment, feelings of having failed as a parent, or traumatic flashbacks to her own school history.

A particularly sensitive situation occurs when a parent is first confronted with a child's serious disability. What is just another day in the evaluator's professional life (albeit a challenging one) may have lifelong implications for the parent—a devastating message that can crush hopes and dreams and foretell long-term heavy responsibilities. Since the information will have an enduring effect, the feedback session should be regarded as the beginning or continuation of an ongoing process. If the evaluator is presenting new and surprising information, it may be pointless to expect the reeling parent to process detailed findings. The emotional needs of the parent instead become the primary focus of the meeting. Assuming more of a therapeutic role, the evaluator must gauge the parent's reactions and allow ample opportunity to address questions and concerns. The evaluator should be prepared to identify available resources, such as websites, books and articles, support groups, and local parents who have coped with a similar situation. Browning Wright and Gronroos (n.d.) provide valuable tips for sensitively engaging parents when conveying the "hard news" of a child's intellectual disability. They emphasize that such discussions should take place in a safe and supportive environment, rather than in a large meeting.

Determining what the parent knows or believes about a serious diagnosis is critical. Parents may be burdened by troubling assumptions about what caused the disability, thinking they are somehow to blame. The evaluator might explore these associations by first asking, "What do you expect to hear?" or "Is there anything in particular that you fear I will tell you?" These expectations and associations may need to be reexamined. Does the parent understand what is meant by an "intellectual disability" or "severe developmental delay"? Has the parent received assurance from a physician or preschool teacher that the child "will grow out of it"? In some cases, it is useful to ask a parent, "Do you ever feel responsible for your child's condition?" We have heard parents share painful and irrational burdens of guilt and shame, such as autism being caused by a parent's medical illness when a child was young or a serious learning disability being the result of a parent spending too much time at work. In such discussions, the evaluator has the opportunity to lighten the parent's load by providing accurate scientific information about the known causes of a condition.

Parents may misunderstand the severity of a child's disability for years because an evaluator has soft-pedaled findings or cloaked them in technical language. Failure to explain a serious disability is an abdication of professional responsibility and a disservice to parents. Evaluators must resist the inclination to soften the message in order to ease their own discomfort. They must be prepared to accept consumers' reactions and provide both helpful information and emotional support.

Communicating with Teachers

Teachers are critically important collaborators. They have an enormous influence over a child's performance and well-being, and play a major role in the process of assessing the child and implementing recommendations.

To establish an effective working relationship with the child's teacher, the evaluator must respect a teacher's time and expertise. Teachers are busy professionals. They experience constant demands and make countless "micro-decisions" throughout the school day. The relationship with the teacher is nurtured during the information-gathering phase of the assessment. Being considerate of the teacher's time, the evaluator should come prepared to an information-gathering meeting prepared, having reviewed referral information and records. By using good listening skills (nonverbal attention, door openers, reflective listening, etc.), the evaluator conveys that he values the teacher's input. It is particularly important to ask what strategies the teacher has tried and with what results, and to register this information uncritically.

Although teachers have expertise in curriculum and instruction and acquire extensive knowledge of their students, they may have a different perspective than the evaluator regarding the interpretation of student behavior. The child who lacks social skills may be regarded as a bully or as antisocial. The child who interrupts may be considered rude and insensitive, rather than impulsive or unable to read social cues. Hence, there is much to be gained by the evaluator eliciting the teacher's impressions and then offering a complementary or contrasting understanding of the child.

The evaluator might meet individually with a teacher to discuss assessment findings and recommendations or to develop a behavioral intervention plan. This may involve proposing that the teacher try a new approach or carry out some additional activity. The likelihood of gaining a teacher's support is greatly enhanced by employing a problem-solving process founded upon shared goals, willing participation, and a common understanding of the process (Kratochwill et al., 2014). In a team meeting at which assessment feedback is provided, the evaluator should take advantage of opportunities to value the teacher's input. The evaluator might look to the teacher to elaborate on or confirm important points. Similarly, the evaluator might relate her own key findings to information that the teacher has provided. When teachers contribute their own ideas and forthrightly discuss what is practical and acceptable on their part, their investment in the plan increases. The collaborative relationship is furthered as the evaluator arranges to follow up with the teacher and consider needed adjustments to the plan. Throughout the process, the evaluator is well served to prioritize results over her ego. This attitude is epitomized by the advice of a former clinical supervisor of ours: "If the plan works, credit the teacher; if it doesn't, take the blame."

Sometimes a teacher is unreceptive to the evaluator's input. One possible reason for rejecting the evaluator's recommendations is that the teacher is intent on having the child receive additional services *outside* of the classroom or having him removed from the classroom altogether. Thus, the evaluator who is trying to make the child more successful in the current classroom setting is working at cross-purposes with the teacher. Or, a teacher who has had little success with a student may respond defensively to assessment feedback, interpreting the evaluator's analysis and recommendations as critical of the teacher's work. A particularly touchy situation arises when the referral concerns are the result of problematic teaching practices that affect the entire class. (Perhaps the teacher has referred several children for this same reason.) Working with this teacher in a consultative role may be the optimal course of action; however, shifting to a classwide focus must be approached with care and may be rejected outright. If the teacher is unreceptive to addressing his teaching practices, it may be necessary to instead discuss interventions for the referred child, while commenting that the teacher may find this intervention to be useful with other students as well.

Communicating with Children and Adolescents

The relationship established during the assessment process sets the stage for a productive feedback meeting with the child. Establishing rapport, listening attentively and nonjudgmentally, and being responsive to the child's needs help establish a sense of trust and make it more likely that the child will actively engage in a discussion of the findings.

There are several reasons to discuss assessment findings with a child or adolescent when the assessment has concluded. Such a conversation allows for a deliberate debriefing of the assessment experience. It also allows the evaluator to learn more about the child's perception of his difficulties. Furthermore, in discussing assessment feedback, the evaluator can check whether the child accepts her explanations and recommendations, and whether he will be a willing participant in the intervention efforts that are proposed. A follow-up meeting also provides an opportunity to preview and facilitate the next steps in the process, such as the child's involvement in an IEP team meeting or in intervention planning. This objective is in keeping with NASP's (2010b) ethical principles.

> **Standard II.3.11.** School psychologists discuss with students the recommendations and plans for assisting them. To the maximum extent appropriate, students are invited to participate in selecting and planning interventions.

The discussion of assessment findings should be adapted for the child's age and developmental level. For a very young or intellectually disabled child, it might consist of a few simply worded statements at the close of the last assessment session. For older children, this interaction may be more prolonged, and possibly take place in a separate meeting, during which the evaluator and student discuss findings, interpretations, and recommendations that might be presented to parents or at a team meeting. Box 6.3 features examples of developmentally appropriate language that can be used to convey messages about assessment findings. Regardless of how the discussion goes, the child's reactions, both verbal and nonverbal, are noteworthy and help the evaluator gauge how to present the findings at a feedback conference and how to follow up with the parties involved.

IN CONCLUSION

The face-to-face presentation of assessment findings to consumers has a major bearing on the value of an assessment and its subsequent impact. Feedback meetings may be confusing or illuminating, adversarial or productive, disconcerting or satisfying. It is highly advisable for the evaluator to dedicate considerable time and thought to these meetings, anticipating the needs and reactions of consumers. The evaluator cannot control every variable, but much can be done to obtain the best possible outcome.

BOX 6.3. Discussing Assessment Findings with Children

Assessment findings and follow-up procedures can be productively discussed with children of all ages, adapting messages accordingly for the developmental level of the child. For each level below, a generally applicable message is provided, followed by several examples of case-specific messages.

EARLY CHILDHOOD AND ELEMENTARY LEVEL, OR VERY-LOW-FUNCTIONING SECONDARY LEVEL

"I got to know you pretty well in the time we spent together. Here are some things I learned that I think are important for your teacher and parent(s) to know. You can tell me if you agree or not, and if you think these ideas will be helpful."

- "You are a person who has good ideas, but sometimes you can't find the right words to let people know what you are thinking."
- "You like being at school; you are a friendly person and other kids like to play with you. But some things in school aren't fun for you, like sounding out words and reading out loud. You avoid these things or get them over with as quickly as possible. But if you want to get better at these things, you may need to slow down and work on them."
- "You have a lot of energy, and your mind goes really fast. Sometimes you do stuff without thinking first, and that gets you into trouble. We can talk about some ways to help you calm down so you don't get into trouble."

MIDDLE AND HIGH SCHOOL LEVEL

"I think I learned a lot about you that could be helpful going forward, but I wanted to share my impressions with you first before I meet with your parents and teachers. It's important that I get it right, so it would help if you clarify or correct anything that you think is incorrect or problematic. I expect you care what I say about you and what I recommend to parents and teachers, so I really encourage you to attend the meeting where I'll present my findings, and to speak up about things that matter to you. So, here are the important things that I would be telling people at this meeting:"

- "Now that you are in sixth grade and things are moving faster, school has become more difficult for you, especially in subjects like science and social studies. The teacher covers a lot of information in each lesson, and it's hard to keep up. If we can build in some opportunities for you to have extra preparation or practice, it will help you to hold your own in classes where you need to hold on to a lot of information."
- "You seem to find it hard to concentrate—to block out distractions and stay focused on the same activity for long periods of time. Some people do that easily, but you're not one of those people. You may find it exhausting to apply the mental energy it takes for you to concentrate for long period of time. There are some things that you can do, or that teachers might do, that may be helpful. For example, . . ."
- "Life has gotten pretty complicated for you. Things are tense at home, you're experiencing a lot of pressure in your social life, and you don't feel like things are going well. Your feeling stressed and discouraged makes it hard to concentrate on school or to be patient with other kids. It doesn't take much to set you off, and when you lose your temper, you do things that cause even more problems for you. Maybe we could talk about some things that will help you break out of this cycle."

CHAPTER 7

Variations on a Theme
Reports for Special Purposes

Psychological assessments are conducted in assorted settings and for varied purposes. The settings include schools, hospitals, community health and mental health centers, court clinics, private practice offices, and others. Assessment purposes range from understanding learning difficulties, to predicting postsurgery functioning for those with neurological diseases, to informing custody decisions in cases of divorce. The guiding principles of consumer-responsive assessment are applicable, regardless of the setting or emphasis. Thus far, we have written primarily about comprehensive assessments that address a wide variety of cognitive, social–emotional, developmental, and educational referral concerns. We now turn our attention to assessment reports that have a more specific focus or distinctive nature.

SCHOOL-BASED ASSESSMENT ALTERNATIVES

Certain types of school-based assessments have features that distinguish them from the modal assessments discussed to this point. Evaluators must modify their approach when they undertake screening and progress monitoring, special education re-evaluation, and assessment of children with severe intellectual disabilities.

Screening and Progress Monitoring

As discussed in Chapter 3, MTSS makes use of solution-focused screening and assessment data to identify and address early-stage learning and behavior problems within the general education program. These assessments may be integrated into the general education curriculum, such as benchmark assessments that periodically ensure that children are making expected progress toward literacy and numeracy goals or tests and checklists that are pegged to the Common Core State Standards. Such universal (i.e., Tier 1) curriculum-based assessments are an integral part of the educational program and do not require parental consent or written reports for individual children. A general notification to the parent community, such as a description of screening procedures and MTSS in the school's parent handbook, will adequately addresses procedural requirements. Parents of children who meet expectations may be informed of the results of curriculum-based assessment measures through quarterly report cards, parent–teacher conferences, or other regular means of communication.

Some general education assessments clearly necessitate parent contact, such as individual data collection efforts that are not a standard feature of the school curriculum program (e.g., a functional behavioral assessment) or supplemental supports or services that represent a change in the child's program. In keeping with the "Golden Rule standard," (i.e., What would you want for *your* child?), these situations call for school personnel to communicate proactively and openly with parents. Parents expect to be informed when their children are slated for more specialized services within general education, and may wish to know about data collection efforts that inform behavioral or social–emotional interventions, such as mental health screening.[1]

There are clear advantages to contacting parents when concerns first arise. While the distinction between discretionary procedures in general education and mandate-driven procedures in special education may be significant for school personnel, it is an arbitrary distinction for parents, who are concerned about their children regardless and wish to be informed and included in remediation plans. Engaging proactively with parents in the initial stages of problem identification enables school personnel to establish the kind of rapport and trust that is essential to a consumer-responsive approach. It also reduces the likelihood of adverse reactions when parents are "kept in the dark" or are opposed to the supports or strategies provided.

The type of parent contact may vary with the nature and degree of the child's issues. Communication with parents may involve a written notification, a phone call, an in-school conference, or a brief written report. In the absence of mandates or clear-cut guidance, a school district may be faced with a range of options regarding whether or how to provide such information to parents. Reporting procedures for academic assessments conducted within general education assessments are discretionary, and subject to varying practices. However, if and when an educational disability is suspected, a special education referral necessitates a comprehensive evaluation and the prescribed assessment procedures and reporting practices that accompany it.

The delivery of increased supports or services within general education calls for some sort of record keeping or documentation. School personnel might keep track of assessment

---

[1] In school districts where parent response is spotty, a passive consent procedure (i.e., notifying parents and allowing them to reject the offered services) may be advisable, so that children are not unnecessarily deprived of a beneficial service.

findings and problem-solving efforts using a form or chart, or brief progress monitoring reports, such as those described by Brown-Chidsey and Andren (2013). They identify three major components of a progress monitoring report—an intervention plan, progress monitoring activities, and intervention discontinuation—and propose using a worksheet, such as the one shown in Figure 7.1. Progress monitoring relies on conducting repeated measures over a period of time and thus may consist of a series of brief reports that include updated progress monitoring data. Such documentation may be shared with parents at any of several stages in the process.

Parents of children who are identified by a benchmark assessment as being at risk or performing below expectations could be notified by means of a template-generated brief report, which might include an offer to discuss the matter with school personnel (see a sample letter in Box 7.1). The report might also include a description of the screening process, identification of the skills or areas that need additional support, a description of the services to be provided, and an explanation of what further information will be provided as the child receives remedial instruction. It may be noted that the example in Box 7.1 describes CBM data in language that parents can understand and steers clear of technical terms like benchmark, cut score, and aimline. The written notification is best paired with a personal contact, such as a phone call, to ensure that parents understand the report and to address any questions and concerns they may have. The parent contact might be undertaken by a classroom teacher to normalize the process and to ensure that the discussion is conducted by someone with thorough knowledge of the curriculum and the child.

For children receiving Tier 2 or Tier 3 services, progress reports should be prepared at regular intervals, perhaps every 6–10 weeks. These reports should indicate in objective terms (e.g., correct words read per minute, rate and type of writing errors) what the target goal is and what progress the child has made. Again, charts and tables can be highly useful for showing performance over time. The progress report might be summarized in a letter to parents, along with the offer to speak or meet with school personnel (see Box 7.2). A meeting is certainly advisable if the child's progress with Tier 2 services is unsatisfactory, and more intensive services or supports are proposed. At this stage, parents should not only be notified, but also invited to discuss the child's educational progress and needs at a school conference. At this conference, school personnel should also discuss whether a referral for special education is warranted and the reasoning behind this decision. When a child receives Tier 3 services, parents should be kept apprised of progress through brief periodic reports or other means of documentation.

If general education services are followed by a referral for special education, the ensuing educational evaluation should document the services provided in general education and the child's response to the intervention. Given its relevance, CBM data are likely to figure prominently in written and oral reports. The CBM data that informed decision making at each tier should be included in the Background Information section of the report. Graphs or tables can be especially effective for reporting trend data to parents and teachers in an understandable format and for describing academic goals for future progress (Miller & Watkins, 2010).

Student: _____

Case Manager: _____

1. **Problem Definition**

   Date of meeting when problem was defined: _____

   State the problem in the space here: _____

   _____

   _____

   _____

   _____

2. **Intervention Activities**

   Teacher/aide responsible: _____

   Specific teaching steps or methods: _____

   _____

   _____

   _____

   _____

   Frequency of instruction: _____

3. **Progress Monitoring Activities**

   Assessment method(s) used to track student's progress: _____

   _____

   _____

   _____

   _____

   Date for next report and/or meeting: _____

   Intervention discontinuation criteria: _____

   _____

   Procedure for phasing out intervention: _____

   _____

   _____

   _____

FIGURE 7.1. Intervention planning worksheet.

CBM can be a valuable component of a psychoeducational assessment, even if a school system does not employ a multitiered model or if the evaluator works outside the school system. The evaluator might administer CBM measures to establish baseline levels against which subsequent educational performance can be compared or to efficiently obtain an independent sample of relevant academic performance without replicating the achievement measures administered by a teacher or educational diagnostician. These findings would be reported in the Assessment Results or Test Results section of the report.

BOX 7.1. Template for Parent Notification of Benchmark Assessment

This is a sample of a letter template that has been customized to report below-cutoff performance on a benchmark assessment. This letter from the classroom teacher uses simple language that should be amenable to translation into other languages.

Dear Parent,

  As you may have read in the Parent Handbook, Central School conducts brief assessment (i.e., *screening*) of all second grade children three times a year to make sure that they are meeting learning goals in reading and math. This allows us to provide extra help without delay if a child is falling behind in an important area.

  The screening in January showed that your child, Abby, was above the minimum expected level in math facts, but below the minimum expected level in reading rate and accuracy. Reading rate is important because it tells us if a child can quickly and easily read words that should be familiar to students at that grade level.

  It is a regular feature of our educational program to provide additional instruction time for children who need to improve key skills. The extra help for Abby will be provided in the regular classroom and will not involve any changes in your child's school day schedule. I or another member of the teaching staff will check your child's progress every 2 weeks on the skills that need special attention, and will give you a progress report after 8 weeks of providing this support.

  If you have any concerns or would like more information about this, please do not hesitate to contact me at 123-456-7890 or at laura.spelman@district.state.us.

  Sincerely,

  Laura Spelman

Reading Rate: Correct words per minute

Minimum expected level: 65
Your child's screening score: 52

Reading Accuracy: Words read correctly

Minimum expected level: 93%
Your child's screening score: 90%

Math Calculations: Math Facts answered correctly

Minimum expected level: 90%
Your child's screening score: 95%

BOX 7.2. Sample Progress Monitoring Report to Parents

Dear Parent,

As you may know, your child has been receiving additional instruction and learning time in reading to bring her skills up to expected levels. The letter from your child's teacher in February explained that the teaching staff would be providing extra help to improve Abby's reading rate and accuracy, and that you would receive information about her progress on these key skills after 8 weeks. This is a report on Abby's progress so far.

We set the following goals for Abby to reach by the end of the school year:

1. *Reduce the gap between Abby's reading rate and that of other District second graders by 50%.* Abby's reading rate on the midyear screening was 54 correct words per minute, which is 20 below the District midyear average of 74. The average rate for the end of second grade is 88 correct words per minute, so the target for Abby is 78 correct words per minute (10 below the District average).
2. *The goal for reading accuracy is 96% words read correctly,* which is considered an acceptable level to keep up with regular class instruction. Abby's reading accuracy on the midyear screening was 90% correct.

After 8 weeks of additional instruction (which started on February 13th), Abby is on pace to meet the end-of-year goals. The chart below shows her biweekly progress in reading rate and reading accuracy.

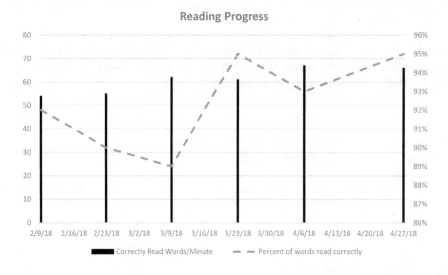

You will receive another report in about 8 weeks. If Abby continues to make current progress, she will be unlikely to need extra support in reading to keep up with classmates next year. However, if she falls short of reaching the goals, we will invite you to meet with her teacher and me to discuss Abby's reading skills and future educational needs.

Please feel free to contact me at 123-456-7890 or at mary.clark@district.state.us with any questions or to arrange a school conference.

Sincerely,

Mary Clark, Reading Specialist

Special Education Re-Evaluation

Federal regulations mandate that every child who receives special education services must have a re-evaluation at least once every 3 years to ensure that, in the course of the day-to-day continuation of the child's educational program, important issues are not overlooked. ("Is Franny making satisfactory progress?"; "Should Seymour be exited from special education?").

For the most part, the federal special education regulations apply the same standards to initial evaluations and re-evaluations.[2] These regulations specify that education evaluations, at a minimum, must fulfill certain purposes, namely, to determine (1) disability status and eligibility for special education, (2) current levels of functioning, and (3) educational needs (see Chapter 3, Box 3.1). The procedures used to produce these results must meet various requirements, such as using a variety of tools and strategies, selecting nondiscriminatory assessment measures, and not basing decisions on any single measure or assessment (see Chapter 3, Box 3.3). These requirements serve as an operational definition of "comprehensive assessment," as cited in the following federal special education regulation:

> In evaluating each child with a disability . . . the evaluation is sufficiently comprehensive to identify all of the child's special education and related services needs, whether or not commonly linked to the disability category in which the child has been classified. (Sec. 300.304(c)(6))

This regulatory language does not resolve questions as to what re-evaluations should involve and how "comprehensive" they must be. The fact that the same requirements are applicable to both initial evaluations and re-evaluations might suggest that they should be more similar than different. Most notably, the requirement that "The child is assessed in all areas of the suspected disability" (Sec. 300.304(c)(4)) could be interpreted to mean that a psychoeducational assessment conducted for a re-evaluation should be as thorough and detailed as an initial evaluation assessment. However, federal regulations neither require nor encourage evaluators to repeat the same assessment procedures in a re-evaluation, nor do state regulations as a rule. On the contrary, federal regulations allow the basic purposes of re-evaluation to be accomplished with minimal assessment, or even none at all; a review of existing data may suffice to meet the purposes of re-evaluation if the IEP team concludes, with parental agreement, "that no additional data are needed to determine whether the child continues to be a child with a disability, and to determine the child's educational needs" (Sec. 300.305(d)).

Consistent with the principle of referral-driven selectivity, a re-evaluation can and often should be briefer and more limited than the evaluation that initially qualified the child for special education. The child's educational needs may be well known to school personnel, and his progress may have been carefully monitored and documented. A minimal

---

[2]There are slight differences in wording. Initial evaluations must determine "whether the child is a child with a disability," while re-evaluations determine "whether the child continues to have such a disability"; initial evaluations determine "whether the child needs special education and related services," while re-evaluations determine "whether the child continues to need special education and related services."

approach to conducting a re-evaluation may be the preferable course of action in cases in which the child's disability is well established, current services are meeting his needs, and educational progress is satisfactory. When student progress toward academic and behavior goals is regularly assessed as a part of the special education program and parents are kept apprised of their child's goals and progress, the appropriate focus of the re-evaluation is more readily known and the need for additional assessment is reduced.

The principle of individualizing assessments to address child-specific referral concerns is also applicable. For some children, extensive assessment is warranted, perhaps to investigate the need for additional services or to explore areas of functioning not previously assessed that may be related to the disability. If substantial questions have arisen about the child's progress, program, or needs, a re-evaluation might be every bit as comprehensive as the initial evaluation, if not more so.

In many school districts, however, re-evaluations routinely consist of the same standard test battery or similar measures that were administered in the initial evaluation. Conducting a standard assessment for all re-evaluations is poor practice, as it assumes that all children have similar needs. Replicating the initial evaluation will, in many cases, be unnecessarily invasive and expend resources that would better be used elsewhere. Cognitive testing in particular can often be reduced or omitted since intellectual functioning tends to be fairly stable over time for school-age children. Re-evaluation of cognitive abilities is best reserved for cases in which there are specific areas of concern or in which there is a reason to suspect clinically significant changes since the initial evaluation. Again, the essential point is to individualize assessments to meet the needs of the given child.

Consumer-responsive re-evaluations should be pursued with the same care and dedication as initial evaluations, albeit with attention to efficiency. Similar to the initial evaluation, the planning phase should involve direct contact with important consumers—certainly parents, usually teachers, and sometimes (especially with older children) the child herself. The objectives of initial data gathering are the same as for initial evaluations: to forge a relationship, share information, and offer support. Interview questions at this stage recognize and make reference to the child's special education history, for example:

- Do the parents fully understand the programs and service being provided?
- Do the parents and teachers believe that the programs and services are appropriate?
- Are they satisfied with the child's progress?
- Do they believe that these services should continue?
- Are there changes that they believe would help?
- Are they concerned about other areas of suspected disability?
- Have there been changes in the child's status—such as a medical condition, a family move, or changes in family composition or functioning—that may affect the child's educational plan or progress?

A consumer-responsive approach will meet the purposes of a re-evaluation more effectively than the perfunctory administration of standardized tests, achieving optimal outcomes with greater efficiency. These individualized re-evaluations may range from little or no direct assessment of the child to extensive multisource data collection. Systematic monitoring of progress toward IEP goals will ensure that key information is routinely available and needn't be generated anew for the re-evaluation. Interviews can be shorter and more focused, as much of the child's history is already known and parents have gained some familiarity with the special education process. When parents are routinely informed about their child's progress, there is less need to generate new assessment data and a greater likelihood of collaborative and productive problem solving. The re-evaluation process will be especially productive when there exists a sound foundation of mutually respectful relationships between the evaluator, school team members, and parents in place.

Assessment of Children with Severe Intellectual Disabilities

School-based educational evaluations are subject to the same mandates and guidelines, regardless of the type or severity of a child's disability. Nevertheless, assessing children with severe to profound intellectual disabilities requires a qualitatively different approach to assessment and will result in reports of a somewhat different nature. Cautions about overreliance on standardized testing and using a standard template for reports are especially applicable with this population.

Individuals with severe to profound intellectual functioning are a small subset of the *intellectual disability* (formerly, mental retardation) category. Their spoken language is usually minimal or nonexistent, and their cognitive and academic skills may be entirely out of testable range. The usual standardized tests will yield very low numbers and very little value.

Assessments need to focus on functional life skills instead, such as the ability to communicate, socialize, and attend to self-care and personal safety. Hence, an account of these adaptive behaviors at home and at school, as reported by parents, teachers, and caretakers, will comprise the core findings regarding the child's capabilities. Comparing and contrasting what the child does in these two settings is also relevant, as is determining the extent to which this information is shared between school personnel and family members. Hence, interviews and rating scales of adaptive behavior by key informants are two major sources of assessment data.

Since the actual behaviors of the child are of primary interest, they should be specifically identified in the assessment report. How does the child communicate his needs, wants, and feelings—hunger, discomfort, frustration? What can the child do for himself with respect to feeding, toileting, and dressing? How does the child relate to others and respond to social contact? Is the child active and excitable, or passive and calm? Rather than providing a table that reports standardized scores on adaptive behavior scales—what, after all, does a score of 40 on self-help skills or a developmental age of 1 year, 6 months, on the socialization scale tell you about the child?—a report might include a table that identifies the most advanced skills that the child demonstrates in each area. For a re-evaluation, it can be instructive to compare current attainments with those at the time of the previous evaluation (see the example in Box 7.3).

Direct observation can also be a valuable assessment tool. Without some guidance, however, the evaluator may glean relatively little from an observation. It may help to check school records before observing the child to learn what were the established performance levels and current education goals. However, it will be far more instructive to speak with a teacher, parent, or service provider who cares for the child on a regular basis. They will know how to interpret subtle but significant behaviors—verbalizations, gestures, and facial expressions—and will be attuned to recent accomplishments and to key targets of developmental growth. The evaluator can then attend closely to behaviors in the zone of proximal development, and also note the extent to which the instructional environment presents the child with activities that promote growth in these areas.

BOX 7.3. Sample Adaptive Behavior Progress Table

This table identifies some of the more advanced adaptive behaviors consistently demonstrated by the child during the current school year and at the time of the previous evaluation, as reported in parent interviews using the Vineland Adaptive Scales, Third Edition.

Adaptive behavior area	November 2018 skills (age 8 years, 4 months)	November 2021 skills (age 11 years, 4 months)
Communication	Identifies at least three named pictured body parts by pointing.	Follows instructions with two unrelated actions (e.g., "Turn off the TV and get my keys").
	Says one-word requests (e.g., "More," "Open").	Uses *and* in phrases or sentences (e.g., "Want ice cream and cake").
Daily living skills	Pulls up clothing with elastic waistbands.	Puts on shoes and pullover garments.
	Drinks from a regular cup.	Feeds self with a spoon without spilling.
	Urinates in a toilet.	Uses the toilet without help and flushes.
Socialization	Smiles in response to praise or compliments (e.g., "Good job").	Uses words to express own emotions (e.g., "happy," "don't like that").
	Plays near another child and copies, without interacting.	Joins a group at play when invited.
	Transitions from one activity to another without getting upset (e.g., play time to bath time).	Recovers quickly from a minor upset or disappointment.
Motor skills	Runs without falling.	Hops on one foot at least once without falling.
	Walks up stairs, putting both feet on each step.	Walks up stairs, alternating feet.
	Opens doors that require only pushing and pulling.	Opens doors by turning a doorknob or handle.
	Marks on paper with a crayon or pencil.	Presses buttons accurately on a small keyboard or touch screen.

The other major component of the assessment and the ensuing report is background information. What is the etiology of the disability, such as a genetic disorder, perinatal trauma, or medical condition? How and when did identification of the disability take place? What has been the history of special services and placements? What gains has the child made over time? What kind of supports or adaptations are provided by the family? What has been the impact of the child's condition on family members? How is the child's time spent at home? School records (including the IEP and previous evaluations) and interviews of parents or caretakers will be the primary sources of this information.

It should be noted that severe to profound intellectual disabilities are not synonymous with low-incidence disabilities. Children with low-incidence conditions, such as autism, deafness, orthopedic impairment, hearing impairment, visual impairment, and "deaf-blindness" (each, a federal disability category under IDEA), whether of normal-range intellectual functioning or far below, also require qualitatively different approaches to assessment. These children are best assessed by an evaluator with specialized training in the respective area.

OTHER ASSESSMENT ALTERNATIVES

Other distinct assessment types involve differences in purpose (independent evaluation, evaluation for disability accommodations), in audience (parent feedback letter), in content focus (neuropsychological assessment, forensic assessment), or in construction (team reports, computer-generated reports).

Independent Evaluation

Most psychological and psychoeducational evaluations of children are completed in schools; however, a sizable number are completed in other settings, such as clinics, hospitals, and private practices. A common reason for evaluations by community-based providers is to provide input into educational decisions. Under federal special education regulations, parents have the right to request an *independent educational evaluation* at public expense (i.e., paid for by the school district) in areas of disability or suspected disability that were previously evaluated by the school district. Alternatively, a family—perhaps at the urging of a pediatrician or social service agency—might seek an independent evaluation prior to having a school district conduct an educational evaluation, although not necessarily at public expense. The principles and practices of consumer-responsive assessment are fully applicable to independent evaluations. Additional cautions, however, are advisable.

The first and most important of these cautions concerns triangulation. In triangulation, two of the three parties (e.g., school, parents, and evaluator) ally with each other and treat the third as a common enemy. For example, the parents and an independent evaluator might decide that the school is entirely responsible for the child's woes. This alliance brings the parent and evaluator closer together at the expense of the school and, possibly, the child. The child is disadvantaged in that a major resource, the school, is villainized, and opportunities for collaboration between home and school are lost. Alternatively, the school and an independent evaluator, perhaps one who often receives referrals from school personnel, might join to blame a family for a child's school difficulties. Once again, the child is disadvantaged, as the potential power of collaboration is lost in a haze of fault finding.

The remedies for triangulation are respectful contact, communication, and collaborative planning among all who make decisions about a child's life. Thus, independent evaluators should reach out and contact school personnel in order to understand the school perspective and plan jointly. Similarly, school personnel should be accessible to independent evaluators, share information freely (within the limits of informed consent), and be open to new ideas. All three parties—the child, the family, and the school— will be well served.

The second caution for independent evaluators concerns the responsibility for making special education disability and program planning decisions. In special education proceedings, it is the IEP team's responsibility to make disability determinations and design special education programs. Parents, older students, and independent evaluators should be valued and active participants in the team process. However, even a highly competent and experienced independent evaluator cannot make a diagnosis or propose a service and expect that the IEP team will automatically accept it without further consideration.[3] As stated in federal regulations (Sec. 300.502(c)), school district personnel are required only to *consider*, rather than accept, the findings and recommendations of an independent evaluation. For an evaluator to suggest that the independent evaluation is the "final say" may raise parents' expectations inappropriately and exacerbate adversarial relations between the school and parents. It is the evaluator's responsibility to explain to the parent that the independent evaluation contributes valuable information, but the actual decisions are made by the IEP team—of which the parent is a member.

A related matter concerns the difference between a clinical diagnosis and an educational disability classification. Clinicians outside of schools are accustomed to making medical diagnoses using the American Psychiatric Association's (2013) *Diagnostic and Statistical Manual of Mental Disorders* (DSM-5) or the World Health Organization's (1992) International Classification of Diseases (ICD-9). However, school teams use a different classification system, making eligibility decisions based on the educational disabilities specified by the IDEA or individual state variants. There are some areas of overlap between the medical and educational categories (e.g., for intellectual disability, autism, and attention deficits), but there are also many differences. It is important for independent evaluators and schools to understand that they use related but different concepts and speak related but different languages. When making school-directed recommendations, independent evaluators must understand that they must work within the parameters of school policies and practices.

There are two additional cautions for independent evaluators. First, conduct only the testing that is needed. As all testing procedures are invasive, use only those that directly help to answer the assessment questions. Unfortunately, independent evaluators often administer too many tests and produce overly long reports.[4] This seems due, at least in part, to the economics of independent evaluations. Independent evaluators are paid an hourly

---

[3]I (B. E.) am reminded of a highly respected but ill-informed community pediatrician who wrote disability designations on a prescription pad (e.g., "ADHD," "Learning Disability") and expected the school IEP team to accept them.

[4]We have seen reports that exceed 50 pages in length!

fee, a fee for each test administered, or one large flat fee—as much as $5,000 and upward in some metropolitan areas—all of which reward the completion of long test batteries. Hefty payments encourage long reports to justify the expense, which may be contrary to the best interests of the child. Parenthetically, these extensive reports are available primarily to the economically advantaged.

Second, long batteries and reports are conducive to identifying numerous problems, many of which have little direct impact on day-to-day functioning. Simply put, if you are paid a lot, you had better come up with a lot of findings. The identification of many problems often leads to a view of the child as being far more disabled than is actually the case. In addition, a focus on weaknesses more than on strengths may cause those who work with the child to neglect important resources—both internal to the child and in the child's school, family, and community—that could be helpful. Since all contributors, at least in theory, are motivated to work in a child's best interest, receptive and respectful communication will be far more responsive to the needs of consumers than disagreement and discord.

Assessment for Disability Accommodations

Some assessments are conducted for the explicit purposes of providing documentation for disability accommodations. Just as Section 504 of the Rehabilitation Act of 1973 ensures that children whose disabilities substantially limit major life activities can receive accommodations to fully access K–12 public education, the Americans with Disabilities Act (ADA) ensures that individuals with disabilities who are "otherwise qualified" can receive accommodations to participate in postsecondary education (e.g., colleges and universities, professional schools, trade schools) and in work settings without discrimination. ADA also entitles individuals with disabilities to accommodations when taking high-stakes standardized tests such as the SAT, ACT, and GRE. The documentation serves (1) to verify that an individual has a disability that substantially limits a major life activity, as defined by the ADA and (2) to establish the types of accommodations needed for the given setting or test. Common standardized test-taking accommodations are having extra time, a separate room, and additional breaks. For higher education courses, a student may be entitled to accommodations, such as extra time for exams, recording of lectures, or a note taker.

School-age children who qualify for Section 504 services (which, by rule, includes all children served under IDEA) already have documentation by virtue of the evaluation procedures and consequent accommodations provided under IDEA or Section 504. However, high school students and young adults who seek accommodations for the first time, must obtain documentation anew, typically in the form of a psychoeducational or neuropsychological assessment. A situation that frequently arises is when a high school student who has gotten by without formal accommodations seeks extra time for taking college entrance tests.

Testing companies, such as ETS [the Educational Testing Service] and the College Board, have published guidelines for documenting specific disabilities, sometimes requiring that the assessment include certain types of tests or be completed within a given period of time. For example, ETS advises that assessments be conducted within 5 years for LD and ADHD and within 12 months for psychiatric disabilities. ETS (2015) provides detailed online guidelines ("Tips for Evaluators of Adolescents and Adults with Disabilities") that describe the pertinent information needed to document each of three categories of disabilities: (1) LD, ADHD, and autism spectrum disorder (ASD); (2) psychiatric disabilities, physical disabilities, and traumatic brain injury (TBI); and (3) blindness/low vision and deaf/hard of hearing. The guidelines advise evaluators to provide functional information, that is, a "discussion of the candidate's limitations due to the disability and its impact on academic performance, employment, and major life activities." Other functional information that evaluators should highlight is the extent to which the individual has relied on and benefited from accommodations.

Historically, each recipient of documentation (a college, professional school, testing company, etc.) has made independent decisions about whether the submitted documentation is sufficient, whether to offer accommodations, and what accommodations to provide. Notably, the U.S. Department of Justice (2015), in response to complaints and concerns about "excessive and burdensome documentation," issued guidelines in September 2015 that direct testing entities that administer high-stakes tests to accept accommodations that were previously granted in similar testing situations or as part of an IEP or Section 504 plan. The department has since stepped up its efforts to ensure compliance with these guidelines.

Since assessments for disability accommodations have a clear and limited purpose, it would seem that some assessment data (e.g., background information) could be omitted for lack of relevance. If anything, however, these assessments tend to be lengthy, detailed, and technical. According to L. Brinckerhoff (personal communication, March 31, 2014), reports submitted to ETS for disability accommodations are often inordinately long—as much as 100 pages! The reason for the tendency to conduct extensive assessments may be to ensure that the documentation includes all required elements. (Testing companies frequently determine from an initial review of submitted documentation that additional information is needed.) Another possibility, as suggested by a documentation reviewer for a testing company, is that the evaluators hope to sway the outcome with an overwhelming amount of verbiage.

In light of the distinctive nature of disability documentation assessments, some principles of consumer-responsive assessment are more applicable than others. Most notably, the primary consumer is the entity from which accommodations are being requested (e.g., the testing company or college). Thus, the criteria of selectivity and relevance are largely determined by the guidelines promulgated by the prospective provider of accommodations. Adhering closely to these guidelines is a top priority. Nonetheless, as with any assessment, the report should be understandable, well organized, and of reasonable length.

Parent Feedback Letter

Recognizing that the typical complexity of an assessment report can befuddle and reduce the engagement of families, Jones (2018) proposed that evaluators summarize key findings for parents in a brief and accessible caregiver (or parent) feedback letter. A sample parent feedback letter that accompanies the related re-evaluation report can be found in Appendix D.

The value of providing parents with a personal and plainly worded document is self-evident. It is likely to have greater impact than a lengthy report by virtue of being wholly relevant, readily understood, and digested with relatively little time and effort. Other consumers—the concerned teacher, counselor, or pediatrician, as well as the evaluated older child—would also benefit from having a brief summary and knowing what was communicated to parents. School personnel and community-based evaluators might routinely propose to parents that they make the letter available to other consumers. Notably, the parent feedback letter admirably fits the description of what Stout and Cook (1999) indicated that physicians prefer: a one- to two-page document focusing on diagnosis and treatment.

The counterargument to preparing a parent feedback letter for every assessment is a logistical one: the duplicate paperwork would significantly expand the time devoted to each assessment case. The challenge of writing a brief, clear message should not be underestimated; as the saying (variously attributed to Pascal, Franklin, and Twain) goes, "If I had more time, I would have written a shorter letter." Increasing the time dedicated to writing leaves less time for direct contact with consumers or for other beneficial psychological services.

Perhaps the most feasible course of action is to produce a single report that is accessible to all consumers, and to consider writing a separate parent feedback letter in select cases.

Neuropsychological Assessment

Clinical neuropsychology is defined as " . . . an applied science concerned with the behavioral expression of brain dysfunction" (Lezak, Howieson, Bigler, & Tranel, 2012, p. 3). Clinical neuropsychology strives to explain human behavior in terms of neurological function and dysfunction. In describing neurological function, it draws from highly specialized knowledge and terminology. Brain locations, brain systems, and highly specific types of behavioral function and dysfunction are the purview of neuropsychology. Neuropsychology is rooted largely in a medical tradition, in which cognitive systems are isolated, attending more to the parts than the whole, and with an emphasis on deficits rather than on normal functioning and strengths. The language of reporting tends to be highly technical. Technical terms, such as associative agnosia, constructional apraxia, procedural memory, stereognosis, and dysgraphia abound in neuropsychological test reports. These functions are critical to the evaluator's case conceptualization, but the use of this terminology communicates little to nonmedical consumers.

The task of using understandable language may be particularly challenging for neuropsychologists given the discipline-specific focus on technical factors, such as neurological locations, cortical systems, and neuropsychological functions. However, explaining phenomena in terms that patients and parents can understand in no way detracts from the communication used with physicians and other specialists. References to brain locations and functions can be supplemented with plain-language explanations of technical terms. For example, the prefrontal cortex might be described as the portion of the brain at the front of the head just above the eyebrows. Similarly, dysfunction may be clarified by describing what kind of systems are operating inefficiently or what parts of the brain are not communicating as they should. Dysgraphia is no less a problem if it described as "difficulty writing or drawing." There is no loss in meaning to state that some function is "weak" rather than "compromised," or if functioning is described as occurring "before the problem started" rather than being "premorbid." Using clear, simple language engages the reader and helps demystify neuropsychological concepts. When explaining concepts in person, neuropsychologists might make use of a brain model as a way of indicating brain locations and systems.

Neuropsychological assessments are distinctive in other respects as well. An implicit expectation is that the assessment will yield a full accounting of the child's neuropsychological functions. Thus, neuropsychologists typically report findings across numerous areas of functioning without focusing selectively on child-specific assessment questions. Furthermore, an overemphasis on dysfunction is common in neuropsychological assessment. Donders and Strong (2016) note that neuropsychologists too often interpret common and normal patterns of strengths and weaknesses as being indicative of pathology. Also, like their psychologist and school psychologist counterparts, neuropsychologists often conclude their reports with a list of treatment recommendations, taken verbatim from computer files, which correspond to the identified disorder or area of dysfunction.[5] These treatment recommendations are typically not prioritized and may be too numerous to realistically implement. They may have some general relevance, but do not provide meaningful guidance for the individual patient being assessed.

In proposing an alternate model that is more aligned with consumer-responsive reporting, Donders and Strong (2016) recommend a neuropsychological report that "communicates relevant information in an evidence-based, orderly and clear manner that is appropriate for the target audience" (p. 6). Consistent with this recommendation, one of the American Board of Clinical Neuropsychology's (2017) criteria for judging the adequacy of reports submitted by candidates for board certification is that "The clinical report is written in a clear, professional style tailored to the background and needs of the identified primary consumer of the report" (p. 5).

Who, then, are the primary consumers of neuropsychological assessments? The question is as relevant for neuropsychologists as it is for school and clinical psychologists. Neuropsychologists must meet the needs of the physicians who often initiate referrals, just as school psychologists must provide useful information to the educators who request psychoeducational assessments. However, neuropsychologists must recognize that parents and teachers may be primary consumers as well. This is particularly true given that, much like psychoeducational assessments, neuropsychological assessments of children are often conducted in order to address learning or behavior problems rather than concerns about brain injury or neurological disorders. They yield findings with educational implications. Hence, the value of a neuropsychological assessment often depends on its relevance to the child's everyday functioning at home or in school.

As with all child evaluators, neuropsychologists should make concerted efforts to communicate with both parents *and teachers* to better understand what is relevant to a child's two major life settings. Parents contribute only part of the picture, and cannot fully convey how the child is performing in school. The essential tasks of collecting background information and developing referral questions must be done at the outset of the assessment with

---

[5]My (B. E.) favorite example of this was a recommendation for help with timely completion of lengthy research papers, found in the report of a 6-year-old girl diagnosed with ADHD.

all who are relevant to the referral questions—be they parents, teachers, physicians, or others—because they can contribute to understanding the child. Communication between the neuropsychologist and school personnel can be accomplished by talking in person or on the phone, and also by administering standardized rating scales (e.g., BASC, ASEBA, BRIEF [Behavior Rating Inventory of Executive Function]).

Lack of communication is most evident when neuropsychologists make unfeasible or unhelpful recommendations for school interventions, which can result from insufficient awareness of what is currently being provided in school and what changes are realistic. For all their training in psychology and neurology, neuropsychologists typically have insufficient knowledge of educational practices. This limitation does not mean that neuropsychologists should refrain from educationally oriented assessment or from advocacy. It does mean that they should consult with teachers, school psychologists, and other educators so that the valuable assessment information that these school-based professionals possess can be converted into educationally relevant recommendations. Such collaboration enormously enhances the value of a neuropsychological assessment. Furthermore, in order to realize the full value of the assessment, the relationship should continue in the form of personalized feedback and subsequent follow-up contacts.

As with psychological and psychoeducational assessments, neuropsychological assessments could benefit from a reconceptualization that ensures being responsive to consumers by emphasizing collaborative relationships, reporting in terms that all can understand, and generating a limited number of recommendations that are individualized and feasible. Genuine helping begins with responsive relationships whereby all consumers—physicians, educators, parents, and children—are engaged, heard, and respected. For maximum impact, neuropsychologists should report findings in a way that informs, enlightens, and helps all primary consumers. As in all types of assessment, the consumer-responsive approach begins and ends with collaboration.

Forensic Assessment

The term "forensic evaluation" refers to various types of assessments that are involved in some way with a court proceeding. As applicable to children, this assessment might involve an evaluation of violence risk, a question of pretrial detention, an evaluation of competence, or the identification of mental health needs of an adjudicated youth. In such cases, the question "Who is the consumer?" is more complex than in many other kinds of evaluations. Is it the court that ordered the evaluation to answer a specific question? Is it the child's attorney, who referred him for evaluation hoping that the results would bolster her case? Is it the state agency responsible for adjudicated youth? Are the child and his family also primary consumers?

Despite the complexity, many principles of consumer-responsive reporting still apply. Even when an unwilling child is required to complete the evaluation by court order and the family resists the process, attempts should be made to build a collaborative working alliance. The child and family are more likely to be forthcoming and to engage in the process if the evaluator takes the time to build rapport and solicit their input. Given the sensitive nature and potentially large legal ramifications of forensic assessments, the initial explanation to the child is especially important. Sattler (2018) provides examples of how to introduce a forensic assessment to a child or adolescent so as to clarify who needs the information and for what purposes, the implications of the findings, and their rights during the process (e.g., to consult an attorney, to not answer questions). Written reports should be concise, use everyday language, and directly address the questions that are asked (Andrews & Hoge, 2010; Zapf & Roesch, 2008). Furthermore, the reasoning used to arrive at conclusions must be explicit and the references to test findings specific. Since these reports are written primarily for legal personnel and not mental health practitioners, the use of psychological jargon should be minimized. However, such reports often include legal jargon, vocabulary, and complex sentence structures that result in reading levels that are beyond those of many families. As with evaluations done for other purposes, the value of forensic reports is increased when adolescent clients and parents understand them.

Some aspects of recognized best practice for forensic reports are consistent with the consumer-responsive approach. Zapf and Roesch (2008) advise forensic evaluators to describe the client rather than the test result or the psychological function. Thus, one would write "John has difficulty organizing his actions," instead of "John's organizational abilities are compromised." In addition, assessment questions should be answered directly in the Summary and Recommendations sections of a forensic report. Finally, the standard of conciseness for forensic reports calls for diligent application of the "So what?" principle in reporting results; only those results that are relevant to the legal questions asked should be included in the report (Andrews & Hoge, 2010).

Team Reports

Some schools, hospitals, and clinics combine the findings from several types of assessments (e.g., psychoeducational, academic, speech-and-language, and occupational therapy) into one team report. The principles and practices of consumer-responsive assessment apply to team reports as well, although with some refinements.

A lead clinician should be identified as the point of contact for parent and teachers throughout the process. To facilitate a working alliance, there should be one intake appointment at which as many of the evaluators as possible are present or at least introduced to the consumer. The purposes of this intake, as for a single-discipline assessment, are to build trust, obtain background information, develop assessment questions collaboratively, and discuss assessment procedures.

The team report should be written in everyday consumer-responsive language. It should begin with a description of the combined team efforts. Optionally, the initial section might include a brief overview of key findings. To maximize clarity and focus, the report should conclude with a single integrated formulation and a set of recommendations that combine the work of all disciplines. As always, recommendations should be specific, relevant, and feasible. These recommendations should also be kept to a reasonable number—which, given the multiple contributing evaluators, may challenge the team to reach consensus in prioritizing the child's most salient needs. Attempts should be made to iron out any disagreements between evaluators before giving feedback to consumers. However, when disagreements persist, the different perspectives should be conveyed to consumers, affording the individual evaluators all due respect. To ensure accuracy and equity, each member of the evaluating team should review and sign off on the final report.

Feedback meetings should proceed much like the initial intake meeting. The lead evaluator, who has established an ongoing relationship with the parent or referring party, should be the primary presenter. Other members of the team should participate if possible. Whereas a full-team presentation may be inefficient or unfeasible, team members other than the lead clinician might attend at the beginning of the meeting to present their results briefly and respond to questions about their particular assessment. The lead clinician can then present overall clinical impressions and recommendations, address any questions or concerns, and help the consumers with their reactions to the information. There is exceptional power, breadth, and often wisdom in such a team approach.

Computer-Generated Reports

Computers and technological innovations have greatly facilitated the work of assessment. Computer scoring saves time and prevents calculation errors. The advantages of computer scoring are so great that some tests with complicated scoring procedures can only be machine scored. Computer-generated tables and graphs help to organize and illustrate findings. Web-based versions of rating scales allow an evaluator to have them completed by sending out a link rather than a paper form. Some tests can now be administered with a synchronized pair of tablets, one for the evaluator and one for the examinee, which may in time become standard procedure for test administration. Such computer-based test administration efficiently manages the challenges of standardized administration: the correct items are given in the right order, with the appropriate instructions and prompts; timing is precise; scoring is instantaneous and accurate. Some tests require such precise timing and sophisticated analysis of responses that they can only be administered by computer— most notably, continuous performance tests, which register the examinee's accuracy and response time as stimuli are flashed on the screen in quick succession.

Computer-generated *interpretation* of assessment findings, however, is a different story. Such interpretations are based strictly on scores, with no knowledge of a child's history, effort, or sensorimotor limitations. They do not incorporate noteworthy qualitative data during testing, such as strategies and extraneous verbalizations. Furthermore, computer-generated interpretations are limited to a single source of assessment data—standardized testing. They fail to integrate relevant findings from records, observations, and interview data, such as cultural and educational advantage or disadvantage, prior remedial and therapeutic services, motivation, persistence, attention and distractibility, frustration tolerance, use of language, and so on. In contrast, the skilled evaluator interprets test performance through the prism of the many and complex factors that account for behavior. As stated in the *Standards for Educational and Psychological Testing* (AERA, APA, & NCME, 2014), "Efforts to reduce a complex set of data into computer-generated interpretations of a given construct may yield misleading or oversimplified analyses of the meaning of test scores" (p. 168).

The evaluator who makes use of computer-generated interpretations also must have knowledge of, and the ability to critically appraise, the source of the interpretations. To what extent are these interpretations evidence based and derived from reputable and current research? The AERA, APA, and NCME (2014) standards specify that "those who use computer-generated interpretations of test data should verify that the quality of the evidence of validity is sufficient for the interpretations" (Standard 10.17, p. 168).

At best, computer-generated interpretations and recommendations should be regarded as hypotheses to be considered in the light of the full array of data available to the evaluator. It is poor, if not unethical, clinical practice to uncritically insert "canned" interpretations into an assessment report or to place undue weight on them to the exclusion of professional judgment that considers the full array of assessment data. As stated in the American Psychological Association's (2017) ethical principles,

> **Standard 9.06.** When interpreting assessment results, including automated interpretations, psychologists take into account the purpose of the assessment as well as the various test factors, test-taking abilities, and other characteristics of the person being assessed, such as situational, personal, linguistic, and cultural differences that might affect psychologists' judgments or reduce the accuracy of their interpretations. They indicate any significant limitations of their interpretations.
>
> **Standard 9.09c.** Psychologists retain responsibility for the appropriate application, interpretation, and use of assessment instruments, whether they score and interpret such tests themselves or use automated or other services.

Similar language appears in the following NASP (2010b) ethical principle:

> **Standard II.3.2.** When using computer-administered assessments, computer-assisted scoring, and/or interpretation programs, school psychologists choose programs that meet professional standards for accuracy and validity. School psychologists use professional judgment in evaluating the accuracy of computer-assisted assessment findings for the examinee.

While computer-generated reports may help the evaluator consider hypotheses and subject interpretations to psychometric rigor, it is inconceivable that a stand-alone computer-generated report can adhere to the principles of consumer-responsive assessment.

CHAPTER 8

Making It Happen
Implications and Impact

In this book we advocate for both an oral and written consumer-responsive approach to assessment reports. The practices we propose differ from prevailing practice in many respects: minimizing jargon and technical terms, emphasizing relevance and plain language, organizing findings by theme, integrating multiple sources of assessment data, and emphasizing direct contact with consumers. We now turn our attention to practical considerations of what might bring about this paradigm shift.

Calls for changes in reporting practices have echoed in the literature for decades (Brenner, 2003; Cates, 1999; Groth-Marnat, 2009; Groth-Marnat & Horvath, 2006; Harvey, 1997, 2006; 2013; Hass & Carriere, 2014; Lichtenstein, 2013a, 2013b, 2014; Ownby, 1997; Ownby & Wallbrown, 1986; Shectman, 1979; Tallent, 1980, 1993; Tallent & Reiss, 1959), but to little effect. This may lead one to conclude that evaluators are disinclined to heed these critiques. Yet, in our discussions with practitioners and trainers in various venues (workshops, conferences, email exchanges, online forums, etc.), we have found widespread support for reporting practices that are responsive to consumers and emphasize positive outcomes. Apparently, efforts to effect changes in reporting practices must be directed toward obstacles other than practitioner attitudes. Significant factors, both at the individual practitioner level and at the organizational (i.e., systems) level, maintain the status quo, and include the following:

- Initial training that emphasizes standardized tests and their psychometric properties.
- Academic environments that reinforce writing for a professional audience.
- Models found in textbooks and in current practice.
- Requirements and expectations of school districts and service agencies.

- Time and caseload pressures.
- Reimbursement policies of third-party payers.
- Assumptions about how to influence high-stakes eligibility and service decisions.

A consumer-responsive approach presumes that having a positive impact is the primary objective of assessment and should ultimately guide practice. If individual practitioners and systems are genuinely dedicated to this purpose, it behooves them to consider the proposals offered in this chapter.

INDIVIDUAL PRACTITIONER ISSUES

Revamping a fine-tuned and frequently used skill is no small undertaking. Making the transition from traditional to consumer-responsive assessment practices requires considerable effort to hone the requisite skills, which include individualizing the assessment design, establishing collaborative relationships with consumers, conveying findings in nontechnical language, integrating data from multiple sources, and following up on recommendations. Consumer-responsive reports, despite their simpler language and greater brevity, are *not* quicker and easier to produce—if anything, quite the contrary. Because consumer-responsive reports are highly individualized, the evaluator relies less on stock phrases and on boilerplate descriptions of assessment measures. The report structure will vary from child to child as the evaluator determines which themes to feature and what findings to minimize or disregard. Clarification of psychological terms will sometimes be limited to a brief definition, and at other times consist of a thorough explanation that includes implications for functioning at school and at home.

Letting go of traditional assessment practices can be difficult in work environments with substantial time pressures since a template-based report is easier to produce. This dilemma was often remarked on by the school psychology doctoral students who conducted consumer-responsive assessments at our university-based assessment clinic, while they were concurrently employed as school district psychologists. They recognized the enhanced value of the consumer-responsive assessments they conducted for the clinic and lamented that time constraints made it difficult for them to implement the approach in their school districts.

Ongoing Professional Development

An essential first step toward modifying one's approach to assessment is making the commitment, knowing that it is a demanding process. The committed evaluator may seek guidance from workshops and conferences, professional texts (such as this one), study groups, and other sources. Professional growth is also facilitated by feedback and encouragement from a like-minded clinical supervisor or peer group. The structure of a *learning community* of colleagues that has clearly established goals and a regular meeting schedule offers multiple advantages: a sounding board to test out ideas, input from multiple perspectives, and the energizing effects of social interaction and a shared commitment to effective practice.

Exercising Flexibility

Consumer-responsive assessment is not a rigid model. While the principles are constant, their application will result in assessments that are *not* uniform. The choice of assessment procedures is tailored to the individual child. The evaluator also exercises flexibility when referral questions need to be adjusted or new hypotheses emerge based on information gained from the child, teacher, or parent.

The loss in efficiency from abandoning a standard approach can be offset, to some degree, by the flexibility of a consumer-responsive approach. In considering the specific questions and concerns of each referral, the evaluator will devote extensive time and effort to some assessment cases and considerably less to others. Assessments with limited or simple referral questions may require fewer data sources and a briefer report. Many school-based assessments, particularly re-evaluations that are conducted primarily to comply with special education mandates, fall into this category.

Consumer Expectations

Consumer expectations also play a role. Parents who have received long and impressive-looking reports in the past may be surprised or even feel shortchanged by a briefer report written in plain language. Hence, the evaluator might explain the consumer-responsive approach in advance, noting its emphasis on clear, solution-focused reporting, ongoing collaboration, and follow-up contacts to support recommendations. Few consumers would choose a lengthy, difficult-to-comprehend written report over a briefer and more relevant one (Hite, 2017).

Issues for Community-Based Evaluators

Community-based providers who work in mental health clinics, hospitals, or social service agencies may face setting-specific constraints. For example, the employing agency's income-generating expectations may discourage assessments that require school visits or involve follow-up activities, or the agency may serve families whose availability for multiple visits is restricted because of transportation issues, child care, or hourly wage jobs. Hence, adaptation of optimal assessment procedures may be necessary. The evaluator may need to be extra selective in choosing which tests to administer or might rely on rating scales and interviews in place of direct observation in a naturalistic setting. Interviews, individual feedback conferences, and follow-up discussions might be conducted by phone or electronic communication, rather than face-to-face. Nevertheless, by keeping a clear focus on both purpose and practicality, the evaluator can conduct a consumer-responsive assessment with integrity, providing high-value written and oral reports and related supports.

Community-based evaluators should be cognizant of the effect they have on assessment practices in general and on school-based assessment reports in particular. School-based evaluators, especially those in litigious communities, may feel compelled to produce long and technical reports, knowing they will be compared to those of "outside experts." In this competition, consumers are the losers.

It may appear that independently practicing psychologists have greater control over their clinical practices and can more readily implement consumer-responsive approaches. However, independent evaluators are also subject to certain limitations and expectations that influence their practice, such as the following:

- The cost of an evaluation is often underwritten by a third-party payer (e.g., an insurance company, a school district, or a government agency) that may cap reimbursement levels or specify that only certain assessment activities will be paid for.
- The consumer may be seeking an assessment that affects a high-stakes decision by a third party, for example, whether a college or medical school will provide disability accommodations or whether a school district will foot the bill for an outside placement. In cases wherein the assessment will play a key role in due process proceedings or an agency decision, the consumer may feel—rightly or wrongly—that a long, jargon-laden report is preferable.
- The economics and logistics of private practice may discourage certain assessment procedures. An uncompensated school visit may require the better part of a day; a phone interview with a teacher or pediatrician may prove difficult to arrange; a parent may be disinclined to make additional appointments for a feedback meeting or follow-up discussion.
- Independent evaluators to whom parents pay large fees, typically $3,000–$5,000 in urban areas, may feel that to earn such income they need to provide very long technical reports with recommendations that they believe align with the parents' perspective.
- The private practice psychologist may have limited opportunity to interact with professional colleagues who challenge their thinking and support practice-enhancing efforts.

Given these obstacles, independent evaluators may be reluctant to engage in activities, such as accessing continuing education opportunities, establishing support networks with colleagues, and introducing innovations to consumers that enable the adoption of more consumer-responsive practices.

Phased-In Implementation

Undertaking an immediate and complete transition to a consumer-responsive approach is a tall order for practitioners. A prudent strategy is to begin by phasing in elements of consumer-responsive assessment. Some practices can be adopted more readily, for example:

- Eliminating uninformative stock phrases and descriptions of tests from reports.
- Using simpler language and reducing reading difficulty of reports.
- Using a Data Summary, rather than inserting tables of test scores in the report narrative.
- Minimizing attention to low-relevance findings in written and oral reports.

Other aspects of consumer-responsive assessment may prove more difficult to implement or may require negotiation with work colleagues or supervisors to ensure acceptability, such as the following:

- Reporting test scores selectively in the report narrative.
- Organizing assessment findings by theme.
- Routinely meeting with parents and teachers at the start and conclusion of an assessment.
- Conducting follow-up consultations with parents and teachers.

The process and pace of adopting consumer-responsive assessment practices will vary, depending on the resources available to the individual practitioner and the expectations and reactions of colleagues, supervisors, and consumers.

SYSTEM ISSUES

Assessment practices are shaped by the policies and priorities of organizations and agencies. In many settings, systemic factors are the major determinants of how evaluators approach assessment reporting.

Consumer-responsive assessment is posited on the assumption that the highest priority of psychological assessment is to effect positive outcomes for children and families. However, this assumption may or may not be shared by the employing agency. Organizational policies may be driven by short-term funding issues, saddled by low expectations, or hampered by tradition and inertia. (As the saying goes, "If you always do what you've always done, you'll always get what you always got.") Hence, consumer-focused concerns may take a back seat to priorities, such as productivity and efficiency, or the defense and documentation of organizational decisions. This state of affairs brings to mind Stephen Covey's (1989) parable about leaders and managers.

> [E]nvision a group of producers cutting their way through the jungle with machetes. . . . The managers are behind them, sharpening their machetes, writing policy and procedure manuals, holding muscle development programs, bringing in improved technologies and setting up working schedules and compensation programs for machete wielders. The leader is the one who climbs the tallest tree, surveys the entire situation, and yells, "Wrong jungle!" But how do the busy, efficient producers and managers often respond? "Shut up! We're making progress." (p. 101)

Making the transition to high-impact assessment practices involves, above all, an idealistic philosophy and the commitment to pursue it. Consumer-responsive assessment requires a shift in emphasis from documentation to outcomes. A particular challenge that will complicate this shift is the commitment of professional time that a consumer-responsive approach necessitates. Administrators who oversee a clinical staff and make work assignments will discover that shorter, plainly written consumer-responsive reports are not easier to produce, and that enhanced engagement with consumers may require greater time and effort on the part of practitioners. Challenges notwithstanding, systems that steadfastly prioritize achieving optimal outcomes for children and families can make significant inroads.

Issues for Schools

A school system's adoption of consumer-responsive practices can be complicated by factors such as complying with mandates, controlling costs, resistance to change, and allocation of resources.

Contending with Mandates

As prescribed by federal special education regulations, educational evaluations provide the requisite input for school teams to make eligibility determinations and design IEPs. School districts, especially those that struggle with budget shortfalls and minimal resources, may dispense with discretionary (i.e., nonmandated) activities of school psychologists and other "specialized instructional support personnel" (e.g., speech and language pathologists and occupational therapists) and allocate only enough professional time and resources to comply with special education mandates. When staffing levels are set at the minimum necessary to comply with mandates, evaluators may have scarce time to conduct comprehensive assessments and to interact with parents and teachers. These conditions favor test-focused reports that can be produced with relative ease and that largely serve to inform eligibility decisions. Such assessments have a limited capacity to promote positive outcomes for children and families.

School district policies and procedures may also be impacted by high levels of due process, which can be costly with respect to funds (e.g., for attorney fees and outside placements), educators' time, and job satisfaction. Frequent involvement with due process activities can prompt a school district to emphasize defensive practice, rather than purposeful and efficient use of professional resources. Evaluators may be expected to conduct extensive assessments, regardless of the referral questions, and to generate elaborate reports that are intended to compete with independent evaluations. In the process, the value of the assessment for the child, the family, and school personnel may become secondary concerns.

There are better ways to contend with mandates and scarce resources. By embracing a consumer-responsive approach, a school district can minimize adversarial interactions and be less vulnerable to due process actions. Ample anecdotal evidence supports this expectation; the notion would benefit from empirical research as well (see Research Idea 8.1).

Controlling Costs

Fiscal problems can be addressed by both short- and long-term solutions. Both are necessary; the latter is critical. Short-term solutions involve meeting basic requirements, and doing so efficiently. However, the potential payoff from long-term solutions is far greater, as they deal with root issues, such as the cost of adversarial relationships with parents and the dearth of prevention programs and services in schools.

RESEARCH IDEA 8.1. Impact of Consumer-Responsive Assessment Services on Due Process and Adversarial Relations

Research question: Will evaluators' consumer-responsive practices result in more positive school–family interactions and reduced involvement in due process?

The study is conducted in school districts with high levels of due process and adversarial interactions. School psychologists are trained to conduct consumer-responsive assessments, including oral and written reporting practices and systematic follow-up activity. Assessment cases with a heightened risk of adversarial activity or a prior history of due process are randomly (e.g., in alternating order) assigned to either a conventional assessment or a consumer-responsive assessment condition. Outcome variables include consumer ratings of satisfaction and consequent levels of due process activity.

Empirical support for the hypothesis that consumer-responsive assessments reduce adversarial interactions could encourage school systems to pursue consumer-responsive practices, both to obtain better outcomes and to reduce unproductive and costly involvement in due process.

School districts may rely on exhaustive assessments and lengthy reports to fend off due process challenges. However, providing direct support to families at critical junctures will reduce conflicts more productively. Consumer-responsive assessment practices are a key component of a school district philosophy that uses resources optimally to achieve better results. The emphasis on productive communication and collaboration with families is a good investment, as it reduces adversarial interactions as well as the need for more intensive services.

In an ideal world, schools would have ample resources and be less likely to make money-saving decisions that shortchange children and families. In the face of fiscal realities, optimal use of professional time is a key element. School administrators can pursue various strategies, such as these, that enable school psychologists and other specialists to devote more time to high-yield activities:

- Reduce the time that specialized personnel spend on clerical activities by assigning tasks such as scheduling appointments, sending out notices, and copying documents to administrative support personnel.
- Invest in time-saving technologies, such as computer scoring of tests, electronic access to records, and web-based administration and scoring of parent and teacher rating scales.
- Encourage IEP teams to be flexible in designing educational evaluations, thereby devoting less time to assessment cases that require little in the way of data collection.

In an effort to reduce their obligations to pay for programs and services, some school districts discourage or even forbid the inclusion of recommendations in assessment reports. By designating recommendations as the exclusive responsibility of the IEP team, to be considered only at formal meetings, a school administration can exert more control over expenditures for programs and services. In the same vein, school-based evaluators may be discouraged from conferring with parents outside of IEP team meetings. Yet, such policies exact a price; they diminish the capacity of school district professionals to extend their expertise to children and families and to establish working relationships founded on trust. Consequently, parents may doubt that the school system has their interests at heart and look to advocacy and adversarial action as the primary means of meeting their children's needs.

A more productive alternative is for school districts to provide direction to school-based evaluators about how to formulate recommendations in a way that accurately identifies a child's needs, but still respects the role of the IEP team as the arbiter of decisions about specific services, placements, or resources (see examples in Box 5.8 in Chapter 5). This approach safeguards school district interests, while making use of evaluators' expertise and enabling them to establish collaborative relationships with families.

School districts commit substantial resources for highly trained professionals to conduct psychoeducational assessments. This investment should be weighed against their impact on the district's educational goals. All too often, the primary function of school-based assessments is to comply with mandates and control costs. Consumer-responsive assessment places greater emphasis on meeting the needs of children and families.

Exercising Options

Regardless of finances, staffing levels, or educational philosophy, schools should allocate professional time wisely. In many school districts, evaluators engage in more assessment activity than is necessary and beneficial. School districts can use resources to best advantage by prompting evaluators to vary the length and nature of assessments strategically. IEP teams should plan educational evaluations on an individual basis and exclude unnecessary components. Intelligence testing is often used indiscriminately. There is neither a procedural requirement under IDEA nor an educational rationale to administer a comprehensive intelligence test as part of every psychoeducational assessment. When cognitive functioning is of lesser concern, a brief cognitive measure or short form may suffice, or cognitive assessment may be dispensed with altogether.

The mandated requirements for educational evaluations enable IEP teams to determine not only what *is*, but also what is *not*, relevant content. In many cases, the required re-evaluations of children in special education services can be relatively brief. Federal special education regulations specify the basic objectives that an evaluation must address: to describe current performance, to establish or confirm eligibility, and to determine educational needs (see Box 3.1 in Chapter 3). For some re-evaluations, existing records and teacher and parent reports provide sufficient data to determine whether the education program is being delivered as intended and whether educational goals are being met. When the child's disability is well understood and the education program is closely monitored and serving the child well, little or no psychological testing may be needed. In these cases, the report can be relatively brief and to the point. (See Appendix D for an example of such a re-evaluation report.) Notably, a re-evaluation is not required under federal regulations when a student exits special education because of high school graduation or exceeding the age of eligibility, only a "summary of the child's academic achievement and functional performance" (Sec. 300.305(e)(3)).

School systems should exercise the option to forgo an individualized assessment entirely in some situations. IDEA expressly allows school districts to avoid unnecessary assessments. As stated in the federal special education regulations, a review of existing records (i.e., previously conducted assessments, information from parents, and observations by school personnel) may suffice for the IEP team, subject to parent agreement, to "determine that no additional data are needed to determine whether the child continues to be a child with a disability, and to determine the child's educational needs" (Sec. 300.305(d)). The NASP (2010b) ethical principles support and elaborate upon this option.

> **Standard II.3.7.** It is permissible for school psychologists to make recommendations based solely on a review of existing records. However, they should utilize a representative sample of records and explain the basis for, and the limitations of, their recommendations.

Exercising Flexibility

Since consumer-responsive assessment involves additional work and consumer-responsive reports may take longer to write than conventional reports (especially for evaluators who are in the process of revising their practices), school systems may opt to use this approach selectively. Priority might be given to cases for which optimal outcomes are critical, or when sensitive handling will save time, trouble, and expense in the long run. School systems are especially advised to implement consumer-responsive practices when (1) a serious disability is first identified, (2) a preschool child with established disabilities is first evaluated by a school district, or (3) family dynamics figure prominently in the referral concerns.

Similarly, it may be critical to employ specific aspects of a consumer-responsive approach in certain situations. Follow-up consultation is especially warranted for a teacher who is struggling with behavior management and is likely to make multiple referrals over time. Or, an evaluator might set aside extra time for postassessment discussion with a high school student who is determined to remain in, or return to, a less-restrictive environment that will pose challenges.

Optimizing Psychological Services

All too often, the assessment function of school psychologists is narrowly defined and practiced, and is primarily focused on informing eligibility decisions. The functioning of the IEP team may be similarly confined, with the particulars of the IEP being overly determined by the child's educational disability category. For example, a child identified as having emotional disturbance may automatically receive individual counseling as a related service, even though a behavioral intervention program or family consultation may be the more productive intervention. When program planning is largely decided by the disability category, the assessment role of school-based evaluators will likely emphasize labeling and gatekeeping. Consequently, the school district will value the timely completion of psychological assessments that contribute to the eligibility decisions, more so than their effect on children and families.

School systems devote so much staff time to compliance with special education mandates that they may be hard pressed to enable school psychologists to engage in other roles for which they are trained. These roles, as described in the NASP (2010a) Practice Model, include consultation to families, teachers, and other school personnel; individual and group counseling; behavioral interventions; development of social–emotional learning and prevention programs; evaluation of programs and services; staff development; progress monitoring; and crisis prevention and response. Hence, an exclusive emphasis on assessment can come at the expense of other valuable services that promote student learning and social-emotional development.

Redefining the assessment role of school psychologists can significantly improve outcomes for children and families. Capitalizing on the collaborative relationships with consumers that are established over the course of assessments, evaluators can then apply their repertoire of clinical skills to help parents and teachers implement recommendations, evaluate their effects, and propose modifications as needed. These follow-up activities make good use of the evaluator's expertise in intervention planning, data analysis, counseling, and consultation. These augmentative activities could be formalized and assured by including consultation services in a student's IEP. Rather than regarding the evaluator's assessment role as being mutually exclusive with other roles, this service model magnifies its impact by connecting it with other domains of practice.

The broader issue concerning the optimal use of psychological services is that devoting extensive resources to mandated assessment activities can come at the expense of other educational goals. School psychologists are uniquely qualified to conduct the psychoeducational assessments that are essential to the special education evaluation process. They can also provide services that promote the development of personal, social, and emotional attributes that are critically important for students' academic success in school, as well as subsequent success in the workplace and in the community. K–12 schools have a singular capacity to promote these key social–emotional outcomes (Durlak, Weissberg, Dymnicki, Taylor, & Schellinger, 2010; Hawkins, Kosterman, Catalano, Hill, & Abbott, 2008; Rimm-Kaufman, Fan, Chiu, & You, 2007). Teachers and school-based administrators are acutely aware of the need for such programs and services. Although school psychologists and other school-based mental health professionals can contribute substantially to social and emotional learning goals, school systems may opt not to allocate resources to this end.

Whereas school systems inevitably dedicate staff resources to students' behavioral and social–emotional issues, there are more and less productive ways of doing so. Responding reactively only when problems escalate or crises occur is both costly and ineffective. Forward-thinking school systems use a multitiered service model to reduce both learning and behavior problems. Multitiered systems produce better outcomes by strategically distributing resources to different levels of services (i.e., prevention, early intervention, and intensive services). A critical element, patterned after public health programs, is to dedicate ample resources to primary prevention (i.e., universal academic and behavioral supports). Engaging school psychologists and other specialized personnel in prevention and early intervention programs and services can enhance student learning and reduce the time and expense devoted to disciplinary actions, out-of-district placements, crisis response, parent complaints, due process and attorney fees, corrective action plans, and the like. This approach has long been championed by the UCLA Center for Mental Health in Schools, which proposes that schools adopt a systematic structure for reducing barriers to learning and increasing student engagement in classroom instruction (Adelman & Taylor, 2012).

To recap, school administrators can expand a system's capacity to accomplish educational goals by taking steps to optimize the value of school psychological services, namely,

- Enable and encourage school psychologists and other specialists to establish collaborative relationships with, and provide ongoing support to, families.
- Establish procedures whereby school-based evaluators routinely follow up with teachers and parents to ensure understanding of assessment findings and promote effective implementation of recommendations.
- Establish a "learning supports" component of the school structure that systematically engages school mental health professionals in supporting students' behavioral health and in reducing barriers to learning.
- Advocate for sufficient instructional support services personnel (e.g., school psychologists, counselors, social workers, and speech and language pathologists) to effectively contribute to the pursuit of important educational goals.

Issues for Community Agencies

Psychological assessment is often part of the array of mental health services provided by community health centers, mental health clinics, and hospitals. The cases referred to community agencies are often complicated and may be assigned to specialized evaluators, such as neuropsychologists or autism experts, or to a multidisciplinary diagnostic team. Community providers often have long waiting lists, resulting in delays for services. Children and families may suffer as community-based or school services are deferred, pending assessment results. Assessments that involve an extensive battery of tests and a long, technical report contribute to the backup. But what is the value of unnecessary tests or of incomprehensible reports? Wouldn't simpler, focused assessments that are completed in a timely fashion for the benefit of more children and families better serve the greater good?

Fiscal realities also play a part. Community agencies that rely on third-party payments (e.g., commercial insurance, school districts, and Medicaid) must provide services within budgetary restraints. Fee-for-service payment structures also impose tight caps on reimbursement for psychological assessment. Similar pressures affect the emerging medical home model, whereby health centers receive flat per-patient funding, regardless of the amount of service provided. These fiscal environments require a focused and efficient assessment that has maximum impact. That impact is maximized when assessment is fully responsive to the needs of consumers, with collaborative activities yielding the best return on invested effort.

Issues for Third-Party Payers

The entity that foots the bill for an assessment typically imposes parameters and limitations, such as provider qualifications, reimbursement amounts, types of services reimbursed, and a time period for completion. We typically associate third-party payment with health care insurance, either private (e.g., as an employment benefit) or public (e.g., as a Medicaid benefit). However, school systems also function as third-party payers when they underwrite the cost of an independent educational evaluation. They, too, are entitled to specify examiner qualifications and to establish parameters regarding scope, duration, or cost.

Reimbursement Patterns

Third-party payers influence assessments by allowing reimbursement for certain services (e.g., testing and report writing) and not for others (e.g., observation in naturalistic settings and school visits), and by imposing reimbursement caps that discourage time-consuming assessment methods. These constraints tend to result in assessments that rely largely on standardized testing, for which the main product is often a long and impressive-looking psychological report of limited value. Furthermore, since the written report serves as the deliverable product, follow-up activities are not systematically pursued, and there is much uncertainty as to whether the findings are put to good use.

A more beneficial funding model would encourage the evaluator to use a wide array of assessment sources, feedback mechanisms, and follow-up services. This could be accomplished by giving the evaluator more latitude to apportion services under a flat reimbursement rate or by having a managed care option to complement assessments with follow-up services, similar to the process whereby a psychotherapist can request coverage for additional sessions. A more flexible and comprehensive menu of assessment services would benefit children in particular, since their functioning and needs are best investigated through multiple sources of assessment data and contact with multiple parties (e.g., child, parents, school personnel, and service providers). The ideal is for third-party payers to adopt a value-driven philosophy, recognizing that consultative and follow-up services can greatly enhance the impact of an assessment and reduce long-term problems and costs.

Prevention Pays

Consumer-responsive assessment may require a greater initial investment of evaluator time and system resources, but the enhanced value should reduce long-term costs for therapeutic services, restrictive placements, crisis intervention, and the like. Studies attest to both better results and net savings with preventive approaches (Bierman et al., 2008; Marx, Wooley, & Northrop, 1998). In recognizing the value of this approach, health care insurers now incorporate prevention into their service model, providing incentives for fitness club memberships and participation in wellness maintenance programs. The same logic applies to behavioral health. Just as an annual physical exam allows for the screening of incipient problems and encourages healthy habits, mental health screening can be used to similar advantage.

K–12 schools offer an unmatched opportunity to promote the behavioral health of children in a nonstigmatizing setting. Forward-thinking school systems use a multitiered service model to prevent or minimize learning and behavior problems. Consumer-responsive assessment can be a valuable component of this model. School systems that invest in consumer-responsive practices make good use of resources and can expect reduced levels of adversarial interactions and due process activity. Ample anecdotal evidence supports this expectation; the issue would benefit from empirical research as well (see Research Idea 8.1).

Consumer Feedback

The central tenet of consumer-responsive assessment is to provide beneficial outcomes for consumers. Whether service providers do so successfully, however, should not be left to chance. Soliciting feedback from consumers is not a difficult matter. This might take the form of a web-based survey, like those used by businesses, that can be answered quickly and easily. (How would you rate your hotel stay? Was your appliance repair satisfactory? How long did you have to wait to see your health care provider?) A request for consumer feedback has the added advantage of prompting the consumer to give further attention to assessment findings and recommendations.

Consumer satisfaction feedback should be requested perhaps a week to a month after written and oral reporting has been completed, rather than immediately afterward. Delayed feedback allows consumers time to reflect on the process, and reduces possible bias that may result from the consumer's desire to please or stay on good terms with the evaluator. A sample consumer satisfaction survey developed for use in a university-based assessment clinic is offered in Appendix C. The format and content of a consumer satisfaction survey may look different for a school district, a mental health clinic, or a private practice.

Issues for Graduate Training Programs

Consumer-responsive assessment involves honing a wide repertoire of professional skills that continue to develop over time. How, then, might graduate programs optimally design curriculum and instruction to supports these skills?

Course instructors would be ill advised to reduce the emphasis on foundational data collection skills, such as test scoring and administration, structured observation, and interviewing. However, an introductory course should also provide an overview of larger philosophical and professional issues, for example:

- Who is the client?
- What are the main goals of psychological assessment?
- How do we know if these goals are achieved?
- What skills are required, and how are they attained?

Awareness of these issues can instill an appreciation of the ultimate goals of assessment and the requisite expertise needed to accomplish them.

Report writing is high on the list of assessment skills that evolve through years of practice. Assessment courses at each level should advance students' ability to write in a clear, readable, jargon-free manner, to be selective about what to report, and to organize findings by themes. Unfortunately, the best efforts of instructors are often undermined, as trainees are influenced by examples found in textbooks and in the field and by the temptation to rely on templates that overly simplify case conceptualization.

Oral reporting of assessment findings is an important, but oft-neglected skill. Curry and Hanson (2010), in a large national survey of practicing psychologists, found that only 27% received formal training in their doctoral program that sufficiently prepared them to deliver assessment feedback to clients, while over one-third of the sample reported receiving little or no training in this area. Some carryover from written reports to oral reporting will naturally occur. The core principles of a consumer-responsive approach (e.g., simple, clear language and selective, relevant, strength-based content) are applicable to both written and oral reports. However, oral presentation skills are best developed through explicit instruction, guided practice, and feedback. A feedback conference simulation assignment used in an introductory-level psychoeducational assessment course is provided in Appendix H. This training activity mainly focuses on effective communication and fostering collaborative relationships.[1] These interactional skills, which have even greater impact on consumer satisfaction than content skills such as data analysis and interpretation (Quine & Rutter, 1994), are fully within the grasp of first-year graduate students. Subsequent training on how to deliver feedback might place more emphasis on content skills, such as managing difficult situations (e.g., breaking the news about a child's severe disability or providing feedback to resistant or impaired individuals) and maximizing the likelihood of compliance with recommendations.

A training program curriculum should ensure that trainees continue to improve those assessment skills that require sustained learning, practice, and feedback. Most psychology and school psychology graduate programs include multiple assessment courses that are distinguished by content area, with separate courses for cognitive and for social–emotional assessment, and possibly for educational, behavioral, or neuropsychological assessment. The course sequence should also ensure ongoing development of long-evolving skills, such as writing theme-based reports, integrating multiple data sources, presenting findings orally, and formulating recommendations. These skills might be revisited in advanced level courses or in seminars that support students' practicum or internship fieldwork. Advanced assessment skills can also be incorporated into related coursework; for example, courses on consultation or working with families might include explicit guidance on how the material would be applied to conducting assessments.

A VISION FOR FUTURE PRACTICE

In this book, we have proposed an approach to assessment that is guided by a sense of purpose, with the overriding goal of generating positive results. To this end, we have advocated for giving greater attention to the impact-enhancing aspects of the assessment process: collaborative working relationships with consumers, understandable reports that emphasize implications for everyday functioning, effective oral presentation of findings, and follow-up

---

[1]I (R. L.) found this activity to be the single most important learning activity in my first-year psychoeducational assessment course. Since it served as the final exam, students prepared thoroughly. Student performance on this activity was appreciably stronger when I added the element of modeling a feedback conference presentation after introducing the rubric.

activities that facilitate implementation of recommendations and evaluate their effectiveness.

Nothing in the natural order of things dictates why psychological assessment is conducted the way it is. Current practice is largely a function of history and convention, influenced by mandates, funding patterns, and human nature. Hence, one might take a step back and envision ideal circumstances, in effect, posing the question "What would best serve the public good?" If psychological assessment were reconceptualized from scratch, with positive impact as the goal, what would it look like? This question leads us to envision a paradigm shift that would have major implications for how evaluators are trained and how practitioners conduct assessments.

It is instructive to compare the assessment activities of psychologists with that of medical doctors. Assessment (or diagnosis) is an essential component of health care, as it is indispensable for informing treatment. Doctors engage in diagnostic activities with extreme efficiency. They rely on the same set of data sources as psychologists: records, interviews, observation, and tests. They conduct complex tests themselves (e.g., a spinal tap or colonoscopy), and delegate routine tests to nurses and lab technicians (e.g., blood tests, EKGs, and X-rays). And, they optimize the value of every minute spent in direct contact with patients. In relatively brief time, they conduct a clinical interview, observe the patient first-hand, convey a diagnosis, and explain options and recommendations. Though brief, their direct contact with the patient is essential and serves multiple purposes: to gather data, to assess the patient's attitude toward self-care, and to establish the kind of trust and confidence that will lead the patient to comply with medical advice and continue to access health care services. Time spent on documentation is kept to a minimum. Doctors don't write elaborate reports, as doing so would come at the expense of the higher-priority activity: that of providing treatment.

How, then, can evaluators justify the time devoted to extensive testing and analysis of test results when time spent interacting with parents, teachers, the child, and other consumers reaps greater benefits? How can school psychologists and school systems justify the time devoted to writing long and technical reports when there is such a pressing unmet need for children's mental health services and prevention programs?

There is no requirement in IDEA to produce a comprehensive written report, only to document the findings of an educational evaluation. Other educational evaluators (e.g., speech and language pathologists and occupational therapists) produce briefer reports. Special education teachers who administer achievement tests typically share the results at the IEP team meeting with no written report. The NASP (2010a) Practice Model makes no explicit mention of report writing, the closest being "School psychologists effectively communicate information for diverse audiences, such as parents, teachers and other school personnel." (p. 4). The NASP (2010b) *Principles for Professional Ethics* has only the following statement about documenting work:

> **Standard II.4.2.** School psychologists maintain school-based psychological and educational records with sufficient detail to be useful in decision-making by another professional and with sufficient detail to withstand scrutiny if challenged in a due process or other legal procedure.

Similarly, the *Ethical Principles of Psychologists and Code of Conduct* of the American Psychological Association (2017) only stipulates, in this regard, that "psychologists take reasonable steps to ensure that explanations of results are given to the individual or designated representative" (Standard 9.10).

Consider what would be lost, and what gained, if evaluators were to apply the "So what?" principle in the extreme. As noted by Ownby and Wallbrown (1986), a brief narrative report—no more than a single-spaced page or two—might serve adequately in some situations. Such a report might resemble a parent feedback letter as proposed by Jones (2018) and described in Chapter 7 (see also the example in Appendix D), or might consist mostly of the Clinical Impressions and Summary and Recommendations sections of a consumer-responsive report as described in Chapter 5. Either way, it would advisably include a Data Summary as an addendum to establish the basis for interpretations and recommendations and to enable other professionals to review the findings and consider other conclusions. This approach is largely in accord with the principles of consumer-responsive assessment and offers the practical advantages of using practitioners' time to best advantage.

Scaling back on documentation can yield substantial cost–benefit advantages. Brief reports need not be a disservice to consumers, as long as they contain the information that consumers are most apt to need, remember, and use (see Research Idea 8.2). They offer the further advantage of reducing any guesswork about what the evaluator regards as truly relevant. Furthermore, the time spared from report writing could be dedicated to activities that have high value in producing positive outcomes for schoolchildren and other consumers. There is, however, a potential downside to this approach. A report that consists mainly of "punch lines" will likely stint on delineating the connection between the assessment data and the evaluator's interpretations and conclusions, thus diminishing an important check against undue subjectivity.

RESEARCH IDEA 8.2. Length of Assessment Reports and Consumer Retention of Content

Research question: What is the relationship between the length of assessment reports and consumers' retention and understanding of key assessment content?

The participants in this study are parents or teachers who have prior familiarity with special education assessment reports. Each participant reviews fictitious assessment reports of two children: one that is brief and limited to key findings, and the other that elaborates at greater length on key findings and addresses other assessment findings as well. (There are two versions of the assessment reports for each of the two children—one brief and one elaborated—and these are assigned randomly in counterbalanced order.) After reading each report, participants complete a questionnaire to assess their recall and conceptual understanding of key content. It is hypothesized that participants will read the shorter report with greater care and will retain more key information with comparable understanding of constructs and their practical implications.

Empirical support for this hypothesis would reassure evaluators that consumers are not disadvantaged by briefer, more-focused assessment reports.

Nevertheless, the ultimate value of selective, accessible, child-focused reporting lies not in economy of effort or in a better-written product, but rather in how a consumer-responsive approach increases the evaluator's ability to effect positive outcomes. The benefits of assessment are greatly enhanced by clear communication and productive relationships with primary consumers. Perhaps the greatest enhancement comes from the ongoing support and monitoring of recommendations and interventions in keeping with the NASP (2010b) *Principles for Professional Ethics:*

> **Standard II.2.2.** School psychologists actively monitor the impact of their recommendations and intervention plans. They revise a recommendation, or modify or terminate an intervention plan, when data indicate the desired outcomes are not being attained.

By comparison, the conventional model, whereby evaluators propose recommendations and intervention plans and hope for the best, is a shaky proposition with respect to impact. Follow-up activities that ensure that findings are understood, that support implementation of recommendations, that evaluate outcomes, and that propose adjustments or changes as needed add enormous value. Systematic monitoring of interventions is ethical and evidence-based practice at its best.

Toward a Tipping Point

Consumer-responsive assessment practices offer the promise of better use of resources with better outcomes. The obstacles are many and substantial, but the potential benefits of changing practices are great. Both individuals and institutions with a stake in optimal outcomes can take various steps to promote reforms:

- A graduate training program reexamines its curriculum.
- A health care insurer allows reimbursement for school visits.
- A children's hospital surveys consumers about their satisfaction with assessment services.
- An evaluator devotes less attention to test administration and more time to conducting interviews with parents and teachers.
- Consumers are exposed to, and appreciate the enhanced value of, reports that are easily understood and relevant to their needs.
- A school district directs evaluators to conduct follow-up inquiries about the use and impact of recommendations.
- Evaluators interact with family members throughout the assessment process and derive satisfaction from working collaboratively and having a greater impact.

There are many actions, large and small, that can move the field toward a tipping point. Adoption of more consumer-responsive practices is long overdue, but within our collective reach.

APPENDIX A

Readability Measures

Readability measures have been around for some time, and came into wide usage through the work of Rudolph Flesch in the mid-1900s. Flesch (1948) advocated for documents to be written at a level commensurate with the literacy of a document's intended audience. He developed a reading difficulty scale based on readily measurable features of text (i.e., word length and sentence length). Flesch regarded *standard* reading material as text at the eighth-to-ninth grade reading level on this scale.

The Flesch grade level was adapted by Kincaid, Fishburne, Rogers, and Chissom (1975) for use by the U.S. Navy. Flesch–Kincaid grade levels run about a grade or two lower than Flesch grade level. The Flesch–Kincaid grade level is intended to reflect what the average U.S. student at the given grade level can read and understand. For example, a score of 7.5 suggests that a passage can be understood by the average seventh-grade student. Writing above the level of grade 13 is considered unreasonably dense and subject to being misunderstood or ignored.

The widely used indicators of reading difficulty are readily generated by computer programs. However, they are relatively crude measures that apply mathematical formulas to basic elements: syllables per word and words per sentence. Knowing how readability indicators work, an author can lower the scores by simple means, such as breaking up long sentences and avoiding long words. Other characteristics, such as usage frequency of the actual words, are not figured in. Consider, for example, that many familiar multisyllabic words can be easily read (e.g., *understanding, opportunity, responsibility*) while short, uncommon words (e.g., *angst, blithe, eschew*) can be difficult.

The usual precautions about the use of grade-level scores are less applicable to readability indicators. On norm-referenced achievement tests, the actual differences between performance levels of the average 10th grader and the average 12th grader are slight. (This is one reason why grade-equivalent scores are misleading and best avoided.) The Flesch and Flesch–Kincaid reading levels, however, are interval scales, so there are notable differences between grade levels of, say, 10.5 and 12.5.

The Flesch reading ease score (Flesch, 1979) is derived from the same elements as the Flesch–Kincaid grade level, but uses a scale that reflects how easily material can be read. These scores range from 0 to 100, with higher scores indicating easier reading, although the formula for generating scores can actually produce negative numbers. In the table below (adapted from Flesch, 1979), the grade level indicates the level of schooling at which a passage would expectedly be read easily, and the descriptor conveys how an average adult would regard the passage.

Reading ease score	Grade level	Descriptor
90–100	5th grade	Very easy
80–90	6th grade	Easy
70–80	7th grade	Fairly easy
60–70	8th and 9th grade	"Plain English"
50–60	10th to 12th grade	Fairly difficult
30–50	College	Difficult
0–30	College graduate	Very difficult

The Flesch reading ease scale is frequently used by the publishing industry, and also for evaluating technical writing (e.g., for government publications or life insurance policies). Newspapers and magazines aim for readability levels in the 50s or 60s. As analyzed by Flesch (1979), the average reading ease score for the *Reader's Digest* was 65; for *Time* magazine it was 52; and for *The New York Times* it was 39. The Internal Revenue Code scored a –6.

Test Administration and Scoring Rubric

Note. Some elements in the Near Proficiency and In Need of Attention columns cite multiple issues. The evaluator or supervisor should circle issues that are applicable to clarify the basis for these ratings.

	MASTERY (2)	**NEAR PROFICIENCY (1)**	**IN NEED OF ATTENTION (0)**
1. Preparation	Room free of distractions (auditory and visual), comfortable seating, adequate lighting, etc.	Some effort to reduce distractions and create a conducive work environment, but could be improved	Inadequate testing conditions for lack of effort to reduce distractions and create a conducive work environment
2. Preparation	Optimal positioning of people and materials in accordance with test manual and best practice	Less than optimal positioning of people and materials; some unnecessary inconvenience	Significant shortcomings in the positioning of materials and people; highly inconsistent with test manual

	MASTERY (2)	NEAR PROFICIENCY (1)	IN NEED OF ATTENTION (0)
3. Preparation	All testing materials present and in place; advance preparation as needed	Some testing materials are nonstandard or out of place or not adequately prepared in advance	Testing materials are missing or out of place; lack of preparation significantly detracts from administration
4. Initial steps	Appropriate rapport established: friendly and supportive, but professional	Adequate rapport established, but overly casual or distant	Failure to establish adequate rapport because of poor practice
5. Initial steps	Accurate and developmentally appropriate explanation of testing purpose and procedures	Explanation of testing purpose and procedures is misleading, unclear, or not suited to developmental level	No explanation of testing purpose and procedures, or explanation is highly counterproductive
6. Administration	Fluent, natural tone of voice	Stilted, halting, or unnatural tone of voice; pace is too fast or too slow	Critical or threatening tone of voice
7. Administration	Subtest instructions given verbatim	Some minor deviations from verbatim instructions	Major deviations from instructions or serious omission of instructions
8. Administration	Fluid transitions between subtests, with no previewing description of tasks that follow	Minor confusion or delay in transitions between subtests; some description of tasks that follow	Long or disorganized transitions between subtests; excessive description of tasks that follow
9. Administration	Sample/demonstration items given exactly per instructions	Minor deviations from instructions in administering sample/demonstration items	Significant deviations from instructions or failure to provide sample/demonstration items
10. Administration	Items given in the prescribed sequence according to test manual instructions	Some minor deviation from the prescribed sequence of items, or errors self-corrected	Significant deviations from the prescribed sequence of items

	MASTERY (2)	NEAR PROFICIENCY (1)	IN NEED OF ATTENTION (0)
11. Administration	Accurate timing with stopwatch in accordance with manual instructions (e.g., unobtrusive)	Slight errors in timing or minor deviations from manual instructions (e.g., timing is obtrusive or secretive); failure to use stopwatch, if required	Significant errors in timing or major deviations from manual instructions, failure to time when required, or failure to use a timing device
12. Administration	Wrong answers accepted without cueing (no verbal feedback, telltale pauses, nonstandard queries, etc.)	Wrong answers accepted, but with occasional or slight/subtle cues that answers are incorrect	Feedback repeatedly provided that answers are wrong, when not permitted
13. Administration	Right answers accepted without cueing (verbal feedback, nodding, smiling, etc.)	Right answers accepted, but with occasional or subtle cues that answers are correct, when not permitted	Feedback repeatedly provided that answers are right, when not permitted
14. Administration	Correct querying (Q) of responses: when required or only when permitted, using acceptable wording	Mostly accurate querying: some omitted queries, or querying when not permitted, or nonstandard wording	Many instances of failing to query when required or querying when not permitted; inappropriate wording
15. Administration	Correct prompts (P) and teaching items when required, and only as permitted by instructions	Mostly correct use of prompts and teaching items; occasional oversight or minor errors in prompting or teaching	Serious errors or oversight in prompting or teaching
16. Administration	Items repeated only when permitted and in accordance with instructions	One or two minor errors in repeating items when not allowed or in not repeating items when required	Serious or several errors in repeating items when not allowed or not repeating items when required
17. Administration	Starting point and discontinuation rules followed in accordance with instructions	Minor deviations from starting point and discontinuation rules on one or two subtests	Major deviation from starting point and discontinuation rules, or many minor deviations

	MASTERY (2)	NEAR PROFICIENCY (1)	IN NEED OF ATTENTION (0)
18. Recording	Accurate and complete recording of key information (name/identifier, age, etc.) on record form face sheet	Minor error or omission of key information on face sheet	Major omission of key information on face sheet, or serious error (e.g., test-age error that affects scoring)
19. Recording	Verbal responses recorded in full, in accordance with instructions	Mostly complete recording of verbal responses as required	Failure to record verbal responses as required, or overly abbreviated recording.
20. Recording	Noteworthy behavioral observations recorded (effort, attention, affect, response to failure, quirks, etc.)	Behavioral observations recorded, but some noteworthy behaviors missed	No behavioral observations recorded
21. Recording	Noteworthy extraneous verbalizations recorded, including the point at which they occurred	Some noteworthy extraneous verbalizations recorded	No recording of noteworthy extraneous verbalizations
22. Scoring	Individual items correctly scored	Occasional mistakes in scoring individual items	Many mistakes in scoring individual items
23. Scoring	Subtest raw scores correctly tallied	Minor errors in tallying subtest raw scores	Multiple errors in tallying raw scores that affect scaled scores
24. Scoring	Subtest scaled scores accurately determined	Minor errors in deriving one or two subtest scaled scores	Major error or multiple errors in deriving subtest scaled scores
25. Scoring	Composite scores accurately determined	Minor errors in deriving one or two composite scores	Major error or multiple errors in deriving composite scores

Name: _____

Date: _____

Observer: _____

Score: _____ of 50

Comments: _____

Psychological Assessment Follow-Up Procedures

At the evaluation feedback meeting, inform the client that you will conduct a routine follow-up phone call in about 2–3 weeks. The call should take about 15–30 minutes. Minor paraphrasing of the text below is acceptable, but avoid substantive revision of the content.

OPENING EXPLANATION

"Hello . . . , this is _____, who conducted the evaluation of _____ at the University Assessment Clinic [last month]. As I mentioned to you at the feedback meeting, this is the follow-up call to make sure everything is in order, and to see if there are any concerns or questions about the evaluation that was done."

DISCUSSION QUESTIONS

Each of the following questions may result in some discussion. Feel free to engage clients in a discussion about the use and interpretation of the evaluation findings and closely related issues (e.g., making the evaluation available to others or special education rights and procedural safeguards). If the client brings up new or long-term issues, you might offer suggestions about seeking further assistance (e.g., from school personnel, an advocate, or a community provider).

- "How are things going with _____?"
- "Have you looked at the written report since I gave it to you and we discussed it? Did you have any questions about it, or is there anything I might explain further?"
- "Have you shared the written report with anyone? What came of that?"

- "Did the recommendations make sense? Have they been helpful?"
- "Have the results of the evaluation been put to use in any other way?"
- "Is there anything else about the evaluation that I can help you with?"

CLOSING

"It's important for the Assessment Clinic to get feedback about how well we serve clients. I hope you would be willing to complete a brief online survey, with just a few questions, about the service you received. Would you be willing to have us send this survey by email? [Obtain the client's email address; reassure the client that the address will not be shared or used for other purposes.]

"Thanks so much for your time and for bringing your child to the Assessment Clinic. It was a pleasure working with you."

CONSUMER SATISFACTION SURVEY

Note. The survey is sent to clients who provide an email address for this purpose. The email message with the link to the web-based survey (e.g., Survey Monkey, Qualtrics) below reads as follows:

To: [Parent of child]
Subject: Assessment Clinic Satisfaction Survey

Dear Assessment Clinic Client,

It is important for the Assessment Clinic to get feedback about how well we serve clients. We would greatly appreciate your taking a few minutes to complete a brief survey about the services you received. To complete the survey, please click here.

Many thanks,
[Clinic Director]

Assessment Clinic Consumer Satisfaction Survey

Name of evaluated individual: _____

Your relationship to this individual: _____

Date: _____

A. When the **evaluation results were discussed at the feedback meeting,** how clear was the information you received?

1. It was DIFFICULT to understand the information.
2. I was able to PARTLY understand the information.
3. I was able to MOSTLY understand the information.
4. I was able to COMPLETELY understand the information.

B. When you read the **evaluation report,** how clear was the information?

    1. I was UNABLE to understand the report.

    2. I was able to PARTLY understand the report.

    3. I was able to MOSTLY understand the report.

    4. I was able to COMPLETELY understand the report.

C. How well did the evaluation **address your questions or concerns?**

    1. Questions and concerns were NOT addressed.

    2. Questions and concerns were PARTLY addressed.

    3. Questions and concerns were MOSTLY addressed.

    4. Questions and concerns were COMPLETELY addressed.

D. How useful were the **recommendations** you received?

    1. Recommendations were NOT useful.

    2. Recommendations have been SLIGHTLY useful.

    3. Recommendations have been SOMEWHAT useful.

    4. Recommendations have been VERY useful.

    5. Cannot say—recommendations have received little or no attention.

E. Do you have any other feedback or comments about the services you received from the Assessment Clinic or the evaluator?

APPENDIX D

Sample Assessment Reports and Parent Feedback Letter

APPENDIX D1

This is an example of a psychoeducational assessment report for an independent evaluation by a licensed psychologist.

PSYCHOEDUCATIONAL ASSESSMENT REPORT

Name: Leonard B.

Date of Birth: 7/9/10

Date of Assessment: 6/30/18

Age: 7 years, 11 months

School: Melody Elementary School

Grade: 2 (entering)

Reason for Referral

Leonard (who goes by "Lenny") is a pleasant and hard-working nearly 8-year-old boy who has struggled to make academic progress. He was referred for assessment to aid in educational planning. The referral was made in response to a recent recommendation for a substantially separate special education placement. The referral was placed by Lenny's parents, who sought a school-funded independent evaluation.

Assessment Procedures

Record review

Stanford–Binet Intelligence Scale, 5th Edition (SB5)

NEPSY, 2nd Edition—selected subtests

Wechsler Individual Achievement Test, 3rd Edition

Gray Oral Reading Test, 5th Edition

ASEBA Child Behavior Checklist and Teacher Report Form

ADHD Rating Scale

Revised Child Manifest Anxiety Scale, 2nd Edition

Background Information

Background information was obtained from Lenny, his mother, Jennifer B., his teachers at the Melody School, and prior school and assessment reports.

Lenny is described by his mother as a kind and polite boy who works hard to do well. His rote memory is strong. He is skilled at doing puzzles. He does well when asked to do one thing at a time. However, Lenny has trouble with comprehension and inferencing. He becomes distracted easily. He struggles when needing to combine tasks. Lenny's mother reported also that he has weak paper-and-pencil skills. He also has trouble organizing the placement of words and pictures on a page.

Lenny is the younger of two children of Jennifer and Sam B. Mr. and Ms. B. divorced approximately 2 years ago; they maintain an amicable relationship. Lenny lives primarily with his mother, seeing his father every weekend. He has an older brother Burt, age 11. There is no known family history of learning disabilities, attention-deficit/hyperactivity disorder (ADHD), or other psychiatric disorder.

Lenny's first-grade teacher, Ms. Copeland, noted that Lenny is a pleasant and cooperative boy who works hard. He needs help understanding directions. It is hard to know whether he has problems with attention or with understanding language. Ms. Copeland rated Lenny's reading accuracy as being "somewhat above grade level." She rated his reading comprehension, math, and writing skills as being "somewhat below grade level." Lenny's grade 1 report card noted that he mastered the required skills in mathematics and reading accuracy. Weaknesses were noted in reading comprehension and writing. According to his current individualized educational plan (IEP), Lenny has received specialized interventions since being diagnosed as having apraxia prior to his second birthday. Apraxia is a problem of motor coordination that often affects speech articulation in young children.

Lenny has received special education services in the form of daily instruction in reading (40 minutes) and written language (30 minutes) since January of the current school year. The reading curriculum used in special education is broad based (i.e., focusing on reading accuracy, rate, and comprehension). The written language curriculum is the same as used in his mainstream class. No formal in-classroom accommodations have been tried. Lenny also receives once weekly speech/language and occupational therapies. School personnel reported that Lenny is slated to enter a substantially separate program this coming fall for students with language-based learning disabilities. It is noted that Lenny started kindergarten a year later than most children his age. His parents wished to give him some extra time to develop.

When not at school, Lenny enjoys playing sports, as well as doing jigsaw and word search puzzles. He has several household chores. He plays with friends regularly. While described as quiet and shy at times, he has no significant symptoms of anxiety or depression. He has no history of temper or behavior problems. He sleeps well. He had what appeared to be vocal tics for a 2-week period approximately 1 year ago. He has no history of traumatic experience.

Regarding developmental and medical histories, Lenny was born full term and at a good birth weight following a normal pregnancy. His early development was slow in all areas. He has no history of seizure, concussion, loss of consciousness, chronic illness, or surgery. As noted above, Lenny was diagnosed with apraxia prior to age 2. His pediatrician is Dr. Jonathan Bach at Pediatric Associates of Tanglewood County.

Lenny had a series of school-based assessments in January of this year. A cognitive assessment was done with the WISC-V by school psychologist, Betsy Debussy NCSP. Results indicated average verbal, spatial, and fluid reasoning abilities (approximately 25th to 40th percentiles). Working memory and processing speed were weaker. An educational evaluation was done with the WIAT-III by special education teacher, Laura Schubert. Results indicated low average to average skills in reading and mathematics. Reading accuracy was average and stronger than reading comprehension, which was low average. Lenny's skills were average in spelling and written expression. In the speech and language evaluation by Edward Ives CCC-SLP, Lenny's performance on measures of language understanding and expression fell in the low average to average ranges. He had low scores on some language understanding subtests that suggested problems in attention or language processing.

Behavioral Observations

Lenny is an appealing nearly 8-year-old boy with a good sense of humor. He described his likes and dislikes both at home and at school, expressing a strong preference for playtime. Lenny was fully cooperative in testing, although he sought to avoid difficult work. He was also troubled by his struggles (e.g., crying at one point when he was aware of his reading errors). He hated being timed. He seemed to expect that he would be wrong even before he attempted a difficult test item. At times, he seemed overwhelmed by the volume of information he was given on a task (e.g., when asked to remember a short story that was read to him). Lenny made speech articulation errors, although I could understand him easily.

Test Results

Intellectual Abilities

Lenny's current cognitive functioning, as assessed with the Stanford–Binet Intelligence Scale, 5th Edition, is overall in the low average range. This is within the range of normal, but weaker than many other children his age. This finding is similar to his performance on his recent school-based assessment with the WISC-V. Lenny's abilities were consistent across the different areas assessed by the Stanford–Binet. These areas included problem solving, vocabulary, verbal, quantitative (numerical), working memory, and spatial reasoning. He showed a relative strength in factual knowledge over problem solving. Qualitatively, Lenny was impulsive at points, jumping through a problem rather than reasoning it out.

Language

Lenny's vocabulary knowledge is average for his age, as measured on the Stanford–Binet. The speed with which Lenny can produce simple language, such as words and sounds, was found to be average on the NEPSY-II Word Generation subtest. However, he did not do well in generating written sentences (see Academic Achievement section below). He also had difficulty understanding directions at points (NEPSY-II Comprehension of Instructions).

Memory

Lenny's memory is average in most areas. These included his ability to remember series of words (NEPSY-II List Memory), one type of verbal memory, and his ability to remember designs on a page (NEPSY-II Memory for Designs) and pictures of peoples' faces (Memory for Faces), two types of visual memory. However, his memory is much weaker when he needs to remember more complex verbal information, such as information contained in a story read to him (NEPSY-II Narrative Memory).

Lenny's working memory—the ability to hold information in mind long enough to apply it or combine it with other information—is mildly weak. This was found on the Stanford–Binet (approximately 25th percentile). This finding is consistent with the results of his school-based assessment.

Sensory–Motor and Visual–Motor Skills

Lenny wrote using a four-finger pencil grasp. Consistent with the results of school-based testing, Lenny's understanding of visual images is accurate (NEPSY-II Arrows). Further, his paper-and-pencil hand–eye coordination is average (NEPSY-II Design Copying). However, Lenny does have weaknesses in fine motor coordination, with similar very low performance with both hands (NEPSY-II Imitating Hand Positions). In addition, he had difficulty following a simple pattern of finger movements quickly. He made errors in speed, in sequencing, and in his knowledge of which finger he is using without looking, termed his proprioceptive sense (Fingertip Tapping). These findings are consistent with his earlier diagnosis of apraxia.

Attention

Lenny's abilities to maintain and to shift his attention are mildly weak, but not to the level that indicates a diagnosis of ADHD. His scores on the NEPSY-II Auditory Attention and Response Set were solidly average under simple conditions and in the low average range under more complex ones. He made several impulsive errors, later correcting them.

Lenny's mother and teachers completed the ADHD Rating Scale. Ms. B. indicated the presence of two of the nine symptoms of the inattentive type of ADHD. His classroom teacher, Ms. Copeland and his special education teacher, Ms. Schubert, indicated the presence of 5/9 and 6/9 inattentive symptoms, respectively. Ms. B. and Ms. Copeland both indicated 0/9 symptoms of the hyperactive–impulsive type. Ms. Schubert indicated the presence of 3/9 hyperactive–impulsive symptoms. Mild attention problems were indicated in Ms. B.'s ratings on the ASEBA, but not in Ms. Copeland's. Overall, these ratings suggest that Lenny's attention is likely not as good as that of many children his age. However, it is not at a level indicative of ADHD. The ratings of hyperactive–impulsive symptoms are well within average range.

Academic Achievement

Lenny's academic basic skills were assessed with the Wechsler Individual Achievement Test (WIAT-III) and the Gray Oral Reading Test (GORT-5). Lenny has strong skills in reading accuracy. He reads phonetically. On the GORT-5, he occasionally read the same text over and over again without making errors in the words themselves. Lenny's reading rate was at the lower end of the average range. His comprehension scores were average on the WIAT-III, where little understanding of text is required, and weaker on the GORT-5. These results suggest that he has good skills in showing his understanding of simple text, but has weakness in understanding more complex text. Lenny seemed anxious when he read.

Lenny's spelling skills were very strong. Nonetheless, he showed some weakness in other areas of writing. Although his Sentence Composition score was average overall, it likely overestimates his true writing skills. Lenny correctly copied sentences. He had difficulty generating sentences on his own.

Lenny showed good skills in basic math reasoning. He used numerals to represent quantities, solve basic addition and subtraction word problems, and tell time to the hour. His math computation skills were very weak. For example, he correctly added 3+3 and subtracted 4–2, but stumbled over 8+5 and 10–6.

Behavior and Adjustment

Lenny's mother's rating of his adjustment on the ASEBA indicated that he is a cooperative and upbeat boy, with no undue signs of aggression or depression. He relates well with others. According to his mother's ratings, Lenny has mild problems with anxiety. Ratings by Lenny's teacher, Ms. Copeland, suggested normal functioning across the board with the exception of anxiety. Ms. Copeland indicated that Lenny is anxious to please, that he is perfectionistic in fearing to make mistakes, and that he is self-conscious.

Lenny's self-ratings of anxiety symptoms on the Revised Child Manifest Anxiety Scale—2nd edition were within normal range in all areas. These included social anxiety and the physical aspects of anxiety. He showed a mild tendency to worry more than others his age.

Conclusions

Lenny is a pleasant and hard-working nearly 8-year-old boy who seeks to please. He will enter the second grade in the coming fall of 2018. Current results suggest the presence of mild learning problems that, in combination with feeling anxious and discouraged, have impeded Lenny's progress in school. In presenting these findings, I note that the development of young children such as Lenny sometimes changes more than we expect. Thus, current results might not accurately predict his functioning in 2 to 3 years.

Lenny's skills in reading, decoding, and spelling are very strong at present. However, he struggles with reading comprehension and math computations. He has not committed basic arithmetic facts to memory. He has trouble understanding complex directions. He becomes overwhelmed when asked to remember stories or large amounts of verbal material. He does far better learning specific facts than general principles.

Several factors contribute to Lenny's academic struggles. These include low average aptitude for school learning and a weakness in remembering and perhaps understanding long strings of language. He has greater ease in learning one-step tasks than those that are lengthier or involve independent reasoning. He also shows continuing problems with fine motor coordination. He has difficulty with attention. This not to the degree that warrants a diagnosis of ADHD. Lenny's weaknesses are made worse by self-doubt. He wants to do well, becomes quite anxious when he is aware of errors, and then does worse. These difficulties, as well as his task anxiety, likely started with mild to moderate early delays in some developmental areas, notably apraxia. Also, like younger children, he is more play- than work-oriented, and is prone to avoid that which is hard for him.

While I note several weaknesses, here, I also note that there is ample reason for hope. First, Lenny's development improved substantially since he was first identified as having broad delays, including apraxia as a very young child. Second, he has shown significant academic gains in some areas. They include reading accuracy, reading comprehension, and spelling, assessed previously in January of this year. Third, he is a willing learner who carries on, despite some anxiety.

Recommendations

The following recommendations are best considered with the input and collaboration of parents, teachers, and clinicians.

1. Lenny is slated to start a substantially separate special education program in the coming fall. I can understand why that placement was recommended, given Lenny's low achievement scores in January. However, this does not seem the appropriate program for him. His learning difficulties at this point are present but mild. I fear that enrollment in such a program might not challenge him sufficiently. In addition, this placement might contribute to a self-image of being educationally disabled. Given his learning profile, Lenny might have difficulty in later grades, when material is more content oriented and conceptual. However, the need for more intensive supportive services can be considered at that time.

2. In place of a substantially separate program, I suggest that Lenny's IEP team consider providing Lenny with inclusion services in addition to separate individual and small-group support. The goal of small-group support is to reinforce the skills covered in his general education classroom. Lenny's progress should be monitored with brief curriculum-based measures monthly. A full academic evaluation should be done in 1 year. The IEP team should reconsider placement if he is not making expected progress. His IEP should also include consultation time between regular and special educators.

3. Lenny needs to learn better strategies in several academic areas, in line with the suggestions offered here.

   a. Lenny needs to learn to better understand what he reads. He would likely benefit from learning organizing techniques, such as a story grammar chart. The story grammar technique asks the reader to identify the characters, the setting, and the story problem. It continues with questions about how the problem developed and how the problem was resolved. For nonfiction, where this type of story grammar chart does not fit, the reader is asked to list the facts he has learned. It will be important to use the same kinds of organizer tools consistently so that Lenny learns to use them routinely.

   b. Lenny needs to learn basic math facts more reliably. Extra practice in a low-stress nonjudgmental manner (e.g., in computer-based games or without counting his errors), might work well. Use of objects to help demonstrate concepts and solve arithmetic problems might be helpful as well. Once he demonstrates mastery with objects, they should be removed so that he can learn to solve problems more quickly.

   c. Lenny needs help learning to think about what to write on his own. Given his anxiety, it is important that writing lessons be conducted in a calm and accepting manner. In addition, it would be helpful to begin with brief sentence-level assignments. He could then learn to combine sentences into a paragraph. He could also learn to use graphic organizers, much like those used for reading, to organize the writing process for him.

   d. Lenny's apraxia might make writing slow and effortful for him. He should be given as much time as he needs. Alternatively, he might be taught to use a keyboard and then use a computer for most writing assignments.

4. The following accommodations may be helpful for Lenny:

a. To help Lenny better pay attention and understand what is said in the classroom, it is advisable for teachers to check in with him often. Teachers could also provide explanation or repetition as needed. Similarly, Lenny might need someone to talk through and review stories or other lengthy verbal information. This would compensate for his weakness in remembering language.

b. Lenny would benefit from accommodations that increase attentiveness. They include the use of standard prompts, seating near the instructional area, and the use of a daily agenda. Special incentives for work completion should also be considered.

c. Lenny needs to learn to slow down at times when he does academic work. He seems to become anxious and then responds impulsively. Calmly asking him to go back over his work and then praising him for his efforts, rather than his performance, should be effective.

5. Lenny becomes discouraged when he is aware of his mistakes. It is important for those who work with him to take a positive approach. This involves pointing out his successes and ignoring or minimizing his failures. Warm and nurturing guidance will be helpful in maintaining his motivation.

6. Lenny's academic interventions should be coordinated with the work done by the speech-and-language clinician and occupational therapist who help him at school.

7. I encourage Lenny's mother to share these results with school personnel as soon as possible. An IEP team meeting should be held in order to reconsider his assignment for the fall.

Thank you for allowing me to participate in planning for Lenny. Please feel free to contact me with any additional thoughts or questions.

Bruce Ecker, PhD
Licensed Educational Psychologist
Licensed Psychologist (Clinical)

DATA SUMMARY

The following descriptors are generally applicable interpretations of composite scale *standard scores* that are based on a mean of 100 and a standard deviation of 15, and of subtest *scaled scores* that are based on a mean of 10 and a standard deviation of 3.

Standard score	Percentile rank	Descriptor
Above 130	> 98	Extremely high
116–130	85–98	High
110–115	75–84	High average
91–109	27–73	Average
85–90	16–25	Low average
70–84	2–15	Low
Below 70	< 2	Extremely low

Scaled score	Descriptor
16 and above	Far above average
13–15	Above average
8–12	Average
5–7	Below average
4 and below	Far below average

Stanford–Binet Intelligence Scale—5th Edition (SB-5)

Domain	Standard score	Confidence interval (95%)	Percentile rank
Verbal IQ	85	80–92	16th
Nonverbal IQ	88	83–95	21st
Full Scale IQ	86	82–90	18th
Factor Index			
Fluid Reasoning	82	76–92	12th
Knowledge	91	84–100	27th
Quantitative Reasoning	92	85–101	30th
Visual–Spatial	85	78–94	16th
Working Memory	86	79–95	16th

SB-5 SUBTEST SCALED SCORES

Subtest	Verbal domain	Nonverbal domain
Fluid Reasoning	7	7
Knowledge	10	7
Quantitative Reasoning	7	10
Visual–Spatial Processing	7	8
Working Memory	7	9

NEPSY-II

Subtest	Scaled score	Percentile	Comments
Arrows	11		
Auditory Attention: Total Correct	9		All error types within
Auditory Response Set: Total Correct	8		expected range
Design Copying	10		Motor Score = 7
Comprehension of Instructions	7		
Fingertip Tapping: Repetitions	7		Dom. = Non-dom.
Fingertip Tapping: Sequences	6		
Imitating Hand Positions	5		Dom. = Non-dom.
List Memory: Total	9		
List Memory Delayed	10		
List Memory Interference Effect		Approx. 37th	
Memory for Designs: Total Score	8		
Memory for Designs: Content-Spatial Contrast	8		
Memory for Designs: Delayed	9		
Memory for Faces	8		
Memory for Faces Delayed	10		
Narrative Memory: Free Recall	6		Free-Cued Contrast at
Narrative Memory: Cued Recall	7		Expected Level
Narrative Memory: Recognition		26–50th	
Word Generation: Semantic	8		
Word Generation: Initial Letter	9		

Wechsler Individual Achievement Test—3rd Edition (WIAT-III), Age-Based Norms

Subtest	Standard score	Confidence interval (95%)	Percentile
Word Reading	108	104–112	70th
Reading Comprehension	96	87–105	39th
Numerical Operations	78	69–87	7th
Math Problem Solving	101	91–111	53rd
Sentence Composition: Total	93	84–102	32nd
Sentence Composition: Sentence Combining	108		70th
Sentence Composition: Sentence Building	80		9th
Spelling	117	110–124	87th

Gray Oral Reading Test—5th Edition (GORT-5)

Reading function	Scaled score
Rate	8
Accuracy	10
Comprehension	7

The following descriptors are generally applicable interpretations of clinical rating scales that use T scores, which have a mean of 50 and a standard deviation of 10.

T score	Descriptor
≥ 70	Very elevated—many more concerns than typically reported
60–69	Elevated—more concerns than typically reported
40–59	Average—typical levels of concern
< 40	Low—better than average; fewer concerns

ASEBA Child Behavior Checklist and Teacher Report Form

	Parent rating		Teacher rating	
Scale	T^*	Percentile	T^*	Percentile
Anxious/Depressed	64	92	73	> 97th
Withdrawn/Depressed	58	79	53	62nd
Somatic Complaints	50	50	50	50th
Social Problems	60	84	50	50th
Thought Problems	51	54	50	50th
Attention Problems	66	95	54	65th
Rule-breaking Behavior	50	50	50	50th
Aggressive Behavior	52	58	50	50th

$^*T$ scores of 65–70 indicate a borderline problematic score; T scores above 70 indicate a problematic score.

Revised Child Manifest Anxiety Scale—2nd Edition

Type of anxiety	T score	Percentile
Physiological	54	65th
Worry	57	76th
Social	52	58th
Total	56	72nd
Defensiveness	52	58th

APPENDIX D2

This report is an example of a school psychologist's initial assessment with a primary emphasis on academic functioning and a secondary concern with social–emotional status.

PSYCHOEDUCATIONAL ASSESSMENT REPORT

Student's Name: Millie Slade   **Grade:** 5

School: Monroe Elementary   **Age:** 11 years, 1 months

Dates Assessed: 3/18 & 3/21, 2019   **Date of Birth:** 2/14/2008

Reason for Referral

Millie was referred for an evaluation because of teacher and parent concerns about her school performance. Millie attended parochial school prior to this school year, where she received extra help in reading and writing. Her current classroom teacher feels that Millie is not making sufficient academic progress. Her parents feel that the transition to public school has been difficult for her, both socially and academically.

Assessment Procedures

Review of records

Teacher, parent, and student interviews

Classroom observation

Bender Visual–Motor Gestalt Test, 2nd Edition

Wechsler Individual Achievement Test, 3rd Edition— selected subtests

Wechsler Intelligence Scale for Children, 5th Edition

Conners Comprehensive Behavior Rating Scales— parent and teacher reports

Background Information

Background information was obtained from school records and from interviews with her mother (Helaine Slade), her teacher (Ms. Hamilton), and Millie.

School records provided information about Millie's educational history. She is an 11-year-old fifth grader who is in her first year at Monroe School, having attended Our Lady of Grace Lower School through the fourth grade. Records from her previous school indicate that she received passing grades, with B's in most subjects and an occasional A in math, but lower grades (mostly C's) in English and language arts. Millie's mother, Mrs. Slade, indicated that she and her husband helped her with her reading in first and second grade, and the school supplemented her reading instruction with tutoring by school volunteers in second and third grade.

Mrs. Slade reported that Millie's attendance was excellent through third grade, but she missed about 10 days of school in fourth grade with minor illnesses and "the occasional stomach bug." School records indicate that for the current school year, with about 3 months remaining, Millie has been absent 12 times and tardy another 2 times.

Millie's classroom teacher, Ms. Hamilton, praised Millie's excellent attitude, noting that she tries hard and is an active participant in class. Millie volunteers answers whenever she can, but usually responds in very few words and at times with some confusion. Ms. Hamilton reported that Millie clearly enjoys math, but struggles with science. Millie occasionally asks for extra help after school, which Ms. Hamilton is very willing to provide. She noted that Millie takes longer than her classmates to complete assignments, in part because she checks her work carefully.

Mrs. Slade described Millie as a lively, caring child with a positive attitude. Millie has many friends in the neighborhood and from her prior school. She enjoys active pastimes (e.g., jump rope, tumbling, soccer) and creative activities (e.g., art projects and putting on plays). Millie spends long hours doing her homework, with little prompting. She often looks to her mother and older sister for help with schoolwork. Mrs. Slade is concerned that keeping up with schoolwork has taken a toll on Millie, leaving little time for friends and recreation. She reported that Millie declines invitations to play with friends when she is working on a major school assignment or preparing for a test.

Millie reported she likes school, but prefers the nonacademic subjects (art and music) to reading and writing. She acknowledged that she is a slow reader and "not good at explaining things." She is excited about joining the school chorus next year. She has many friends at school and socializes with them outside of school "as much as I can."

Mrs. Slade indicated that Millie was born prematurely, but reached most developmental milestones at typical ages. Her medical history is unremarkable, except for ear infections as a preschool child.

Behavioral Observations

Classroom

Millie was observed briefly on two separate occasions, once in English and language arts and once in science class. During whole class instruction, she looked intently at the teacher whenever she or he was speaking. While doing seat work, Millie worked steadily with occasional brief interruptions, either to chat with a classmate or to raise her hand to ask a teacher for help. She sought the teacher's help about once every 10 to 15 minutes.

Testing Sessions

Millie was evaluated in two sessions, each approximately 90 minutes long. She was friendly, cooperative, and cheerful from the start. At the first session, she expressed concern about being out of the classroom for a long time, but set aside her worries when told that she would not be expected to make up the work she missed. She smiled easily in response to the examiner's smiles and lighthearted remarks. Millie willingly responded to questions, sometimes asking for them to be repeated.

Millie appeared to try her best throughout each testing session, but seemed tired and less focused after an hour or so. She never requested a break, but welcomed the opportunity when it was offered and appeared more relaxed and engaged afterward. She made comments about the activities that were presented, typically in brief phrases, and asked for clarification of instructions on several occasions. Early on during testing, she asked to have instructions clarified a couple of times and was disappointed when assistance could not be provided because of test procedures. She did not continue to make such requests, relying instead on a puzzled look and an expectant pause when she couldn't come up with an answer.

Assessment Results

A complete list of test scores is provided in the Data Summary at the end of this report. Key findings are discussed below.

General Cognitive Functioning

Millie was administered the Wechsler Intelligence Scale for Children (WISC-V) to assess her current general cognitive functioning. The variability in her performance across the different areas assessed by the WISC-V was so large that her overall cognitive ability cannot be meaningfully summarized in a single score. Her scores on most composite scales, or "indexes" (which are composed of two or more related subtests) fell within the low average or average range—approximately the 20th–60th percentile—but there were notable exceptions. She displayed an overall pattern of lower performance on tasks that emphasized language skills, and of average to high average performance on tasks involving nonverbal reasoning and visual–spatial skills.

LANGUAGE AND VERBAL COMPREHENSION

Millie exhibited low average verbal abilities for her age, scoring at approximately the 15th percentile on the Verbal Comprehension Index of the WISC-V. Her difficulties with language were especially noticeable on tasks that placed high demands on expressive language, such as the WISC-V Vocabulary subtest that called for her to supply definitions. Even when she knew what a word meant, she often struggled to provide a clear, well-worded definition. For example, she defined *pilot* by saying, "That's who drives the plane and tells the people about it." Her expressive language difficulties were also apparent on the WISC-V Similarities subtest, as she tried to explain how two words were alike. In several cases, she was unable to come up with the single word for a category (for example, "transportation" to describe how different types of vehicles are alike), and tried to convey the idea with common words in poorly constructed sentences ("They're both things that move and get people to a place"). Similarly, on the WISC-V Comprehension subtest, she showed good understanding of social and practical situations but had difficulty expressing herself.

NONVERBAL REASONING AND PROBLEM SOLVING

Millie demonstrated typical performance for her age on measures of nonverbal reasoning, problem solving, and pattern recognition, with a solidly average score (50th percentile) on the WISC-V Fluid Reasoning scale. She showed mental flexibility (i.e., coming up with, and trying out, multiple solutions) and persistence in solving puzzle-like tasks. She was pleased with herself and eager to continue after each success.

VISUAL PERCEPTION AND SPATIAL ABILITIES

Millie demonstrated a strength in tasks involving visual and spatial abilities, such as figuring out how parts fit together to form a shape or design. Her performance on the WISC-V Visual Spatial scale was at approximately the 80th percentile for children her age. Similarly, she earned above average scores on the Bender Visual–Motor Gestalt Test (Bender– Gestalt II), which involved copying various designs from a model and drawing them again from memory.

INFORMATION PROCESSING

Basic skills of reading, writing, and math are learned more easily when a student can process information quickly and accurately. This involves being able to pay attention to details, shift attention, and efficiently recognize, remember, and organize bits of information, such as numbers, letters, and words. Millie earned scores in the low average to average range on the WISC-V Cognitive Proficiency and Naming Speed subtests, which tap these skills. On timed tasks that require rapid processing of visual material (Symbol Search, Coding, and Naming Speed Literacy), she worked slowly and carefully, and made no errors. Two of these subtests (Symbol Search and Naming Speed) came near the end of a testing session when Millie was visibly tired, so these scores may underestimate her abilities.

Academic Functioning

The Wechsler Individual Achievement Test—Third Edition (WIAT-III) was administered to assess her current levels of academic achievement in reading, math, and writing. Millie performed below, but close to, average for her age on subtests that involve reading individual words. She adequately read individual sight words (Word Reading), and applied basic rules of phonics in sounding out "non-words" (Pseudoword Decoding). She had some difficulty, however, when asked to read a passage (Oral Reading Fluency). She read slowly, often pausing at long or unfamiliar words, although with good accuracy for the most part. Her understanding of what she read was also weak (Reading Comprehension). She correctly answered most factual questions about the passages she read, but often made mistakes in explaining what occurred or why. These two reading scores together (Reading Comprehension and Fluency) place her passage reading in the below average range, at approximately the 10th percentile.

Millie had considerable difficulty with writing tasks, both in composing single sentences with correct grammar and word usage (Sentence Composition), and in writing a short essay (Essay Composition). She was able to write short, simple sentences (e.g., "I like soccer"), but she struggled to produce complex sentences (writing, for example, "Soccer is my favorite that I am really good at") and did not attempt them for the most part. She used capitalization and punctuation correctly. In her written essay, she made more spelling errors than would be expected given her near-average performance in spelling single words on the Spelling subtest.

Compared to reading and writing, Millie demonstrated strength in math skills. Her knowledge of math facts and arithmetic operations (Numerical Operations) and her ability to apply these operations to math problems (Math Problem Solving) were at, or just above, average for her age. She has a good understanding of how to work with fractions. She solved problems involving time, spatial relations, and geometry with ease.

Ratings by Millie's mother (Mrs. Slade) and teacher (Ms. Hamilton) on the Conners Comprehensive Behavior Rating Scales (Conners CBRS) were consistent with these academic achievement measures. Both raters made note of significant learning problems, with their ratings on the Language items of the Academic Difficulties scale falling at the 99th percentile (lowest 1% for children at her age level). They rated her as average, however, on the Math items of the Academic Difficulties scale.

Social–Emotional Functioning

Ratings by Mrs. Slade and Ms. Hamilton on the Conners CBRS provided information about Millie's social–emotional functioning and behavior. Their ratings were similar for the most part and indicated that Millie, despite her learning problems, is a well-adjusted child. Their ratings of behavior and emotional problems (e.g., aggression, hyperactivity, perfectionist tendencies, and physical symptoms) placed her well within normal range. Her mother rated her level of worrying as slightly higher than typical for age, at approximately the 75th percentile. Overall, parent and teacher ratings were not indicative of emotional distress.

Clinical Impressions

Millie's pleasant and engaging manner, social skills, and social interests have served her well. Her upbeat attitude was apparent during testing and consistent with teacher reports and classroom observations. She welcomes adult help, and does not hesitate to seek it out. Her wish to be like other children her age has motivated her to work hard and to make good use of individualized (i.e., one-to-one) learning opportunities. Keeping up with classmates in regular education classes has made her feel that she is a "capable enough" learner and has helped her to stay motivated and have a positive attitude about school.

Millie has significant difficulty with understanding and use of language, both spoken and written. This was seen in her performance on tests that involved complex sentences and less common vocabulary words and was consistent with teacher reports of using simple language in class. Her language impairment interferes with reading and writing and limits her ability to understand the kind of spoken language that takes place in a middle school classroom.

Millie performed below expected levels for her age in reading rate, reading comprehension, and writing. These are areas that will become even more of a challenge as school subjects become more difficult. In the classroom, Millie tries to make her language problems less obvious by using short, simple sentences when she speaks and writes. By doing so, however, she is not working to improve her language skills.

Test results revealed mild difficulties with information processing. However, it is hard to say how much this contributes to her language-related problems with language and reading. There is little to be learned or gained from further testing of processing difficulties at this time, and it would have little if any bearing on recommendations.

Millie's displayed sound cognitive skills in areas that are less dependent on language. Millie has good math skills. She knows her math facts and understands how to carry out numerical operations. This is consistent with her adequate grades in math over the years. Her visual–spatial skills are an area of strength, and she performed well within average range on tasks requiring nonverbal, logical, mathematical, and social reasoning. These relative strengths are consistent with her artistic and social interests.

Despite her language difficulties, Millie has made adequate progress in academic subjects—enough to allow her to follow along with, and learn from, most regular classroom lessons. However, doing this requires a great deal of effort on her part. She is apt to miss important information when the pace is too rapid or the language is too dense.

Millie is a hard worker and is not easily discouraged. Given the extent of her language difficulties, it is a good sign that she is not further behind academically. This suggests that she has made good use of the modest academic supports available to her in past years.

Summary and Recommendations

Millie has a language impairment that has interfered with her development of reading, writing, and speaking skills and her ability to understand complex and fast-paced language. She has benefited from limited instructional assistance in the past, but will require more consistent and intensive supports to keep up with the academic demands of middle and high school.

Despite the difficulties with language, Millie has cognitive and personal strengths that have helped her to make modest but steady academic progress and to maintain a positive attitude about school. She has solid nonverbal reasoning ability, and her relative strengths in math and in visually based tasks help her to feel competent. She works hard, is not easily discouraged, and participates in classroom activities to the best of her ability. She interacts positively and easily with classmates and adults. Millie is motivated by the desire to be included in regular classroom settings as much as possible.

Given these findings, recommendations are as follows:

1. Millie will need individualized instructional support on a regular basis to keep up in school subjects that involve complex language or challenging reading. In preparation for reading assignments and the introduction of new terms and concepts in class, she will benefit from previewing vocabulary and key words.

2. Millie may need extra time to complete writing assignments of any length or complexity. She should be given extra time to complete tests that place moderate to high demands on language.

3. Millie should be encouraged to read at home. Adults should help her select reading material that is of high interest to her and at an appropriate level of difficulty (i.e., no more than one or two unfamiliar words per paragraph). It may be helpful for her to read aloud to a parent or other individual who can correct errors and engage her in discussion about what she reads.

4. Millie may lose focus as she works on assignments or homework for a long period of time. Teachers and parents might encourage her to take breaks as needed and to reflect on whether this improves her performance.

5. Teachers should be alert to opportunities for Millie to excel at activities that tap into her strong visual–spatial and artistic abilities.

Respectfully submitted,

Robert Lichtenstein, PhD, NCSP

Data Summary

Test scores on the WISC-V, the WIAT-III, and the Bender–Gestalt II are reported below. No set of test score descriptors is universally used by all tests, even though test scores are based on the same statistical model (i.e., a normal curve). While the following descriptors are not an exact match with those proposed by the respective test publishers, they are generally applicable interpretations of *standard scores* that are based on a mean of 100 and a standard deviation of 15, and of *scaled scores* that are based on a mean of 10 and a standard deviation of 3.

Standard Score Descriptors		*Subtest Scaled Score Descriptors*	
Above 130	Extremely high	16 and above	Far above average
116–130	Above average	13–15	Above average
110–115	High average	8–12	Average
90–109	Average	5–7	Below average
85–89	Low average	4 and below	Far below average
70–84	Below average		
Below 70	Extremely low		

Wechsler Intelligence Scale for Children—Fifth Edition

FULL SCALE AND PRIMARY INDEX SCALES

COMPOSITE SCALE	Standard score	Confidence interval (95%)	Percentile rank
Full Scale IQ	99	93–105	47th
Verbal Comprehension Index	84	78–93	14th
Visual Spatial Index	114	105–121	82nd
Fluid Reasoning Index	105	98–112	62nd
Working Memory Index	91	84–99	27th
Processing Speed Index	89	81–99	23rd

PRIMARY INDEX SUBTEST SCORES

Scores in parentheses do not contribute to Primary Index Scales. Subtests in **bold** comprise the Full Scale IQ.

Verbal Comprehension Subtests

SUBTEST	Scaled score
Similarities	9
Vocabulary	5
Comprehension	*(9)*

Fluid Reasoning Subtests

SUBTEST	Scaled score
Matrix Reasoning	10
Figure Weights	12
Arithmetic	*(8)*

Visual Spatial Subtests

SUBTEST	Scaled score
Block Design	14
Visual Puzzles	11

Processing Speed Subtests

SUBTEST	Scaled score
Coding	10
Symbol Search	6

Working Memory Subtests

SUBTEST	Scaled score
Digit Span	9
Picture Span	8
Letter–Number Sequencing	*(7)*

ANCILLARY INDEX AND COMPLEMENTARY INDEX SCALE SCORES

COMPOSITE SCALE	Standard score	Confidence interval (95%)	Percentile rank
Ancillary Index Scales			
Quantitative Reasoning Index	100	94–106	50th
Auditory Working Memory Index	89	83–97	23rd
Nonverbal Index	110	104–115	75th
General Ability Index	100	94–106	50th
Cognitive Proficiency Index	87	81–95	19th
Complementary Index Scale			
Naming Speed Index	89	82–98	23rd

ANCILLARY INDEX SUBTEST SCORES

Quantitative Reasoning Index Subtests

SUBTEST	Scaled score
Figure Weights	12
Arithmetic	8

Auditory Working Memory Index Subtests

SUBTEST	Scaled score
Digit Span	9
Letter–Number Sequencing	7

Cognitive Proficiency Index Subtests

SUBTEST	Scaled score
Digit Span	9
Picture Span	8
Coding	10

Nonverbal Index Subtests

SUBTEST	Scaled score
Block Design	14
Visual Puzzles	11
Matrix Reasoning	10
Figure Weights	12
Picture Span	8
Coding	10

General Ability Index Subtests

SUBTEST	Scaled score
Similarities	8
Vocabulary	6
Block Design	14
Matrix Reasoning	10
Figure Weights	12

COMPLEMENTARY INDEX SCALE SCORES

Naming Speed Index Subtests

SUBTEST	Standard score
Naming Speed Literacy	87
Naming Speed Quantity	96

Wechsler Individual Achievement Test—Third Edition (Age-Based Norms)

COMPOSITE SCALE	Standard score	Confidence interval (95%)	Percentile rank
A. Total Reading	86	81–91	18th
B. Basic Reading	94	90–98	34th
C. Reading Comprehension and Fluency	80	72–88	9th
D. Written Expression	79	72–86	8th
E. Mathematics	103	97–109	58th

SUBTEST*	Standard score	Confidence interval (95%)	Percentile rank
Word Reading (A, B)	92	87–97	30th
Pseudoword Decoding (A, B)	97	92–102	42nd
Oral Reading Fluency (A, C)	82	75–89	12th
Reading Comprehension (A, C)	86	74–98	18th
Sentence Composition (D)	77	66–88	6th
Essay Composition (D)	81	71–91	10th
Spelling (D)	91	85–97	27th
Math Problem Solving (E)	99	91–107	47th
Numerical Operations (E)	107	101–113	68th

*Letters indicate composite scales to which subtests contribute.

Bender Visual–Motor Gestalt Test—Second Edition

PHASE	Standard score	Confidence interval (95%)	Percentile rank
Copy	125	115–131	95th
Recall	110	103–1117	75th

Conners Comprehensive Behavior Rating Scales (CBRS)

The CBRS uses *T* scores, which have a mean of 50 and a standard deviation of 10. Descriptors corresponding to these scores are as follows:

≥ 70   Very elevated—many more concerns than typically reported

65–69   Elevated—more concerns that typically reported

60–64   High average—slightly more concerns than are typically reported

40–59   Average—typical levels of concern

<40   Low—fewer concerns than are typically reported

Scales/Subscales	Parent Report		Teacher Report	
	T score	Percentile	*T* score	Percentile
Emotional Distress	44	27th	41	18th
Upsetting Thoughts	45	31st	N/A	
Worrying	56	73rd	N/A	
Social Problems	43	24th	41	18th
Defiant/Aggressive Behaviors	42	21st	41	18th
Academic Difficulties	68	96th	69	97th
Language	76	99th	75	99th
Math	52	58th	48	42nd
Hyperactivity/Impulsivity	43	24th	41	18th
Separation Fears	44	27th	40	16th
Perfectionist and Compulsive Behaviors	43	24th	41	18th
Violence Potential	44	27th	42	21st
Physical Symptoms	42	21st	40	16th

APPENDIX D3

This report is an example of a focused re-evaluation by a school psychologist, with limited and specific referral questions.

PSYCHOEDUCATIONAL ASSESSMENT REPORT

Student's Name: Millie Slade   **Grade:** 8

School: Madison Middle School   **Age:** 13 years, 11 months

Date Assessed: 1/19/2022   **Date of Birth:** 2/14/2008

Reason for Referral

Millie was referred for a 3-year re-evaluation. While there are no current concerns about her special education services or her academic performance at this time, her parents requested a psychoeducational assessment to review her academic progress and to inform planning for her transition to high school.

Assessment Procedures

Review of records

Teacher, parent, and student interviews

Wechsler Individual Achievement Test, 3rd Edition— selected subtests

Assessment Results

Background information was obtained from school records and from interviews with her mother (Mrs. Slade), two teachers (Ms. Franklin and Ms. Hancock), and Millie.

Background Information and Interview History

As indicated by school records, Millie has received special education services since fifth grade, following an evaluation that identified her as having a significant language impairment. A psychoeducational assessment by this evaluator (R. L.) at that time found that she had difficulty understanding complex and fast-paced language, but showed strengths in nonverbal reasoning, visuospatial abilities, and math. Her initial individualized education program (IEP) included 90 minutes a day of resource room services and weekly individual speech–language therapy. The amount of direct special education services has decreased over the past 2 years. Millie is now included in general education classes for most of the school day, with a single period of resource room support to preview upcoming material in her academic classes and to help her organize homework assignments. Speech and language services have been reduced to teacher consultation only. Her IEP includes the accommodation of extra time on tests and to complete written assignments. Millie has earned passable grades in math and science (mostly B's with some C's) and lower grades (C's and D's) in language arts and social studies. As recommended by her school counselor, Mr. Adams, she does not take a foreign language.

Millie reported that she finds the resource room support to be very helpful. It takes her "a couple hours, maybe longer" to do her homework each night, and she thinks it would be frustrating and "take forever" were it not for the in-school support. In addition to the daily resource room period, she reported that she seeks help after school from one teacher or another about once a week. Millie's science teacher, Ms. Hancock, observed that Millie struggles with the material, but works very hard and, with the aid of the resource room support and the occasional after-school help session, should earn a C grade, possibly even a B– or B.

Her resource room teacher, Ms. Franklin, concurred that Millie makes good use of the resource room support. She spends some resource room time previewing homework assignments, but devotes more time to advance preparation for upcoming lessons in English, science, and history classes. Since Millie is often stumped by academic course vocabulary words, a primary focus of this preparation is looking up unknown words and keeping a written record of them, which she reviews weekly. Ms. Franklin assists Millie with written assignments prior to her submitting them in class. Rather than correcting her work, Ms. Franklin indicates the type of error made, for Millie to then correct. Ms. Franklin reported that Millie's writing continues to be problematic, although the number and severity of errors have decreased somewhat.

Millie acknowledged that the preview and review of academic vocabulary has been helpful. What she finds especially helpful is conferring with Ms. Franklin about how to budget and prioritize her time on homework assignments. She has also found certain study techniques to be helpful, such as reading her written responses out loud and anticipating likely questions on quizzes and tests. She is occasionally invited to study for tests with classmates, but has found that to be less helpful because "I need to work at my own pace."

In a brief phone interview with Millie's mother, Mrs. Slade indicated that Millie's parents are generally satisfied with her school performance and social adjustment. Mrs. Slade noted that Millie has come to accept as necessary the special education services that "keep her on track." She no longer asks to stay home from school at times when she is feeling overwhelmed by schoolwork. Her attendance has been adequate, with approximately 5 to 10 absences each year.

Millie reported that she had played in a recreation league soccer team, but has switched to field hockey and plays on the school team. She sings in the choir and enjoys being part of the group, but says her voice is "nothing special." She hasn't given much thought yet to high school, but hopes it will not present a lot of changes, that is, she hopes to keep the same friends and to remain in general education classes. When asked about postsecondary education and career interests, she said she would like to attend college but had no idea what she wants to study.

Observations

Millie was seen on two occasions—one for testing and for obtaining background information and one for discussing assessment findings and her future plans. She was cooperative with all requests, but was serious and looked worried for the most part. When asked about what worried her, she said she was concerned that if she did poorly, she would be recommended for even more special education services. At our second meeting, Millie appeared cautious and confined herself to brief answers. She was in agreement with, and seemed relieved by, the recommendations that I planned to present.

Test Results

Selected subtests from the Wechsler Individual Achievement Test—Third Edition (WIAT-III) were administered to assess her current levels of academic achievement in reading, math, and writing.

These WIAT-III scores, with a side-by-side comparison to the scores from March 2019, can be found in the Data Summary that accompanies this report.

In comparing current achievement scores with those of her initial evaluation in March 2019, Millie has improved modestly in reading and math, gaining some ground relative to same-age children. Her reading of individual words (i.e., Basic Reading) is solidly at average level for age. She has made good gains in reading comprehension, now scoring well within the average range. However, reading fluency—the rate at which she can read accurately—continues to lag behind.

Overall writing skills remain in the below average range, with scores hovering around the 10th to 20th percentile. Millie showed good improvement in Sentence Composition, largely because she accurately applied the basic rules of punctuation and grammar. However, she still made many syntax errors, as she relies on the slow and effortful strategy of applying learned rules for putting words together correctly, rather than having a sense of what sounds right. She continues to struggle with spelling and with organizing her thoughts in an essay.

Millie again demonstrated good math skills, with scores in the upper part of the Average range. She made moderate gains relative to other children in Math Reasoning.

Conclusions

Millie is compensating well for her language impairment through hard work and good use of available supports in special education (i.e., resource room and speech–language consultation) and in general education (i.e., extra help sessions with teachers). She has managed passing grades in general education courses, which is a considerable accomplishment. Millie is highly motivated to remain in general education courses; in fact, she is troubled by the very thought of not doing so.

Millie showed modest improvements in academic skills of basic reading, reading comprehension, sentence composition, and math reasoning. Writing is now the area of greatest concern. Given her language impairment, she must devote considerable attention to word selection and sentence construction, which leaves her with less mental energy to apply toward organizing ideas. Similarly, her difficulties with spelling consume much mental effort and interfere with her train of thought.

As Millie considers the transition to high school, her clear priorities are to continue in general education and to stay connected with her current group of friends. She has managed to balance school work, extracurricular activities, and socializing, but not without difficulty. These challenges will only intensify in high school. Millie may be inclined to cut back on her high-interest activities in order to keep up with schoolwork. However, this could make for a dismal high school experience and discourage her from academic pursuits in the long run. Alternative solutions, such as a reduced course load, should be considered if and when she is faced with this dilemma.

Recommendations

1. For Millie to remain in general education classes, it is essential that she continue to receive academic support to preview vocabulary and concepts that come up in language-heavy classes and to assist with writing assignments. It will also be important for a special educator to consult with her academic subject teachers at the beginning of each semester to coordinate this support and to ensure they are aware of her special needs.

2. Given Millie's language impairment, she should begin high school with a light load of academic courses and no foreign language. Her school counselor and/or the IEP team should monitor her academic status to determine whether a reduced course load should be continued over time. Similarly, her counselor and/or IEP team should review her academic standing and her interests and consider waiving the foreign language requirement altogether.

3. Millie should be encouraged to pursue electives and extracurricular activities in areas that she enjoys and has experienced success (e.g., graphic arts, choir, and sports).

4. Millie should continue to receive extra time to complete tests with significant written language demands. It may prove that other accommodations, such as a note taker or audio recording of lecture material, are more beneficial. Millie should confer with her school counselor, with input from teachers, about the value and necessity of various accommodations.

Respectfully submitted,

Robert Lichtenstein, PhD., NCSP

DATA SUMMARY

Wechsler Individual Achievement Test—Third Edition (Age-Based Norms)

COMPOSITE SCALE	Current (January 2022)			Previous (March 2019)		
	Standard score	Confidence interval (95%)	Percentile	Standard score	Confidence interval (95%)	Percentile
A. Total Reading	93	88–98	32nd	86	81–91	18th
B. Basic Reading	101	97–105	53rd	94	90–98	34th
C. Reading Comprehension and Fluency	86	78–94	18th	80	72–88	9th
D. Written Expression	82	75–89	12th	79	72–86	8th
E. Mathematics	110	93–117	75th	103	97–109	58th

SUBTEST*	Standard score	Confidence interval (95%)	Percentile	Standard score	Confidence interval (95%)	Percentile
Word Reading (A, B)	103	97–109	58th	92	87–97	30th
Pseudoword Decoding (A, B)	101	96–106	53rd	97	92–102	42nd
Oral Reading Fluency (A, C)	84	77–91	14th	82	75–89	12th
Reading Comprehension (A, C)	96	85–107	39th	86	74–98	18th
Sentence Composition (D)	88	78–98	21st	77	66–88	6th
Essay Composition (D)	82	72–92	12th	81	71–91	10th
Spelling (D)	87	80–94	19th	91	85–97	27th
Math Problem Solving (E)	110	102–118	75th	99	91–107	47th
Numerical Operations (E)	108	99–117	70th	107	101–113	68th

*Letters indicate composite scales to which subtests contribute.

WIAT-III Standard Score Descriptors

Above 145	Very superior
131–145	Superior
116–130	Above average
85–115	Average
70–84	Below average
55–69	Low
Below 55	Very low

APPENDIX D4

This is an example of a letter to parents that briefly summarizes the findings of a special education re-evaluation.

PARENT FEEDBACK LETTER

Dear Mr. and Mrs. Slade,

I am writing to provide you with this brief summary of the findings from my recent re-evaluation of your daughter Millie at age 13 years, 11 months. It is my understanding that you wanted to know how she is doing academically and what would help her successfully transition to high school.

I previously evaluated Millie 3 years ago and found that she has a significant language impairment for which special education service are warranted. In conducting the current re-evaluation, I reviewed her school records, interviewed Millie and two of her teachers, and administered some academic achievement tests. You should have received a copy of the full report of this re-evaluation.

Millie's progress has been commendable—the result of a positive attitude and hard work. She has earned passing grades, with better performance in math and science than in language arts and social studies. Millie does the same work as other students in her classes, aided by supplemental special education services and extra time on tests and writing assignments. She has made good use of resource room support. She has found especially helpful teacher assistance with previewing homework assignments and studying vocabulary words that will come up in classes with high language demands (i.e., English, history, social studies, and science). What has also been helpful is the resource room teacher, Ms. Franklin, pointing out errors in written assignments for Millie to correct prior to submitting in class.

Since her initial evaluation in March 2019, Millie has shown some nice gains in reading. Her ability to read individual words and to comprehend what she has read is now within average range for her age. However, she continues to read slowly. Written language is her biggest challenge. Sentence construction does not come easily to her, and she continues to struggle with spelling and with organizing her thoughts in an essay. Millie continues to do well in math, with average or better skills in calculation and reasoning.

Millie is very invested in taking regular education courses like her friends. She has worked hard and taken advantage of all available help in order to make this possible. It is important to her that she continue to be in "mainstream" classes in high school. I strongly support this goal. It is beneficial to Millie's self-esteem, and it helps her to maintain a positive attitude about school and to stay connected with friends. Keeping her life in balance and supporting her sense of well-being should be a high priority. Millie should be encouraged to pursue elective courses and extracurricular activities in areas that she enjoys and has experienced success (e.g., graphic arts, choir, and sports).

Keeping up with class assignments may become more difficult when she is faced with more challenging material at the high school level. It will be important to monitor how well she is keeping up, and with how much support needed and how much effort on her part. It may be advisable at some point to consider a reduced course load, additional accommodations such as audio recording of lecture presentations, and waiving the foreign language requirement altogether. With special education supports in place and with her continuing hard work, good attitude, and receptiveness to instructional aids, I am optimistic that Millie will continue to learn and to progress in school.

I have enjoyed working with Millie and have appreciated your concerted efforts to understand and support her educational needs. Please do not hesitate to contact me with any questions or concerns.

Kind regards,

Robert Lichtenstein, PhD
Nationally Certified School Psychologist

Background Information Outline and Case Example

BACKGROUND INFORMATION OUTLINE

The topics below should be routinely considered for inclusion in the Background Information section. Start by identifying the sources of information. For example, "Background information was obtained from Kristina, from her parents, Robert and Whitney Gray, from her pediatrician, from her teachers at Southwest High School, and from prior evaluation reports."

Then, address relevant topics, in separate paragraphs, in approximately the order shown. Sample material that may fall under broad topics is also listed.

1. Introduction

Identify the child with one or two positive descriptors and provide basic identifying information (e.g., age, grade, school or program placement, family structure, town).

2. Current Functioning

Start with presenting issues, either cognitive/academic or behavioral/psychiatric, depending on which ones are more relevant to the referral questions. Note the onset, frequency, duration, and severity of symptoms, as needed.

Cognitive/Academic Functioning

Educational disability (e.g., learning disability, speech and language impairment)

Cognitive ability

Academic performance

Productivity in school; homework completion

Attention; concentration

Vision, hearing, or sensorimotor impairment

Behavioral/Psychiatric Functioning

Psychiatric diagnosis (e.g., ADHD, psychosis) – According to whom? When?

Symptoms (e.g., tics, mania)

Areas of dysfunction (e.g., anxiety, depression, disruptive behavior)

Trauma

Peer relations

School-related anxiety or depression

Behavior problems; discipline infractions

3. Assets

Strengths

What is the child good at?

Admirable qualities/characteristics

Activities

Friendships/peers

Group membership

Hobbies, special interests

Extracurricular activities: athletics, performing arts, etc.

4. Family History

Who is in the family?

Parent employment

Ages and personalities of siblings

How do they all get along?

Family stressors that may contribute to current concerns

Family history of learning; psychiatric problems

5. Educational History

Schools attended

Areas of strength and weakness

Early difficulty in reading or math?

Grade retention?

Special services (e.g., special education, 504 services, Tier 2 or 3 supports)

Related services (counseling, speech/language therapy, social skills group, etc.)

6. Mental Health History

Treatment history—now and past

Psychotherapy—Who, when, focus, etc.

Medication—What and how frequent? Anything else tried? Who prescribed?

Other treatment (e.g., home mentor, hospitalization, group treatment)

7. Developmental History

Pregnancy and birth history

Milestones: Gross motor, fine motor, language

Early temperament

Early stressors (e.g., separation, family stress, maternal depression)

8. Medical History

Current health status (healthy; any problems?)

Name of pediatrician, if cited as information source

History of seizure, concussion, loss of consciousness, chronic illness (e.g., asthma, diabetes), hospitalization, surgery

Sleep and eating habits

9. Summary of Prior Evaluations

Summarize key points, or state, "X has had no prior evaluations."

CASE EXAMPLE

Reason for Referral

Shawn is a friendly 10-year-old boy who has been receiving special education and related services since first grade. He has been diagnosed with attention-deficit/hyperactivity disorder (ADHD). His parents initiated this re-evaluation to better understand why he is not performing well in school.

Background Information

Background information was obtained from Shawn, from his parents A. and G. Carter, from his primary teacher at King School, Ms. E., from his pediatrician, Dr. M., from school records, and from prior evaluation reports.

Shawn was described by his parents as a sociable, compassionate, and cooperative boy. However, he struggles with many tasks both at school and at home. His parents feel that his factual memory is fine but he has trouble applying skills. He follows only the first step when given multistep directions. Shawn's current classroom teacher, Ms. E., described him as a kind boy, eager to please, who is perceptive regarding the feelings of others.

Shawn's parents reported that he was diagnosed as having ADHD by Dr. M in 2014. They report that he has frequent worries, such as what will happen if someone breaks into his family's house (this has not previously happened) and whether or not his brother will get hurt if he tips back in his chair. He tends to overfocus on a topic or concern. Peer relationships are hard for him, as he tends to act in immature ways. He has one ongoing friend and he has begun to play with two children in his neighborhood. Shawn has a history of vocal tics that were precipitated by stimulant medication. He has no history of traumatic experience.

As reported by Shawn's parents, his father and his current adoptive mother married in 2014. They then had a son, Eric, who is now 2 years of age. Mr. Carter works as a system engineer for a large retail business. Mrs. Carter works as an educator. Shawn's biological mother, Z., provided for him lovingly, although she was ill for some time prior to her death, when he was 4. Shawn has received much attention from his grandparents. There is no family history of learning, developmental, or psychiatric disorders.

School records indicate that Shawn is currently repeating the fourth grade. Shawn has received special education services since first grade. His initial disability category of developmental delay was changed to other health impairment/ADHD in 2016. According to his current individualized educational plan (IEP), dated 2/11/19, he receives specialized instruction in mathematics, speech/language therapy, and school-based counseling. Several instructional accommodations are listed as well. Ms. E. reported that his oral reading is accurate, but his comprehension is weak. He also omits small words when reading. He has difficulty moving from basic knowledge to higher-level problem solving. Ms. E. rated his performance in social studies as being "at grade level," with performance in reading, writing, and science being "somewhat below grade level," and performance in grammar and mathematics being "far below grade level."

Shawn has received counseling off-and-on from the school adjustment counselor. He has had no other behavioral health intervention, other than a short period of medical treatment for ADHD.

Regarding developmental and medical histories, Shawn was born premature at 31 weeks, with a birth weight of 3 pounds, 2 ounces. He spent 2 months in the neonatal intensive care unit, with common complications of lung problems and mild vision problems (retinopathy). Shawn's early motor development was delayed. His language development was normal. Shawn has no history of seizure or head injury. He is healthy at present. Shawn wears eyeglasses to improve his acuity. He sometimes has problems with eye convergence, which cause him to see double. His pediatrician is Dr. T.

Shawn had a series of school-based evaluations in late 2016. The results of a psychological evaluation, done by school psychologist, S. M., indicated that his general aptitude for academic learning was average, at approximately the 50th percentile, with much stronger nonverbal/spatial than verbal abilities. Shawn's working memory was exceptionally strong (at approximately the 90th percentile). Problematic attention and anxiety were noted as well. Shawn's academic basic skills were assessed by the King School special education teacher, M. K. Shawn showed strong reading decoding but mildly weak comprehension. His math skills were also mildly weak. Shawn's writing skills were average at the level of writing sentences and low average when asked to write a brief essay. His spelling skills were average. The results of a speech-and-language evaluation, done by M. J., yielded largely normal results, including age-appropriate phonological awareness and naming speed, but with some weakness in using words to describe relationships between concepts.

Data Summary Template

No set of test score descriptors is universally used by all tests, even though test scores are based on the same statistical model (i.e., a normal curve). While the following descriptors are not an exact match with the descriptors proposed by the respective test publishers, they are generally applicable interpretations of *standard scores* that are based on a mean of 100 and a standard deviation of 15, and of *scaled scores* that are based on a mean of 10 and a standard deviation of 3.

Standard score	Percentile rank	Descriptor
Above 130	> 98	Extremely high
116–130	85–98	High
110–115	75–84	High average
91–109	27–73	Average
85–90	16–25	Low average
70–84	2–15	Low
Below 70	< 2	Extremely low

Scaled score	Descriptor
16 and above	Far above average
13–15	Above average
8–12	Average
5–7	Below average
4 and below	Far below average

Note. When using the format above, the test-specific descriptors listed below are deleted.

Wechsler Intelligence Scale for Children—5th Edition (WISC-V)

Full Scale and Primary Index Scales

These composite scores are based on a mean of 100 and standard deviation of 15. Scores of 90–109 are considered to be within the Average range (see descriptors below).

SCALE	Composite score	Confidence interval (95%)	Percentile rank	Range
Full Scale IQ				
Verbal Comprehension Index				
Visual Spatial Index				
Fluid Reasoning Index				
Working Memory Index				
Processing Speed Index				

Ancillary Index and Complementary Index Scale Scores

These composite scores are based on a mean of 100 and standard deviation of 15. Scores of 90–109 are considered to be within the Average range.

SCALE	Composite score	Confidence interval (95%)	Percentile rank	Range
Ancillary Index Scales				
Quantitative Reasoning Index				
Auditory Working Memory Index				
Nonverbal Index				
General Ability Index				
Cognitive Proficiency Index				
Complementary Index Scales				
Naming Speed Index				
Symbol Translation Index				
Storage and Retrieval Index				

WISC-V Composite Score Range Descriptors

130 and above	Extremely high
120–129	Very high
110–119	High average
90–109	Average
80–89	Low average
70–79	Very low
69 and below	Extremely low

Primary Index Subtest Scores

Subtest scaled scores are based on a scale of 1–19, with a mean of 10 and standard deviation of 3. Scores of 8–12 are considered to be within Average range. (See descriptors below.)

Supplemental subtests, shown in *italics,* do not contribute to Primary Index scores. Only the subtests shown in **bold** contribute to the Full Scale IQ.

Verbal Comprehension Subtests

SUBTEST	Scaled score
Similarities	
Vocabulary	
Information	( )
Comprehension	( )

Fluid Reasoning Subtests

SUBTEST	Scaled score
Matrix Reasoning	
Figure Weights	
Picture Concepts	( )
Arithmetic	( )

Visual Spatial Subtests

SUBTEST	Scaled score
Block Design	
Visual Puzzles	

Working Memory Subtests

SUBTEST	Scaled score
Digit Span	
Picture Span	
Letter–Number Sequencing	( )

Processing Speed Subtests

SUBTEST	Scaled score
Coding	
Symbol Search	
Cancellation	( )

Ancillary Index Subtest Scores

Quantitative Reasoning Index Subtests

SUBTEST	Scaled score
Figure Weights	
Arithmetic	

Auditory Working Memory Index Subtests

SUBTEST	Scaled score
Digit Span	
Letter–Number Sequencing	

Nonverbal Index Subtests

SUBTEST	Scaled score
Block Design	
Visual Puzzles	
Matrix Reasoning	
Figure Weights	
Picture Span	
Coding	

General Ability Index Subtests

SUBTEST	Scaled score
Similarities	
Vocabulary	
Block Design	
Matrix Reasoning	
Figure Weights	

Cognitive Proficiency Index Subtests

SUBTEST	Scaled score
Digit Span	
Picture Span	
Coding	
Symbol Search	

Subtest Score Range Descriptors

16 and above	Far above average
13–15	Above average
8–12	Average
5–7	Below average
4 and below	Far below average

Complementary Index Subtest Scores

Naming Speed Index Subtests

SUBTEST	Standard score
Naming Speed Literacy	
Naming Speed Quantity	

Symbol Translation Index Subtests

SUBTEST	Standard score
Immediate Symbol Translation	
Delayed Symbol Translation	
Recognition Symbol Translation	

Wechsler Individual Achievement Test—3rd Edition (WIAT-III)

WIAT-III composite and subtest scores are based on a mean of 100 and a standard deviation of 15. Scores of 90–110 are considered to be within the Average range (see descriptors below).

COMPOSITE SCALE	Composite score	Confidence interval (95%)	Percentile rank	Range
A. Total Reading				
B. Basic Reading				
C. Reading Comprehension and Fluency				
D. Written Expression				

SUBTEST[a]	Standard score	Confidence interval (95%)	Percentile rank	Range
Early Reading Skills				
Word Reading (A, B)				
Pseudoword Decoding (A, B)				
Reading Comprehension (A, C)				
Oral Reading Fluency (A, C)				
Alphabet Writing Fluency (D)				
Sentence Composition (D)				
Spelling (D)				

[a]Letters indicate composite scales to which subtests contribute.

Composite Score Range Descriptors

Above 145	Very superior
131–145	Superior
116–130	Above average
85–115	Average
70–84	Below average
55–69	Low
Below 55	Very low

Comprehensive Test of Phonological Process—2nd Edition (CTOPP-2)

COMPOSITE SCALE	Composite score	Confidence interval (95%)	Percentile rank	Range
Phonological Awareness				
Phonological Memory				
Rapid Naming				

CTOPP-2 composite scores are based on a mean of 100 and a standard deviation of 15. Scores of 90–110 are considered to be within the Average range.

Phonological Awareness Subtests		Rapid Naming Subtests	
SUBTEST	**Scaled score**	**SUBTEST**	**Scaled score**
Elision		Rapid Digit Naming	
Blending Words		Rapid Letter Naming	
Phoneme Isolation		Rapid Color Naming	
		Rapid Object Naming	

Phonological Memory Subtests	
SUBTEST	**Scaled score**
Memory for Digits	
Nonword Repetition	

Subtest Score Range Descriptors

17–20	Very superior	6–7	Below average
15–16	Superior	4–5	Poor
13–14	Above average	1–3	Very poor
8–12	Average		

Bender Visual–Motor Gestalt Test—2nd Edition (Bender–Gestalt-II)

Bender–Gestalt standard scores are based on a mean of 100 and a standard deviation of 15. Scores of 90– 109 are considered to be within the Average range.

PHASE	Standard score	Confidence interval (95%)	Percentile rank	Range
Copy				
Recall				

Standard Score Range Descriptors

145 and above	Extremely high	80–89	Low average
130–144	Very high	70–79	Low
120–129	High	55–69	Very low
110–119	High average	54 and below	Extremely low
90–109	Average		

Differential Ability Scales—2nd Edition (DAS-II)

SCALE/Subtest	Standard score	*T* score	Confidence interval (95%)	Percentile rank	Qualitative range
General Conceptual Ability (GCA)					
[Special Nonverbal Composite]					
Verbal Ability					
Verbal Comprehension					
Naming Vocabulary					
Verbal Similarities					
Word Definitions					
Nonverbal Reasoning Ability					
Picture Similarities					
Matrices					
Sequential and Quantitative Reasoning					
Spatial Ability					
Recall of Designs					
Pattern Construction					
Copying					
DIAGNOSTIC SUBTESTS					
Recall of Objects— Immediate					
Recall of Objects—Delayed					
Recall of Digits Forward					
Recognition of Pictures					
Phonological Processing					
Working Memory					
Recall of Sequential Order					
Recall of Digits Backward					
Processing Speed					
Speed of Info. Processing					
Rapid Naming					
School Readiness					
Early Number Concepts					
Matching Letter-Like Forms					
Phonological Processing					

Standard Scores for the DAS-II have a mean (average) of 100 and a standard deviation of 15.

T scores have a mean of 50 and a standard deviation of 10. For the DAS-II, T scores from 43 to 57 (approximately the 25th– 75th percentile) are considered to be within the average range.

INTERPRETATION OF RATING SCALE SCORES

The following descriptors are generally applicable interpretations of clinical rating scales that use *T* scores, which have a mean of 50 and a standard deviation of 10.

T score	Descriptor
≥ 70	Very elevated—many more concerns than typically reported
60–69	Elevated—more concerns than typically reported
40–59	Average—typical levels of concern
<40	Low—better than average; fewer concerns

Note: When using the format above, the test-specific descriptors listed below are deleted.

Behavior Rating Inventory of Executive Function—2nd Edition (BRIEF–2)

The BRIEF–2 (and/or Conners–3) uses *T* scores, which have a mean of 50 and a standard deviation of 10. Descriptors corresponding to these scores are as follows:

T score	Descriptor
≥ 70	Very elevated—many more concerns than typically reported
60–69	Elevated—more concerns than typically reported
40–59	Average—typical levels of concern
<40	Low—better than average; fewer concerns

SCALE/INDEX	Teacher Report		Parent 1 Report		Parent 2 Report		Self-Report	
	T	Percentile	T	Percentile	T	Percentile	T	Percentile
Inhibit								
Shift								
Emotional Control								
Behavioral Regulation Index								
Initiate								
Working Memory								
Plan/Organize								
Organization of Materials								
Monitor								
Task Completion								
Metacognition Index								
Global Executive Composite								

Conners 3rd Edition (Conners–3)

SCALE/INDEX	Parent Report		Teacher Report		Self-Report	
	T	Percentile	T	Percentile	T	Percentile
CONTENT SCALES						
Inattention						
Hyperactivity/Impulsivity						
Learning Problems						
Executive Functioning						
Aggression						
Peer/Family Relations						
SYMPTOM SCALES						
ADHD Inattentive						
ADHD Hyperactive–Impulsive						
Conduct Disorder						
Oppositional Defiant Disorder						
ADHD Index						
Global Index						

Behavior Assessment System for Children—Third Edition (BASC-3)

The BASC-3 uses T scores, which have a mean of 50 and a standard deviation of 10. Descriptors corresponding to these scores differ for clinical scales and for adaptive scales, as follows:

T score	Clinical scales	Adaptive scales
≥ 70	Clinically significant	Very high
60–69	At-risk	High
41–59	Average	Average
31–40	Low	At-risk
≤ 30	Very low	Clinically significant

	Teacher Report		Parent Report	
SCALE/INDEX	T	Percentile	T	Percentile
COMPOSITE SCORES				
Externalizing Problems				
Internalizing Problems				
School Problems				
Adaptive Skills				
Behavioral Symptoms Index				
Clinical Scales				
Hyperactivity				
Aggression				
Conduct Problems				
Anxiety				
Depression				
Somatization				
Attention Problems				
Learning Problems				
Atypicality				
Withdrawal				
Adaptive Scales				
Adaptability				
Social Skills				
Leadership				
Study Skills				
Functional Communication				

(continued)

	Teacher Report		Parent Report	
SCALE/INDEX	*T*	Percentile	*T*	Percentile
Content Scales				
Anger Control				
Bullying				
Developmental Social Disorders				
Emotional Self-Control				
Executive Functioning				
Negative Emotionality				
Resiliency				
Clinical Indexes				
ADHD Probability Index				
EBD Probability Index				
Autism Probability Index				
Functional Impairment Index				

BASC-3 Self-Report of Personality

SCALE/INDEX	*T*	Percentile
COMPOSITE SCORES		
School Problems		
Internalizing Problems		
Inattention/Hyperactivity		
Emotional Symptoms		
Personal Adjustment		
Clinical Scales		
Attitude to School		
Attitude to Teachers		
Sensation Seeking		
Atypicality		
Locus of Control		
Social Stress		
Anxiety		
Depression		
Sense of Inadequacy		
Somatization		
Attention Problems		
Hyperactivity		

(continued)

SCALE/INDEX	*T*	Percentile
Adaptive Scales		
Relations with Parents		
Interpersonal Relations		
Self-Esteem		
Self-Reliance		
Content Scales		
Anger Control		
Ego Strength		
Mania		
Text Anxiety		
Executive Functioning		
Negative Emotionality		
Resiliency		
Clinical Index		
Functional Impairment Index		

Report-Writing Rubric

Note. Some elements in the Needs Improvement and Problematic columns cite multiple issues. The evaluator or supervisor should circle issues that are applicable to clarify the basis for these ratings.

	PROFICIENT/ SATISFACTORY (3)	NEEDS IMPROVEMENT (2)	PROBLEMATIC (1)
1. Overall Organization	Report includes all sections pertinent to the assessment.	A section is missing or misplaced; some sections contain material that belongs elsewhere.	Report deviates problematically from recommended section organization and content.
2. Reason for Referral	Reason for referral concisely identifies key child-specific questions and concerns.	Reason for referral includes some irrelevant information, omits key points, or is overly generic or detailed.	Reason for referral is highly irrelevant or far too detailed.
3. Assessment Procedures	Selected procedures are appropriate and sufficient to address referral question(s) and hypotheses.	Absence of an important data source reduces the capacity to address referral question(s) and hypotheses, or unnecessary or inappropriate procedures are included.	Selected procedures are clearly inappropriate or insufficient to address referral question(s) and hypotheses.

	PROFICIENT/ SATISFACTORY (3)	NEEDS IMPROVEMENT (2)	PROBLEMATIC (1)
4. Background Information	Background information is well organized.	Some background information is somewhat disorganized.	Background information is highly disorganized.
5. Background Information	Background information fully attributes sources and adequately protects client privacy.	Some background information does not attribute sources.	Background information fails to protect client privacy.
6. Background Information	Background information is sufficient, relevant, and appropriate.	Background information is somewhat insufficient or includes some inappropriate or irrelevant material.	Background information is highly insufficient or inappropriate or includes much irrelevant material.
7. Behavioral Observations	Observations are low inference, and meaningfully and clearly distinguish the child from others.	Some observations are overly inferential, or fail to distinguish the child from others.	Observations are lacking, inappropriate, or highly inferential.
8. Behavioral Observations	Observations are pertinent to referral questions and provide insight into the child's functioning.	Observations provide limited insight into referral questions and the child's functioning.	Observations are lacking or provide little insight into referral questions and the child's functioning.
9. Thematic Organization of Test/Assessment Results	Assessment results are organized by themes or areas of functioning, which are appropriately titled and relevant to the given case.	Assessment results are organized by themes or areas of functioning, but are heavily influenced by test structure or include areas with little relevance to the given case.	Assessment results are organized by tests administered.
10. Test Results	Test results are presented in a manner that appropriately considers measurement error.	Test results are presented with limited or inconsistent recognition of measurement error.	Test results are presented with no recognition of measurement error.
11. Test Results	Test results are reported selectively, with emphasis on key findings and minimal attention to trivial or uninterpretable results.	Test results are reported with some selectivity; too much attention to trivial or uninterpretable results or to description of tests and tasks.	All test results are reported regardless of importance, and with equal emphasis.
12. Test Results	Test results are presented in an understandable and meaningful manner, using sample responses and/or qualitative data to clarify findings.	Test results are presented with some confusion or with insufficient elaboration to understand findings.	Test results are presented in a misleading or incomprehensible manner or with no clarifying elaboration.

	PROFICIENT/ SATISFACTORY (3)	NEEDS IMPROVEMENT (2)	PROBLEMATIC (1)
13. Thematic Organization of Clinical Impressions	Clinical impressions are organized by themes or areas of functioning and are relevant to referral question(s) and concerns.	Clinical impressions are organized by themes or areas, but include material with little relevance to referral question(s) and concerns.	Clinical impressions are very limited or include material that is irrelevant to referral question(s) and concerns.
14. Clinical Impressions	Clinical impressions are highly consistent with findings.	Clinical impressions are somewhat consistent with findings.	Clinical impressions are highly inconsistent with findings.
15. Clinical Impressions	Clinical impressions make optimal use of integrated findings from multiple assessment sources.	Clinical impressions make limited use of integrated findings from multiple assessment sources.	Clinical impressions do not integrate findings from multiple assessment sources.
16. Clinical Impressions	Clinical impressions effectively address all referral questions, and provide valuable insight into the child's life and functioning.	Clinical impressions adequately address most referral questions, and provide some insight into the child's life and functioning.	Clinical impressions inadequately address referral questions, and provide little insight into the child's life and functioning.
17. Summary	Summary is concise, highlights key findings, and addresses referral questions; no new information is introduced.	Summary is too long or short, fails to selectively highlight key finding and referral questions, or introduces new information.	Summary is far too long or short, fails to highlight key finding and referral questions, or introduces much new information.
18. Summary	Summary is selective and concise, with no new information.	Summary is overly long or detailed or introduces some new information.	Summary is far too long or detailed or introduces much new information.
19. Summary	Summary clearly addresses referral questions and key findings; the child, rather than assessment data, is the focus.	Summary does not fully or clearly address referral questions, omits key findings, or includes some irrelevant or confusing material.	Summary fails to address referral questions or key findings or includes much irrelevant or confusing material.
20. Recommendations	Recommendations are consistent with reported findings in Clinical Impressions and Summary.	Recommendations are somewhat inconsistent with reported findings in Clinical Impressions and Summary.	Recommendations are highly inconsistent with reported findings in Clinical Impressions and Summary.
21. Recommendations	Recommendations are clinically or procedurally sound, practical, and applicable to the individual child.	Recommendations could be more clinically sound, practical, or applicable to the individual child, or pose procedural problems.	Recommendations are unfounded, impractical, generic, missing, or pose major procedural problems.

	PROFICIENT/ SATISFACTORY (3)	NEEDS IMPROVEMENT (2)	PROBLEMATIC (1)
22. Data Summary	Data Summary follows the report and includes all scores, clearly labeled, along with essential related data (e.g., percentiles, confidence intervals) and interpretive guidance.	Data Summary has missing or problematically presented scores or related data, or lacks sufficient interpretive guidance.	Data Summary is missing or misplaced, or misinforms the reader because of serious errors.
23. Writing	Avoids jargon, technical terms, and complex language; terms unfamiliar to a teacher or parent are accompanied by definitions or explanations.	Some avoidable use of jargon, technical terms, and complex language; technical terms are not adequately defined or explained.	Much jargon, technical terms, and complex language; no attempt to define or explain technical terms.
24. Writing	Writing is clear and concise, with well-constructed paragraphs and sentences, and is carefully proofread for mechanical errors and typos.	Writing is unclear or confusing in parts, includes some poorly constructed paragraphs and sentences, or is insufficiently proofread for mechanical errors and typos.	Writing is very unclear or confusing, has many poorly constructed paragraphs and sentences, or is replete with mechanical errors and typos.
25. Follow-Up	Follow-up procedures with one or more consumers (e.g., teachers, parents, child) provide detailed information about the value of the assessment and the extent to which recommendations were followed.	Follow-up procedures with one or more consumers provide limited information about the value of the assessment and the extent to which recommendations were followed.	No follow-up procedures were conducted to ascertain the value of the assessment and the extent to which recommendations were followed.

Report Author: _____

Evaluator/Supervisor: _____

Date Reviewed: _____

Readability Level: _____

Score: _____ of _____

Comments: _____

_____

Feedback Conference Simulation

CASE PRESENTATION GUIDELINES

Using one of your assessment case studies, you will simulate providing feedback to an IEP team that consists of typical participants (e.g., parent(s), teacher(s), administrator, other education specialist). Set the stage however you choose. Specify the reason for the meeting (e.g., initial evaluation, 3-year re-evaluation, review of updated assessments) and indicate who is in attendance (assign roles). You can assign parts in the form of general instructions or a script (e.g., what the parent might ask or contribute).

Plan on spending about 6–8 minutes for the presentation, followed by 10–15 minutes of debriefing and case-related discussion. Bring copies of the Data Summary for the group to consider during the debriefing session. Your presentation should address the points below. Each category will be graded on a 5-point scale.

1. Relationship with Parents and Team Members
   a. Establish a welcoming, respectful climate for the parent.
   b. Actively encourage parent participation.
   d. Recognize and support the expertise of other team members.
   d. Use "people skills" (door openers, reflective listening, etc.) in responding to others.

2. Tone and Delivery
   a. Confident, relaxed manner.
   b. Good eye contact.
   d. Engaging, fluid, conversational tone.
   d. Work from an outline or brief notes, rather than from a script or the report.

3. Presentation of Data

    a. Clear, nontechnical description of assessment: general purpose and methods.

    b. Avoid unnecessary jargon; explain relevant terms in everyday language.

    d. Present results in a nontechnical manner (e.g., ranges, approximate percentiles).

    d. Use examples of test performance or behavior to illustrate key points.

4. Findings/Focus (Content)

    a. Convey a sense of the child.

    b. Highlight the child's strengths and positive attributes.

    d. Address referral questions and concerns.

    d. Focus on *key* findings, rather than on trivial and irrelevant data.

    e. Relate findings to the child's school performance and behavior.

    f. Summarize key findings to set the stage for recommendations.

    g. Provide input into IEP team decisions without overstepping the team role.

Post-conference Discussion

- The presenter reflects on her/his performance.
- Classmates and TA offer positive observations and feedback. What was done well?
- Discuss the case, including the interpretation of findings and their implications for presentation.

    The TA or instructor will provide written feedback afterward using the evaluation form.

CASE PRESENTATION EVALUATION FORM

	Inadequate	Weak	Fair	Good	Excellent
	1	2	3	4	5

1. **Relations with Parents and Team Members**   1   2   3   4   5

    a. Establishes a welcoming, respectful climate for the parent.

    b. Explicitly encourages parent participation.

    d. Recognizes and supports the expertise of other team members.

    d. Uses people skills (door openers, reflective listening, etc.) in responding to others.

    Comments:

2. **Tone and Delivery**   1   2   3   4   5

    a. Confident, relaxed manner.

    b. Good eye contact.

    d. Engaging, fluid, conversational tone.

    d. Works from an outline or brief notes, rather than from a script or the report. [Apptext]
    Comments:

3. **Presentation of Data**   1   2   3   4   5

    a. Clear, nontechnical description of assessment: purpose, methods, interactions.

    b. Avoids unnecessary jargon; explains relevant terms in everyday language.

    d. Presents results in a nontechnical manner (e.g., ranges, approximate percentiles).

    d. Uses examples of test performance or behavior to illustrate key points.

    Comments:

(continued)

4. **Findings/Focus**   1   2   3   4   5
   a. Conveys a sense of the child.
   b. Highlights the child's strengths and positive attributes.
   d. Addresses referral questions and concerns.
   d. Focuses on *key* findings, rather than on trivial and irrelevant data.
   e. Relates findings to child's school performance and behavior.
   f. Summarizes key findings to set the stage for recommendations.
   g. Provides input into IEP Team decisions without overstepping the team role.

Comments:

Other observations/comments:

Student: _____

Evaluator: _____

Score: _____

References

Ackerman, M. J. (2006). Forensic report writing. *Journal of Clinical Psychology, 62*(1), 59–72.

Adelman, H. S., & Taylor, L. (2012). Mental health in schools: Moving in new directions. *Contemporary School Psychology, 16*, 9–18.

Allen, R. A., & Hanchon, T. A. (2013). What can we learn from school-based emotional disturbance assessment practices? Implications for practice and preparation in school psychology. *Psychology in the Schools, 50*(3), 290–299.

Allyn, J. B. (2012). *Writing to clients and referring professionals about psychological assessment results: A handbook of style and grammar.* New York: Routledge.

American Board of Clinical Neuropsychology. (2017). Guidelines for practice samples in clinical neuropsychology. Retrieved from *www.abpp.org/i4a/pages/index.cfm?pageid=3403.*

American Educational Research Association, American Psychological Association, & National Council on Measurement in Education. (2014). *Standards for educational and psychological testing.* Washington, DC: Author.

American Psychiatric Association. (2013). *Diagnostic and statistical manual of mental disorders* (5th ed.). Arlington, VA: Author.

American Psychological Association. (2017). Ethical principles of psychologists and code of conduct (2002, Amended June 1, 2010, and January 1, 2017). Retrieved from *www.apa.org/ethics/code/index.aspx.*

Andren, K. J. (2013). Conducting problem-solving interviews. In R. Brown-Chidsey & K. J. Andren

(Eds.), *Assessment for intervention: A problem-solving approach* (2nd ed., pp. 144–156). New York: Guilford Press.

Andrews, D. A., & Hoge, R. D. (2010). *Evaluation for risk of violence in juveniles.* New York: Oxford University Press

APA Presidential Task Force on Evidence-Based Practice. (2006). Evidence-based practice in psychology. *American Psychologist, 61*(4), 271–285.

Belk, M. S., LoBello, S. G., Ray, G. E., & Zachar, P. (2002). WISC-III administration, clerical, and scoring errors made by student examiners. *Journal of Psychoeducational Assessment, 20*, 290–300.

Bierman, K. L, Domitrovich, C. E., Nix, R. L., Gest, S. D., Walsh, J. A., Greenberg, M. T., et al. (2008). Promoting academic and social–emotional school readiness: The Head Start REDI program. *Child Development, 79*(6), 1802–1817.

Bolton, R. (1979). *People skills: How to assert yourself, listen to others, and resolve conflicts.* New York: Simon & Schuster.

Braaten, E. (2007). *The child clinician's report-writing handbook.* New York: Guilford Press.

Bramlett, R. K., Murphy, J. J., Johnson, J., Wallingsford, L., & Hall, J. D. (2002). Contemporary practices in school psychology: A national survey on roles and referral problems. *Psychology in the Schools, 39*, 327–335.

Brenner, E. (2003). Consumer-focused psychological assessment. *Professional Psychology: Research and Practice, 34*, 240–247.

Brown-Chidsey, R., & Andren, K. J. (2013). Solution-focused psychoeducational reports. In R. Brown-

Chidsey & K. J. Andren (Eds.), *Assessment for intervention: A problem-solving approach* (2nd ed., pp. 253–276). New York: Guilford Press.

Browning Wright, D., & Gronroos, N. (n.d.). Pacing a "hard news" session: Key concepts for communicating a mental retardation diagnosis. Retrieved from *www.naspcenter.org/teachers/conferencing.html.*

Carlson, J. F., Geisinger, K. F., & Jonson, J. L. (Eds.). (2017). *The twentieth mental measurements yearbook.* Lincoln, NE: Buros Center for Testing.

Cash, R. E. (2017, February). *Best practices in report writing.* Presentation at the Trainers of School Psychologists Annual Conference, San Antonio, TX.

Castillo, J. M., Curtis, J. J., & Gelley, C. (2012). School psychology 2010—Part 2: School psychologists' professional practices and implications for the field. *Communiqué, 40*(8), 4–6.

Cates, J. A. (1999). The art of assessment in psychology: Ethics, expertise, and validity. *Journal of Clinical Psychology, 55*(5), 631–641.

Charvat, J. (2011). *Ratio of students per school psychologist by state: Data from the 2009–10 and 2004–05 NASP Membership Surveys* (Research report). Bethesda, MD: National Association of School Psychologists.

Christenson, S. L., & Reschly, A. L. (2010). *Handbook of school-family partnerships.* New York: Routledge.

Consortium for Evidence-Based Early Intervention Practices. (2010). A response to the Learning Disabilities Association of America (LDA) white paper on specific learning disabilities (SLD) identification. Retrieved from *www.isbe.net/speced/pdfs/LDA_SLD_white_paper_response.pdf.*

Covey, S. R. (1989). *The seven habits of highly effective people: Restoring the character ethic.* New York: Simon & Schuster.

Cronbach, L. J. (1975). Beyond the two disciplines of scientific psychology. *American Psychologist, 30*(2), 116–127.

Cronbach, L. J., & Snow, R. E. (1977). *Aptitudes and instructional methods: A handbook for research on interactions.* Oxford, UK: Irvington.

Curry, K. T., & Hanson, W. E., (2010). National survey of psychologists' test feedback training, supervision, and practice: A mixed methods study. *Journal of Personality Assessment, 92*(4), 327–336.

Deno, S. L. (1985). Curriculum-based measurement: The emerging alternative. *Exceptional Children, 52*(3), 219–232.

Deno, S. L. (2003). Developments in curriculum-based measurement. *Journal of Special Education, 37*(3), 184–192.

Donders, J. (2001). A survey of report writing by neuropsychologists: II. Test data, report format, and document length. *Clinical Neuropsychologist, 15,* 150–161.

Donders, J., & Strong, C. A. (2016). General principles of neuropsychological report preparation. In J. Donders (Ed.), *Neuropsychological report writing* (pp. 1–29). New York: Guilford Press.

Durlak, J. A., Weissberg, R. P., Dymnicki, A. B., Taylor, R. D., & Schellinger, K. B. (2010). The impact of enhancing students' social and emotional learning: A meta-analysis of school-based universal interventions. *Child Development, 82*(1), 405–432.

Educational Testing Service. (2015). Tips for evaluators of adolescents and adults with disabilities. Retrieved from *www.ets.org/s/disabilities/pdf/tips_for_evaluators_adults_adolescents.pdf.*

Ferguson, C. (2008). *The school–family connection: Looking at the larger picture.* Austin, TX: National Center for Family and Community Connections with Schools.

Finn, S. E., & Tonsager, M. E. (1997). Information-gathering and therapeutic models of assessment: Complementary paradigms. *Psychological Assessment, 9*(4), 374–385.

Flesch, R. (1948). A new readability yardstick. *Journal of Applied Psychology, 32,* 221–233.

Flesch, R. (1979). How to write plain English: Let's start with the formula. Retrieved from *www.mang.canterbury.ac.nz/writing_guide/writing/flesch.shtml.*

Fletcher, J. M., & Miciak, J. (2017). Comprehensive cognitive assessments are not necessary for the identification and treatment of learning disabilities. *Archives of Clinical Neuropsychology, 32,* 2–7.

Floyd, R. G. (2010). Assessment of cognitive abilities and cognitive processes: Issues, applications and fit within a problem-solving model. In G. G. Peacock, R. A. Ervin, E. J. Daly, & K. W. Merrell (Eds.), *Practical handbook of school psychology: Effective practices for the 21st century* (pp. 48–66). New York: Guilford Press.

Geva, E., & Wiener, J. (2015). *Psychological assessment of culturally and linguistically diverse children and adolescents: A practitioner's guide.* New York: Springer.

Gischlar, K. L. (2014). Observing the child. In S. C. Dombrowski, *Psychoeducational assessment and report writing* (pp. 43–62). New York: Springer.

Glazer, A. (2014). Communication matters: Effective oral communication of evaluation results. *Communiqué, 42*(6), 1, 32–33.

Goldfinger, K., & Pomerantz, A. M. (2014). *Psycho-*

logical assessment and report writing (2nd ed). Thousand Oaks, CA: SAGE.

Gresham, F. M., & Witt, J. C. (1997). Utility of intelligence tests for treatment planning, classification, and placement decisions: Recent empirical findings and future directions. *School Psychology Quarterly, 12*, 249–267.

Groth-Marnat, G. (2009). The five assessment issues you meet when you go to heaven. *Journal of Personality Assessment, 91*, 303–310.

Groth-Marnat, G., & Horvath, L. S. (2006). The psychological report: A review of current controversies. *Journal of Clinical Psychology, 62*(1), 73–81.

Groth-Marnat, G., & Wright, A. J. (2016). *Handbook of psychological assessment* (6th ed.). Hoboken, NJ: Wiley.

Hackett, L., Shaikh, S., & Theodosiou, L. (2009). Parental perceptions of the assessment of autism spectrum disorders in a tier three service. *Child and Adolescent Mental Health, 14*(3), 127–132.

Halpern, R. (1984). Physician–parent communication in the diagnosis of child handicap: A brief review. *Children's Health Care, 12*(4), 170–173.

Hammond, K. R., & Allen, J. M. (1953). *Writing clinical reports*. Englewood Cliffs, NJ: Prentice-Hall.

Hart, B., & Risley, T. (1995). *Meaningful differences in the everyday experience of young American children*. Baltimore, MD: Brookes.

Hart, B., & Risley, T. R. (2003). The early catastrophe: The 30 million word gap by age 3. *American Educator, 27*(1), 4–9.

Harvey, V. S. (1997). Improving readability of psychological reports. *Professional Psychology: Research and Practice, 28*, 271–274.

Harvey, V. S. (2006). Variables affecting the clarity of psychological reports. *Journal of Clinical Psychology, 62*, 5–18.

Harvey, V. S. (2013). Communicating test results. In K. F. Geisinger, B. A. Bracken, J. F. Carlson, J. C. Hansen, N. R. Kuncel, S. P. Reise, et al. (Eds.), *APA handbook of testing and assessment in psychology: Vol. 2. Testing and assessment in clinical and counseling psychology* (pp. 35–50). Washington, DC: American Psychological Association.

Hasnat, M. J., & Graves, P. (2000). Disclosure of developmental disability: A study of paediatricians' practices. *Journal of Paediatrics and Child Health, 36*(1), 27–31.

Hass, M. R., & Carriere, J. A. (2014). *Writing useful, accessible, and legally defensible psychoeducational reports*. Hoboken, NJ: Wiley.

Hattie, J. (2009). *Visible learning: A survey of over 800 meta-analyses relating to achievement*. New York: Routledge.

Hawkins, J. D., Kosterman, R., Catalano, R. F., Hill, K. G., & Abbott, R. D. (2008). Effects of social development intervention. *Archives of Pediatric Adolescent Medicine, 162*(12), 1133–1141.

Henderson, A. T., & Mapp, K. L. (2002). *A new wave of school evidence: The impact of school, family and community connections on student achievement*. Austin, TX: National Center for Family and Community Connections with Schools.

Hilton, K., Turner, C., Krebs, G., Volz, C., & Heyman, I. (2012). Parent experiences of attending a specialist clinic for assessment of their child's obsessive–compulsive disorder. *Child and Adolescent Mental Health, 17*(1), 31–36.

Hintze, J. M., Volpe, R. J., & Shapiro, E. S. (2008). Best practices in the systematic direct observation of student behavior. In A. Thomas & J. Grimes (Eds.), *Best practices in school psychology V* (pp. 319–335). Bethesda, MD: National Association of School Psychologists.

Hite, J. (2017). *Parent evaluations of traditional and consumer-focused school psychoeducational reports*. Doctoral dissertation, William James College, Newton, MA.

Ho, H. S. W., Yi, H., Griffiths, S., Chan, D. F. Y., & Murray, S. (2014). "Do it yourself" in the parent–professional partnership for the assessment and diagnosis of children with autism spectrum conditions in Hong Kong: A qualitative study. *Autism, 18*(7), 832–844.

Horvath, A. O., Del Re, A. C., Fluckiger, C., & Symonds, D. (2011). Alliance in individual psychotherapy. *Psychotherapy, 48*(1), 9–16.

Hosp, J. L., & Reschly, D. J. (2002). Regional differences in school psychology practice, *School Psychology Review, 31*(1), 11–29.

Jones, J. (2018, February). *Culturally responsive assessment feedback: Sharing results with culturally diverse families*. Webcast presented at the National Association of School Psychologists Annual Convention, Chicago, IL.

Kaufman, A. S., Raiford, S. E., & Coalson, D. L. (2016). *Intelligent testing with the WISC-V*. Hoboken, NJ: Wiley.

Kincaid, J. P., Fishburne, R. P., Rogers, R. L., & Chissom, B. S. (1975). *Derivation of new readability formulas for Navy enlisted personnel* (Research Branch Report 8-75). Memphis, TN: Chief of Naval Technical Training, Naval Air Station.

Kranzler, J. H., & Floyd, R. G. (2013). *Assessing intelligence in children and adolescents: A practical guide*. New York: Guilford Press.

Kranzler, J. H., Floyd, R. G., Benson, N., Zaboski, B., & Thibodaux, L. (2016). Cross-battery assessment pattern of strengths and weaknesses approach to the identification of specific learning disorders: Evidence-based practice or pseudoscience? *International Journal of School and Educational Psychology, 4*(3), 146–157.

Kratochwill, T., Altschaefl, M., & Bice-Urbach, B. (2014). Best practices in school-based problem-solving consultation: Applications in prevention and intervention systems. In P. L. Harrison & A. Thomas (Eds.), *Best practices in school psychology: Data-based and collaborative decision making* (pp. 461–482). Bethesda, MD: National Association of School Psychologists.

Kuentzel, J. G., Hetterscheidt, L. A., & Barnett, D. (2011). Testing intelligently includes double-checking Wechsler IQ scores. *Journal of Psychoeducational Assessment, 29*(1), 39–46.

Lewis-Fernandez, R., Aggarwal, N. K., Hinton, L., Hinton, D. E., & Kirmayer, L. J. (2016). *Handbook on the Cultural Formulation Interview.* Washington, DC: American Psychiatric Association Press.

Lezak, M. D., Howieson, D. B., Bigler, E., & Tranel, D. (2012). *Neuropsychological assessment* (5th ed.). New York: Oxford University Press.

Lichtenstein, R. (2013a). Writing psychoeducational reports that matter: A consumer-responsive approach. *Communiqué, 42*(3), 1, 28–30.

Lichtenstein, R. (2013b). Writing psychoeducational reports that matter: A consumer-responsive approach, Part 2. *Communiqué, 42*(4), 1, 10–13.

Lichtenstein, R. (2014). Writing psychoeducational reports that matter: A consumer-responsive approach, Part 3. *Communiqué, 42*(6), 1, 30–32.

Lichtenstein, R., & Axelrod, J. (2016). Case 15—Jane, age 8: Consumer-responsive approach to assessment reports. In A. S. Kaufman, S. E. Raiford, & D. L. Coalson, *Intelligent testing with the WISC-V* (pp. 578–586). Hoboken, NJ: Wiley.

Loe, S. A., Kadlubek, R. M., & Marks, W. J. (2007). Administration and scoring errors on the WISC-IV among graduate student examiners. *Journal of Psychoeducational Assessment, 25,* 237–247.

Marx, E., Wooley, S., & Northrop, D. (Eds.). (1998). *Health is academic: A guide to coordinated school health programs.* New York: Teachers Press.

Mazza, J. (2014). Best practices in clinical interviewing parents, teachers and students. In P. L. Harrison & A. Thomas (Eds.), *Best practices in school psychology: Data-based and collaborative decision making* (pp. 317–330). Bethesda, MD: National Association of School Psychologists.

McCain, K. W. (2015, November). *Nothing as practical as a good theory: Does Lewin's Maxim still have salience in the applied social sciences?* Presentation at the Association for Information Science and Technology Meeting, St. Louis. Retrieved from *https://onlinelibrary.wiley.com/doi/abs/10.1002/pra2.2015.145052010077.*

McConaughy, S. (2013). *Clinical interviews for children and adolescents* (2nd ed.). New York: Wiley.

McDermott, P. A., Fantuzzo, J. W., & Glutting, J. J. (1990). Just say no to subtest analysis: A critique on Wechsler theory and practice. *Journal of Psychoeducational Assessment, 8,* 290–302.

Miller, J. A., & Watkins, M. W. (2010). The use of graphs to communicate psychoeducational test results to parents. *Journal of Applied School Psychology, 26*(1), 1–16.

Moh, T. A., & Magiati, I. (2012). Factors associated with parental stress and satisfaction during the process of diagnosis of children with Autism Spectrum Disorders. *Research in Autism Spectrum Disorders, 6,* 293–303.

Monroe, R. (2015). *Thing explainer: Complicated stuff in simple words.* New York: Houghton Mifflin Harcourt.

Mrazik, M., Janzen, T. M., Dombrowski, S. C., Barford, S. W., & Krawchuk, L. L. (2012). Administration and scoring errors of graduate students learning the WISC-IV: Issues and controversies. *Canadian Journal of School Psychology, 27,* 279–290.

National Association of School Psychologists. (2003). *Portraits of children: Culturally competent assessment* [Video]. Bethesda, MD: Author.

National Association of School Psychologists. (2010a). Model for comprehensive and integrated school psychological services. Retrieved from *www.nasponline.org/standards-and-certification/nasp-practice-model.*

National Association of School Psychologists. (2010b). Principles for professional ethics. Retrieved from *www.nasponline.org/standards-and-certification/professional-ethics.*

Nissenbaum, M., Tollefson, N., & Reese, R. M. (2002). The interpretive conference: Sharing a diagnosis of autism with families. *Focus on Autism and Other Developmental Disabilities, 17*(1), 30–43.

Norcross, J. C., & Hill, C. E. (2004). Empirically supported therapy relationships. *Clinical Psychology, 57*(3), 19–24.

Norcross, J. C., & Wampold, B. E. (2011). Evidence-based therapy relationships: Research conclusions and clinical practices. *Psychotherapy, 48*(1), 98–102.

Oppenheimer, D. M. (2006). Consequences of erudite vernacular utilized irrespective of necessity: Problems with using long words needlessly. *Applied Cognitive Psychology, 20,* 139–156.

Ownby, R. L. (1997). *Psychological reports: A guide to report writing in professional psychology* (3rd ed.). New York: Wiley.

Ownby, R. L., & Wallbrown, F. (1986). Improving report writing in school psychology. In T. R. Kratochwill (Ed.), *Advances in school psychology* (Vol. 5, pp. 7–49). Hillsdale, NJ: Erlbaum.

Pearson. (n.d.). Interpretation problems of age and grade equivalents. Retrieved from *www.pearsonclinical.com/language/RelatedInfo/interpretation-problems-of-age-and-grade-equivalents.html*.

Pelco, L. E., Ward, S. B., Coleman, L., & Young, J. (2009). Teacher rating of three psychological report styles. *Training and Education in Professional Psychology, 3*, 19–27.

Postal, K., & Armstrong, K. (2013). *Feedback that sticks: The art of effectively communicating neuropsychological assessment results.* New York: Oxford University Press.

Power, T. J., Eiraldi, R. B., Clarke, A. T., & Mazzuca, L. B., & Krain, A. L. (2005). Improving mental health utilization for children and families. *School Psychology Quarterly, 20*(2), 187–205.

President's Commission on Excellence in Special Education. (2002). *A new era: Revitalizing special education for children and their families.* Washington, DC: U.S. Department of Education Office of Special Education and Rehabilitative Services.

Quine, L., & Rutter, D. R. (1994). First diagnosis of severe mental and physical disability: A study of doctor–parent communication. *Journal of Child Psychology and Psychiatry, 35*(7), 1273–1287.

Reynolds, C. R. (1981). The fallacy of "two years below grade level for age" as a diagnostic for reading disorders. *Journal of School Psychology, 19*(4), 350–358.

Rimm-Kaufman, S. E., Fan, X., Chiu, Y., & You, W. (2007). The contribution of the Responsive Classroom Approach on children's academic achievement: Results from a three year longitudinal study. *Journal of School Psychology, 45*(4), 401–421.

Ryan, C. (2013). Language use in the United States 2011: American community survey reports. Retrieved from *www.census.gov/prod/2013pubs/acs-22.pdf*.

Sattler, J. M. (2018). *Assessment of children: Cognitive foundations and applications* (6th ed.). La Mesa, CA: Author.

Schneider, W. J., Lichtenberger, E. O., Mather, N., Kaufman, N. L., & Kaufman, A. S. (2018). *Essentials of assessment report writing* (2nd ed.). Hoboken, NJ: Wiley.

Schrank, F. A., & Wendling, B. J. (2012). The Woodcock–Johnson III normative update: Tests of cognitive abilities and tests of achievement. In D. P. Flanagan & P. L. Harrison, (Eds.), *Contemporary intellectual assessment: Theories, tests, and issues* (3rd ed., pp. 297–335). New York: Guilford Press.

Shapiro, E. S., & Heick, P. F. (2004). School psychologist assessment practices in the assessment of students referred for social/behavioral/emotional problems. *Psychology in the Schools, 41*(5), 551–561.

Shectman, F. (1979). Problems in communicating psychological understanding: Why won't they listen to me? *American Psychologist, 34*, 781–790.

Shirk, S. R., Karver, M. S., & Brown, R. (2011). The alliance in child and adolescent psychotherapy. *Psychotherapy, 48*(1), 17–24.

Smith, S. R., Wiggins, C. M., & Gorske, T. T. (2007). A survey of psychological assessment feedback practices. *Assessment, 14*(3), 310–319.

Sotelo-Dynega, M., & Dixon, S. G. (2014). Cognitive assessment practices: A survey of school psychologists. *Psychology in the Schools, 51*(10), 1031–1045.

Stout, C. E., & Cook, L. P. (1999). New areas for psychological assessment in general health care settings: What to do today to prepare for tomorrow. *Journal of Clinical Psychology, 55*(7), 797–812.

Styck, K. M., & Walsh, S. M. (2016). Evaluating the prevalence and impact of examiner errors on the Wechsler scales of intelligence: A meta-analysis. *Psychoeducational Assessment, 28*(1), 3–17.

Sue, D. W., & Sue, D. (2016). *Counseling the culturally diverse: Theory and practice* (7th ed.). Hoboken, NJ: Wiley.

Tallent, N. (1980). *Report writing in special education.* Englewood Cliffs, NJ: Prentice-Hall.

Tallent, N. (1993). *Psychological report writing* (4th ed.). Englewood Cliffs, NJ: Prentice Hall.

Tallent, N., & Reiss, W. J. (1959). Multidisciplinary views on the preparation of written clinical psychological reports: III. The trouble with psychological reports. *Journal of Clinical Psychology, 15*, 444–446.

Terman, L. M., & Merrill, M. A. (1937). *Measuring intelligence.* Boston: Houghton Mifflin.

Turnbull, A. A., Turnbull, H. R., Erwin, E. J., Soodak, L. C., & Shogren, K. A. (2015). *Families, professionals, and exceptionality: Positive outcomes through partnerships and trust* (7th ed.). Upper Saddle River, NJ: Pearson.

U.S. Department of Education. (2006, August 14). Assistance to states for the education of children with disabilities and preschool grants for children with disabilities: Final rule. *Federal Register, 71*, 156.

U.S. Department of Justice, Civil Rights Division. (2015). ADA requirements: Testing accommodations. Retrieved from *www.ada.gov/regs2014/testing_accommodations.html*.

van der Oord, S., Prins, P. J. M., Oosterlaan, J., & Emmelkamp, P. M. G. (2006). The association between parenting stress, depressed mood, and informant agreement in ADHD and ODD. *Behaviour Research and Therapy, 44,* 1585–1595.

Wagner, M., Newman, L., Cameto, R., Javitz, H., & Valdes, K. (2012). A national picture of parent and youth participation in IEP and transition planning meetings. *Journal of Disability Policy Studies, 23*(3), 140–155.

Walrath, R., Willis, J. O., & Dumont, R. (2014). Best practices in writing assessment reports. In P. L. Harrison & A. Thomas (Eds.), *Best practices in school psychology: Data-based and collaborative decision making* (pp. 433–448). Bethesda, MD: National Association of School Psychologists.

Ward, R. (2008). Assessee and assessor experiences of significant events in psychological assessment feedback. *Journal of Personality Assessment, 90*(4), 307–322.

Wechsler, D. (1939). *The measurement of adult intelligence.* Baltimore: Williams & Wilkins.

Wechsler, D., Raiford, S. E., & Holdnack, J. A. (2014). *WISC-V technical and interpretive manual.* Bloomington, MN: Pearson.

Weddig, R. A. (1984). Parental interpretation of psychoeducational reports. *Psychology in the Schools, 21,* 477–481.

Wiener, J., & Costaris, L. (2012). Teaching psychological report writing: Content and process. *Canadian Journal of School Psychology, 27*(2), 119–135.

Wiener, J., & Kohler, S. (1986). Parents' comprehension of psychological reports. *Psychology in the Schools, 23,* 265–270.

Wiesel, E. (2000). Oprah talks to Elie Wiesel. Retrieved from *www.oprah.com/omagazine/Oprah-Interviews-Elie-Wiesel.*

Willis, J. O. (2015). Publishers' classification schemes for test scores. Retrieved from *www.myschoolpsychology.com/.../Publishers-Classification-Schemes-for-Test-Scores.*

Wilson, M. S., & Reschly, D. J. (1996). Assessment in school psychology. *School Psychology Review, 25,* 9–23.

World Health Organization. (1992). *The ICD-10 classification of mental and behavioural disorders: Clinical descriptions and diagnostic guidelines.* Geneva: Author.

Zapf, P. A., & Roesch, R. (2008). *Evaluation of competence to stand trial.* New York: Oxford University Press.

Index

Academic functioning, 94, 95, 117–122, 120*f*
Accessibility, 2, 49
Achenbach System of Empirically Based Assessment (ASEBA), 32
Adaptive behavior, 94, 95
Adaptive progress, 125–127
Adolescents, 115, 116
Age-equivalent scores, 81–82
Aptitude-treatment interactions (ATIs), 10–11
Assessment procedures
    assessment design, 22–26
    external pressures on, 139–140, 141–144, 147–148
    interpretation of results, 38, 40–41
    multi-tiered system of supports (MTSS) and, 43–46
    oral reporting of assessment findings and, 112
    overview, 4*t*, 22
    severe intellectual disabilities and, 125–127
    sources of assessment data and, 26–38
    use of findings, 38, 40–41
Assessment Procedures section, 89, 207. *See also* Assessment procedures
Assessment reports. *See also* Oral reporting of assessment findings; Written reporting of assessment findings
    conveying findings, 110–111
    parent feedback letter, 130–131
    report structure and, 94–97, 98
    severe intellectual disabilities and, 125–127
    training and, 14
    types of, 5, 117–136
Assessment Results section, 94–97, 208. *See also* Test Results section of reports
Assessor, 6
Attention-deficit/hyperactivity disorder (ADHD), 129–130
Autism spectrum disorder (ASD), 130

Background information, 26–29, 127, 132–133, 191–194. *See also* Background Information section; History
Background Information section. *See also* History
    assessment results and, 94
    example of, 191–194
    oral reporting of assessment findings and, 112
    overview, 89, 89–91, 90
    report writing rubric, 208
    screening and progress monitoring and, 119, 121
BASC-3 Self-Report of Personality, 205–206
Behavior Assessment System for Children (BASC), 32, 204–206
Behavior Rating Inventory of Executive Function-2nd Edition (BRIEF-2), 202–203
Behavioral factors, 25, 29, 30–31, 52–53
Behavioral intervention plan, 91, 114
Behavioral Observation section, 93–94, 97, 208
Benchmark assessment, 43, 119, 121
Bender Visual–Motor Gestalt Test–2nd Edition (Bender–Gestalt-II), 96, 200
Bender Visual–Motor Gestalt Test, 38
Brain functioning, 131–133

California Verbal Learning Test–Children's Version (CVLT-C), 96
Caregivers, 5. *See also* Parents
Case presentation guidelines, 211–214
Caseload factors, 18–19
Cattell–Horn–Carroll (CHC) theory, 96
Children
    child-focus and, 2, 49, 72–73
    collaborative relationships and, 52
    interaction with, 56, 58, 60–61
    oral reporting of assessment findings and, 115, 116
    terminology, 5

Children's Memory Scale, 96

Clinical Impressions section, 98–99, 209

Cognitive functioning, 94, 95

Cognitive testing, 10–11, 36, 38, 39. *See also* Testing

Collaborative relationships
    bridging the school–family divide and, 67–68
    consumer-responsive assessment and, 48, 50–54, 56–61
    overview, 2

Communication. *See also* Feedback; Language factors
    children and adolescents and, 58, 60–61, 115, 116
    cultural factors and, 65, 67
    neuropsychological assessment and, 133
    oral reporting of assessment findings and, 105–106
    parents and, 111–113
    teachers and, 113–114

Community functioning, 58, 59

Community-based evaluations, 18–19, 139–140, 147

Comprehensive Test of Phonological Process–2nd Edition (CTOPP-2), 199–200

Computer-generated reports, 135–136

Conclusions in written reports, 4t. *See also* Interpretation in written reports

Conners 3rd Edition (Conners-3), 203

Conners Comprehensive Behavioral Rating Scales, 32

Consent, 23–24

Consumer-responsive approach. *See also* Consumer-responsive report writing; Oral reporting of assessment findings; Written reporting of assessment findings
    adopting, 7, 140–141, 153
    bridging the school–family divide and, 67–68
    collaborative relationships and, 50–54
    core principles of, 48–49
    cultural factors, 62–67
    forensic assessment and, 133–134
    future directions, 150–153
    independent evaluations and, 127–129
    individual practitioner issues, 138–141
    neuropsychological assessment and, 132–133
    over the course of the assessment, 54–62
    overview, 2–7, 4t, 21, 47, 137–138
    phased-in implementation of, 140–141
    readability and, 12, 12t
    re-evaluation and, 124–125
    report-writing practices and, 6–7
    system issues, 141–150

Consumer-responsive report writing. *See also* Consumer-responsive approach; Report-writing practices
    characteristics of reports, 70–85, 76t, 78t, 80t
    overview, 69–70
    report structure, 85, 87–103

Conventional assessment, 4t, 8–14, 12t, 63

Costs, 19, 142–144, 147–148

Court proceedings, 133–134

Cultural factors, 10–11, 62–67

Curriculum-based assessment (CBA), 43, 44

Curriculum-based measurement (CBM), 44–45, 46, 91, 119, 121

Data presentation, 73–83, 76t, 78t, 80t

Data sources, 26–38, 49, 195–206. *See also* Multiple sources of assessment data

Data Summary section. *See also* Written reporting of assessment findings
    child-focus and, 73
    data summary template and, 195–206
    overview, 73, 103
    range descriptors and, 81
    report writing rubric, 210
    uninterpretable and invalid findings and, 82–83

Decision making, 102, 119, 121–122, 140

Defensive practice, 20–21, 142

Descriptors, range, 77–79, 78t, 80t

Developmental history, 57

Devereux Student Strengths Assessment, 32

Diagnostic Impressions section. *See* Clinical Impressions section

Differential Ability Scales-2nd Edition (DAS-II), 77–78, 201–202

Direct observations, 30, 125–126. *See also* Observation

Disability accommodation assessments, 129–130

D-KEFS Trail Making Test, 38

Documentation, 119, 152. *See also* Recommendations

Educational Testing Service (ETS), 129–130

Emotional factors, 10–11, 25, 53, 94, 111

Environmental factors, 30–31, 36–37

Ethics, 151–153

Evaluation, 22, 32–33

Evaluator
    adherence to testing procedures by, 34–35
    assessment design and, 23
    consumer-responsive assessment and, 54
    established models of report writing and, 17–18
    external pressures on, 18–21
    independent evaluations and, 128–129
    professional writing and, 41
    terminology, 6, 16
    training and, 14–15

Expectations, 10–11, 21, 139

External pressures, 18–21

Family functioning, 57–58, 59, 67–68. *See also* Parents

Feedback
    collaborative relationships and, 52
    example of parent feedback letter, 189–190
    feedback conference simulation, 211–214
    feedback from consumers, 149, 161–163
    oral reporting of assessment findings and, 106–110
    parent feedback letter, 130–131
    team reports and, 134–135

Financial factors, 19, 142–144, 147–148

Flesch–Kincaid levels, 11–12, 12t, 84, 86–87, 155–156. *See also* Readability

Flexibility, 139, 145

Follow-up
    collaborative relationships and, 52
    consumer-responsive assessment and, 61–62, 102, 145
    overview, 4t, 7
    procedures for, 161–163
    report writing rubric, 210

Forensic assessment, 133–134

Formulaic approaches, 15, 17–18

Free observation, 29–30. *See also* Observation
Functional behavioral assessment (FBA), 45

Goal attainment scales, 91
Grade-equivalent scores, 81–82, 155–156
Graduate training programs, 149–150. *See also* Training to
 become an evaluator
Graphs, 119, 121–122

History, 2, 57. *See also* Background information; Background
 Information section; Intervention History section
Humility, 53–54
Hypothesis testing, 25–26

Identifying Information section, 88
Independent evaluations, 7, 127–129
Individual feedback meetings, 109–110. *See also* Feedback
Individualized assessment, 24–25
Individualized education program (IEP)
 consumer-responsive assessment and, 3, 20, 67–68, 142,
  143–145
 disability accommodation assessments and, 130
 oral reporting of assessment findings and, 107–109, 115
 recommendations and, 40–41
 Recommendations section of a report and, 101
 severe intellectual disabilities and, 127
 terminology and, 22
Inferences, 29–30, 93, 98
Informed consent, 23–24
Instructional approaches, 10–11, 45–46
Intellectual disability, 125–127
Intelligence, 9–10, 36
Internal consistency, 75, 76t. *See also* Reliability
Interpersonal skills, 105–106
Interpretation in written reports, 4t. *See also* Conclusions
 in written reports
Interpretation of test results. *See also* Testing
 computer-generated reports and, 135–136
 data summary template and, 202–206
 integration, 38, 40, 72, 98–99, 209
 overview, 10–11, 30–31, 35–36, 38, 40–41
 psychological terms in report writing, 16
Intervention History section, 91–92. *See also* History
Intervention suggestions, 2, 23, 45–46, 100–103, 114, 115,
 119, 120f
Interviews
 collaborative relationships and, 52
 consumer-responsive assessment and, 54–56, 57–58, 59
 cultural factors and, 65, 66
 report structure and, 92
 sources of assessment data and, 26–29
 types of, 28–29
Invalid findings, 82–83

Jargon. *See also* Language factors
 characteristics of consumer-responsive reports, 85,
  86–87
 community-based evaluations and, 140
 consumer-responsive assessment and, 2
 neuropsychological assessment and, 131–132
 oral reporting of assessment findings and, 110–111
 psychological terms in report writing, 16

Kaufman Assessment Battery for Children–Second Edition
 (KABC-II), 75, 76t

Language factors
 community-based evaluations and, 140
 cultural factors and, 65, 67
 language in written reports, 4t, 83–85, 86–87, 131–132,
  134–135
 neuropsychological assessment and, 131–132
 oral reporting of assessment findings and, 110–111, 116
 report structure and, 94
 severe intellectual disabilities and, 125
 testing and, 10–11
Learning disability, 25, 45–46, 129–130
Legal factors, 19–20, 133–134, 142

Measurement error, 36–37, 74–75, 76t
Medical history, 57
Memory functioning, 94, 95
Multiple sources of assessment data, 2, 26–38, 49. *See also*
 Data sources
Multi-tiered system of supports (MTSS)
 assessment in, 41–46
 external pressures and, 19
 screening and progress monitoring and, 117–122, 120f
 terminology, 6

Narrative observation, 29–30. *See also* Observation
Naturalistic observation. *See* Observation
Neuropsychological assessment, 131–133

Observation, 26–27, 29–31, 93–94, 112, 125–126
Optimal performance, 35
Oral reporting of assessment findings. *See also* Consumer-
 responsive approach
 case presentation guidelines and, 211–214
 children and adolescents and, 115, 116
 consumer-responsive assessment and, 7, 49
 conveying findings, 110–111
 feedback meetings, 106–110
 interpersonal and communication skills and, 105–106
 overview, 1–2, 2, 4t, 7, 105, 115, 137
 parents and, 111–113
 teachers and, 113–114
 training and, 150

Parents
 assessment process and, 1–2, 4t
 bridging the school–family divide and, 67–68
 collaborative relationships and, 52
 community-based evaluations and, 140
 consumer-responsive assessment and, 55–56, 57–58, 62,
  67–68
 feedback and, 7
 feedback letter and, 130–131, 189–190
 independent evaluations and, 127–128
 neuropsychological assessment and, 132–133
 oral reporting of assessment findings and, 108, 109–110,
  111–113
 rating scales and, 32
 screening and progress monitoring and, 118, 121, 122
 terminology, 5

Percentiles, 80–81
Performance level, 77–79, 78t, 80t, 91
Phased-in implementation, 140–141
Prevention, 148–149
Process, 2, 3, 48, 54–62
Professional development, 138
Professional texts, 17
Progress monitoring
    multi-tiered system of supports (MTSS) and, 43, 44,
        45–46
    overview, 117–122, 120f
    re-evaluation and, 124
    report structure and, 91
Psychiatric disabilities, 129–130
Psychoeducational assessment, 24–25, 55, 60, 164–188.
        See also Assessment procedures
Psychological assessment. *See also* Assessment procedures
    consumer-responsive assessment and, 67–68
    follow-up procedures, 161–163
    individualized assessment and, 24–25
    overview, 1–2, 9
    schools and, 145–147
    terminology, 5
    working alliance and, 50–51

Qualitative findings, 38, 39
Questions, 53, 65, 66

Range descriptors, 77–79, 78t, 80t
Rapport
    consumer-responsive assessment and, 56–61
    interpersonal and communication skills and, 106
    oral reporting of assessment findings and, 107, 115, 116
    testing and, 35
    training and, 14–15
Rating scales, 31–32, 112, 133, 202–206
Readability
    characteristics of consumer-responsive reports, 83–85
    examples of reports and, 17
    measures of, 7, 155–156
    overview, 11–13, 12t
    psychological terms in report writing, 16
Reason for Referral section, 88, 89, 90, 207
Reciprocity, 52–53
Recommendations, 40–41, 100–103, 114, 115
Recommendations section, 100–103, 209
Records, 26–27, 119, 125–126
Re-evaluation, 7, 22, 23, 34, 123–125, 144–145
Referral questions
    assessment design and, 22–23, 25, 26
    child-focus and, 73
    Clinical Impressions section and, 98
    community-based evaluations and, 139–140
    consumer-responsive assessment and, 2, 142
    independent evaluations and, 128–129
    overview, 4t
    Reason for Referral section of a report and, 88, 90
    re-evaluation and, 123–124
    testing and, 9, 10
Relevance, 2, 3, 48–49, 100
Reliability, 30, 36–37, 75, 76t
Report structure. *See also* Report-writing practices

Assessment Procedures section, 89
Assessment Results section, 94–97
Background Information section, 89, 89–91, 90
Behavioral Observation section, 93–94
Clinical Impressions section, 98–99
Data Summary section, 103
examples of reports, 164–188
future directions, 152
Identifying Information section, 88
Intervention History section, 91–92
Interview section, 92
overview, 85, 87–103, 104
Reason for Referral section, 88, 89, 90
Recommendations section, 100–103
report writing rubric, 207–210
Summary section, 99–100
theme-based, 49, 71–72, 94–96, 208, 209
Reporting. *See also* Consumer-responsive approach; Oral
        reporting of assessment findings; Written reporting of
        assessment findings
    consumer-responsive assessment and, 61
    examples of reports, 164–188
    future directions, 150–153
    overview, 137
    report writing rubric, 207–210
    terminology, 6
    test results and, 9
Report-writing practices. *See also* Consumer-responsive
        report writing; Report structure; Written reporting of
        assessment findings
    evaluator factors and, 14–21
    multi-tiered system of supports (MTSS) and, 45–46
    overview, 6–7, 21, 69–70
    professional writing and, 41
    readability and, 11–13, 12t
    report writing rubric, 207–210
    training and, 14
Response-to-intervention (RTI) model, 6, 19, 45–46. *See
        also* Multi-tiered system of supports (MTSS)
Rey–Osterrieth test, 96
RIOT acronym, 26–27, 72–73. *See also* Data sources

School-based assessments, 18–19, 117–129, 120f, 139
Schools, 19–20, 57, 59, 67–68, 108, 137–138, 142–147
Screening, 7, 43, 92, 117–122, 120f
Section 504 of the Rehabilitation Act of 1973, 129–130
Selectivity, 25, 70–71, 97, 98
Semistructured interviews, 28, 29. *See also* Interviews
"So what?" principle, 70–71
Social Emotional Assets and Resilience Scales, 32
Social–emotional functioning, 94, 95
Solution-focused assessments, 43–46
Special education
    assessment design and, 23–24
    consumer-responsive assessment and, 63, 144–145, 146
    curriculum-based measurement (CBM) and, 44–45
    evaluation and re-evaluation design and, 23
    external pressures and, 18–19
    multi-tiered system of supports (MTSS) and, 42
    oral reporting of assessment findings and, 107
    re-evaluation and, 123–125
Standardized testing. *See* Testing

Stanford–Binet (SB-5), 77–78

Structure of reports. *See* Report structure

Structured interviews, 28–29. *See also* Interviews

Style factors, 83–85, 86–87

Summary section, 99–100, 209

System issues, 141–150

Systematic observation, 29, 30. *See also* Observation

Tables, 119, 121–122

Teachers
    bridging the school–family divide and, 67–68
    collaborative relationships and, 52
    consumer-responsive assessment and, 1–2, 56, 59–60, 62, 146–147
    neuropsychological assessment and, 132–133
    oral reporting of assessment findings and, 107, 109–110, 113–114

Team-evaluation model, 28, 107–109, 115, 134–135. *See also* Individualized education program (IEP)

Terminology, 5–6, 16, 22, 85, 86–87, 131–132. *See also* Language factors

Test Results section of reports, 72–73, 94–97, 208. *See also* Assessment Results section

Testing
    characteristics of consumer-responsive reports, 72–73
    consumer-responsive assessment and, 2
    cultural factors, 63–64
    data presentation and, 73–83, 76*t*, 78*t*, 80*t*
    data summary template and, 195–206
    disability accommodation assessments and, 129–130
    emphasis on in conventional assessment, 8–11
    interpretation of results, 38, 40–41
    oral reporting of assessment findings and, 112
    overview, 4*t*, 32–38, 39
    Recommendations section of a report and, 103
    sources of assessment data and, 26–27
    test administration and scoring rubric, 157–160
    testing limits, 37–38
    use of findings, 38, 40–41

Test–retest reliability, 75, 76*t*. *See also* Reliability

Three-tiered model. *See* Multi-tiered system of supports (MTSS)

Tiered model. *See* Multi-tiered system of supports (MTSS)

Training to become an evaluator
    consumer-responsive assessment and, 149–150
    individual practitioner issues, 138–141
    interpersonal and communication skills and, 106
    overview, 14–21
    professional writing and, 41
    reporting practices and, 137–138

Uninterpretable findings, 82–83

Unstructured interviews, 28. *See also* Interviews

Validity, 30, 75, 76*t*

Wechsler Individual Achievement Test–Third Edition (WIAT-III), 77–78, 82, 199

Wechsler Intelligence Scale for Children (WISC), 75, 76*t*, 96–97, 196–198

Wide Range Achievement Test-4 (WRAT-4), 75

Wide Range Assessment of Memory and Learning-Second Edition (WRAML-2), 96

Woodcock–Johnson (WJ-IV), 77–78, 96–97

Working alliance, 50–51. *See also* Rapport

Writing style, 41, 83–85, 86–87, 207–210

Written reporting of assessment findings. *See also* Consumer-responsive approach; Report-writing practices
    characteristics of consumer-responsive reports, 70–85, 76*t*, 78*t*, 80*t*
    examples of reports, 164–188
    multi-tiered system of supports (MTSS) and, 45–46
    overview, 1–2, 4*t*, 6–7, 137
    parent feedback letter, 130–131
    professional writing and, 41
    report structure, 85, 87–103
    report writing rubric, 207–210
    test results and, 9
    training and, 149